About This Book

Why is this topic important?

Continuing education and development lie at the very heart of any successful organization. Time and time again, studies show that the best organizations, those that deliver better-than-average return on investment, also happen to be the ones with the highest commitment to training and development. Moreover, training has become a powerful ally in the war for talent. Job seekers frequently cite a strong commitment to development as one of the principal reasons for joining or remaining with an organization.

What can you achieve with this book?

In your hands is a working toolkit, a valuable source of knowledge for the training professional. Offering entirely new content each year, the Pfeiffer Training *Annual* showcases the latest thinking and cutting-edge approaches to training and development, contributed by practicing training professionals, consultants, academics, and subject-matter experts. Turn to the *Annual* for a rich source of ideas and to try out new methods and approaches that others in your profession have found successful.

How is this book organized?

The book is divided into four sections: Experiential Learning Activities (ELAs); Editor's Choice; Inventories, Questionnaires, and Surveys; and Articles and Discussion Resources. All the material can be freely reproduced for training purposes. The ELAs are the mainstay of the *Annual* and cover a broad range of training topics. The activities are presented as complete and ready-to-use training designs; facilitator instructions and all necessary handouts and participant materials are included. Editor's Choice pieces allow us to select material that doesn't fit the other categories and take advantage of "hot topics." The instrumentation section introduces reliable survey and assessment tools for gathering and sharing data on aspects of personal or team development. The articles section presents the best current thinking about training and organization development. Use these for your own professional development or as lecture resources.

About Pfeiffer

Pfeiffer serves the professional development and hands-on resource needs of training and human resource practitioners and gives them products to do their jobs better. We deliver proven ideas and solutions from experts in HR development and HR management, and we offer effective and customizable tools to improve workplace performance. From novice to seasoned professional, Pfeiffer is the source you can trust to make yourself and your organization more successful.

Essential Knowledge Pfeiffer produces insightful, practical, and comprehensive materials on topics that matter the most to training and HR professionals. Our Essential Knowledge resources translate the expertise of seasoned professionals into practical, how-to guidance on critical workplace issues and problems. These resources are supported by case studies, worksheets, and job aids and are frequently supplemented with CD-ROMs, websites, and other means of making the content easier to read, understand, and use.

Essential Tools Pfeiffer's Essential Tools resources save time and expense by offering proven, ready-to-use materials—including exercises, activities, games, instruments, and assessments—for use during a training or team-learning event. These resources are frequently offered in looseleaf or CD-ROM format to facilitate copying and customization of the material.

Pfeiffer also recognizes the remarkable power of new technologies in expanding the reach and effectiveness of training. While e-hype has often created whizbang solutions in search of a problem, we are dedicated to bringing convenience and enhancements to proven training solutions. All our e-tools comply with rigorous functionality standards. The most appropriate technology wrapped around essential content yields the perfect solution for today's on-the-go trainers and human resource professionals.

Pfeiffer
www.pfeiffer.com   *Essential resources for training and HR professionals*

The Pfeiffer Annual Series

The *Pfeiffer Annuals* present each year never-before-published materials contributed by learning professionals and academics and written for trainers, consultants, and human resource and performance-improvement practitioners. As a forum for the sharing of ideas, theories, models, instruments, experiential learning activities, and best and innovative practices, the *Annuals* are unique, not least because only in the *Pfeiffer Annuals* will you find solutions from professionals like you who work in the field as trainers, consultants, facilitators, educators, and human resource and performance-improvement practitioners and whose contributions have been tried and perfected in real-life settings with actual participants and clients to meet real-world needs.

The Pfeiffer Annual: Consulting
Edited by Elaine Biech

The Pfeiffer Annual: Human Resource Management
Edited by Robert C. Preziosi

The Pfeiffer Annual: Training
Edited by Elaine Biech

Call for Papers

How would you like to be published in the *Pfeiffer Training* or *Consulting Annual*? Possible topics for submissions include group and team building, organization development, leadership, problem solving, presentation and communication skills, consulting and facilitation, and training-the-trainer. Contributions may be in one of the following three formats:

- Experiential Learning Activities

- Inventories, Questionnaires, and Surveys

- Articles and Discussion Resources

To receive a copy of the submission packet, which explains the requirements and will help you determine format, language, and style to use, contact editor Elaine Biech at Pfeifferannual@aol.com or by calling 757–588–3939.

Elaine Biech, EDITOR

The *2006*
Pfeiffer
ANNUAL

TRAINING

Pfeiffer
A Wiley Imprint
www.pfeiffer.com

ISBN-10: 0-7879-7821-3
ISBN-13: 978-0-7879-7821-1
ISSN: 1046-333-X

Acquiring Editor: Martin Delahoussaye
Director of Development: Kathleen Dolan Davies
Developmental Editor: Susan Rachmeler
Production Editor: Dawn Kilgore
Editor: Rebecca Taff
Manufacturing Supervisor: Becky Carreño
Editorial Assistant: Leota Higgins
Composition and Technical Art: Leigh McLellan Design

Printed in the United States of America

Printing   10   9   8   7   6   5   4   3   2   1

Contents

Experiential Learning Activities

Editor's Choice

Inventories, Questionnaires, and Surveys

Articles and Discussion Resources

**Topic is cutting edge.

Preface

Beyond Your Own Little World

Worldly wisdom. Those two words continued to buzz in my brain as we read, selected, and edited the submissions during the past nine months for the *2006 Training* and *Consulting Annuals*. Why? Was it that we had more international submissions than ever before? No. I didn't think that was it, even though four of those submissions from Canada, India, New Zealand, and Spain made the final cut.

After some thought, I decided that it was based on the unique variety of submissions. I think you will agree. The *2006 Annuals* offer contributions from music, art, and literature ("Pygmalion" and "El Quixote"). Many of the most interesting submissions in the two volumes test the boundaries of your comfort zones, encouraging you to address difficult subjects such as trust, values, narcissism, and your personal life plan.

Today's trainers, consultants, and facilitators require a broader variety of skills, expertise, and knowledge. To gain new skills, acquire different expertise, and to attain worldly wisdom requires that you push yourself outside your comfort zone beyond your own little world. This is hard work! But it is just what we all need to become better at what we do for our customers, our employers, and our clients. We need to learn and grow and to achieve a more global mindset.

Experiential learning activities in these two volumes test how far you are willing to stretch (try Jameson's relay race). Articles in these two volumes provide you with new way to consider old topics (read Royal's article addressing buy-in). Instruments in the two volumes help you measure your individual development as well as leadership and organizational effectiveness.

What about beyond the *Annuals*? What personal attributes does it take to continue to learn and grow and to keep you on top of the changes and the expectations of your profession? Peter Drucker tells us that we cannot manage change; we can only stay ahead of it. Change creates an environment that forces us to move from our comfortable world to a more comprehensive (or global) mindset. It means that we must continue to learn and grow to stay ahead of change.

The following personal attributes identify perspectives that I have learned from other professionals, my colleagues, and you, our *Annual* contributors. Think about yourself as you read them. What can you do to boost your worldly wisdom?

Know Yourself.   Know your strengths. Know your weaknesses. Know your limitations. Turn your weaknesses into strengths through learning and experience. Invite others to provide their insight and feedback.

Welcome Crises.   You will learn more from the surprises that life brings your way than from any book. Be flexible and innovate. Creative solutions are the mark of a wise and flexible person.

Take Risks.   The more you risk, the greater your chances for success or failure. Risks abound in everything you do, but the riskiest of all is to never take a risk. Risks, and yes, sometimes failure, are a strong foundation for learning.

Stretch.   Try the Impossible. Eleanor Roosevelt said, "You must do the thing you think you cannot do." Anything is possible. You will never know if you do not try. Feel the Fear and Do It Anyway, is one of my favorite book titles. It states what we all must consider before we say "can't."

Broaden Your Perspective.   If you are a big-picture thinker, learn to take care of the details. If you are creative, practice logic. If you focus on tasks, take time to focus on people. Focus on both the future and the history that created it. Argue for and against the same issue. Each of you has natural preferences. Spend time in the opposite mode to help you step outside your comfortable world.

Exude Passion.   Life is simply too short to do something you do not like. I hope that you not only *like* what you do—I hope you *love* what you do. I do not believe that anyone should get up and go to work in the morning; I believe that we should all get up and go to *play* every morning. If you are not playing every day, learn something new, try a new process, meet a new colleague or client. Find something that paints the passion back in the picture.

Know When to Quit.   Training, consulting, and facilitating are all rewarding professions. But when they no longer are rewarding to you, quit. When play becomes work, when fun becomes drudgery, when challenges become formidable obstacles, recognize that it may be time for you to move on.

This is certainly not an exhaustive list of every attribute that will move you to experience the wide world around you, but it is a place to start. And be sure to use the *2006 Annuals* to get started.

A Native American friend shared a quote he attributed to his people. It has echoed in my mind for years, "If you are not living on the edge, you take up too much room." To gain worldly wisdom, we all probably need to do more edge-sitting outside the box in which we find comfort.

What Are the Annuals?

The *Annual* series is published in three volumes: Training, Consulting, and Human Resource Management. The collection of practical materials is written for trainers, consultants, and performance-improvement technologists. We know the materials are practical because they are written by the same practitioners who use the materials.

The *Pfeiffer Annual: Training* focuses on skill building and knowledge enhancement and also includes cutting-edge articles that enhance the skills and professional development of trainers. The *Pfeiffer Annual: Consulting* focuses on intervention techniques and organizational systems. It also includes skill building for the professional consultant. You can read more about the differences between these two volumes in the section that follows this preface, "The Difference Between Training and Consulting: Which Annual to Use."

The *Annuals* have been an inspirational source for experiential learning activities, resource for instruments, and reference for cutting-edge articles for thirty-four years. Whether you are a trainer, a consultant, a facilitator, or a bit of each, you will find tools and resources that provide you with the basics and challenge (and we hope inspire) you to use new techniques and models.

Annual Loyalty

The Pfeiffer *Annual* series has many loyal subscribers. There are several reasons for this loyalty. In addition to the wide variety of topics and implementation levels, the *Annuals* provide materials that are applicable to varying circumstances. You will find instruments for individuals, teams, and organizations; experiential learning activities to round out workshops, team building, or consulting assignments; ideas and contemporary solutions for managing human capital; and articles that increase your own knowledge base, to use as reference materials in your writing, or as a source of ideas for your training or consulting assignments.

Many of our readers have been loyal customers for a dozen or more years. If you are one of them, we thank you. And we encourage each of you to give back to the profession by submitting a sample of your work to share with your colleagues.

The *Annuals* owe most of their success, though, to the fact that they are immediately ready to use. All of the materials may be duplicated for educational and training purposes. If you need to adapt or modify the materials to tailor them for your audience's needs, go right ahead. We only request that the credit statement found on the copyright page (and on each reproducible page) be retained on all copies. Our liberal copyright policy makes it easy and fast for you to use the materials to do your job. However, if you intend to reproduce the materials in publications for sale or if you wish to reproduce more than one hundred copies of any one item, please contact us for prior written permission.

If you are a new *Annual* user, welcome! If you like what you see in the 2006 edition, you may want to consider subscribing to a standing order. By doing so, you are guaranteed to receive your copy each year straight off the press and receive a discount off the cover price. And if you want to go back and have the entire series for your use, then the *Pfeiffer Library*—which contains content from the very first edition to the present day—is available on CD-ROM. You can find information on the *Pfeiffer Library* at www.pfeiffer.com.

I often refer to many of my *Annuals* from the 1980s. They include several classic activities that have become a mainstay in my team-building designs. But most of all, the *Annuals* have been a valuable resource for over thirty years because the materials come from professionals like you who work in the field as trainers, consultants, facilitators, educators, and performance-improvement technologists, whose contributions have been tried and perfected in real-life settings with actual participants and clients to meet real-world needs.

To this end, we encourage you to submit materials to be considered for publication. We are interested in receiving experiential learning activities; inventories, questionnaires, and surveys; and articles and discussion resources. Contact the Pfeiffer Editorial Department at the address listed on the copyright page for copies of our guidelines for contributors or contact me directly at Box 8249, Norfolk, VA 23503, or by email at pfeifferannual @aol.com. We welcome your comments, ideas, and contributions.

Acknowledgments

Thank you to the dedicated, friendly, thoughtful people at Pfeiffer who produced the *2006 Pfeiffer Annual: Training*: Kathleen Dolan Davies, Martin Delahoussaye, Leota Higgins, Dawn Kilgore, Susan Rachmeler, Laura Reizman, and Rebecca Taff. Thank you to Lorraine Kohart of ebb associates inc, who assisted our authors with the many submission details and who ensured that we met all the deadlines.

Most important, thank you to our contributors, who have once again shared their ideas, techniques, and materials so that trainers and consultants everywhere may benefit. Won't you consider joining the ranks of these prestigious professionals?

Elaine Biech
Editor
September 2005

The Difference Between Training and Consulting
Which Annual to Use?

The two volumes of the *Pfeiffer Annuals*—training and consulting—are resources for two different but closely related professions. Each *Annual* serves as a collection of tools and support materials used by the professionals in their respective arenas. The volumes include activities, articles, and instruments used by individuals in the training and consulting fields. The training volume is written with the trainer in mind, and the consulting volume is written with the consultant in mind.

How can you differentiate between the two volumes? Let's begin by defining each profession.

A *trainer* can be defined as anyone who is responsible for designing and delivering knowledge to adult learners, and may include an internal HRD professional employed by an organization or an external practitioner who contracts with an organization to design and conduct training programs. Generally, the trainer is a subject-matter expert who is expected to transfer knowledge so that the trainee can know or do something new. A *consultant* is someone who provides unique assistance or advice (based on what the consultant knows or has experienced) to someone else, usually known as "the client." The consultant may not necessarily be a subject-matter expert in all situations. Often the consultant is an expert at using specific tools to extract, coordinate, resolve, organize, expedite, or implement an organizational situation.

The lines between the consulting and training professions have blurred in the past few years. First, the names and titles have blurred. For example, some external trainers call themselves "training consultants" as a way of distinguishing themselves from internal trainers. Some organizations now have internal consultants, who usually reside in the training department. Second, the roles have blurred. While a consultant has always been expected to deliver measurable results, now trainers are expected to do so as well. Both are expected to improve performance; both are expected to contribute to the bottom line. Facilitation was at one time thought to be a consultant skill; today trainers are expected to use facilitation skills to train. Training one-on-one was a trainer skill; today consultants train executives one-on-one and call it "coaching."

The introduction of the "performance technologist," whose role is one of combined trainer and consultant, is a perfect example of a new profession that has evolved due to the need for trainers to use more "consulting" techniques in their work. The "performance consultant" is a new role supported by the American Society for Training and Development (ASTD). ASTD has shifted its focus from training to performance improvement.

As you can see, the roles and goals of training and consulting are not nearly as specific as they once may have been. However, when you step back and examine the two professions from a big-picture perspective, you can more easily differentiate between the two. Maintaining a big-picture focus will also help you determine which *Pfeiffer Annual* to turn to as your first resource.

Both volumes cover the same general topics: communication, teamwork, problem solving, and leadership. However, depending on your requirement and purpose—a training or consulting need—you will use each in different situations. You will select the *Annual* based on *how you will interact with the topic, not on what the topic might be.* Let's take a topic such as teamwork, for example. If you are searching for a lecturette that teaches the advantages of teamwork, a workshop activity that demonstrates the skill of making decisions in a team, or a handout that discusses team stages, look to the Training *Annual.* On the other hand, if you are conducting a team-building session for a dysfunctional team, helping to form a new team, or trying to understand the dynamics of an executive team, you will look to the Consulting *Annual.*

The Training *Annual*

The materials in the Training volume focus on skill building and knowledge enhancement as well as on the professional development of trainers. They generally focus on controlled events: a training program, a conference presentation, or a classroom setting. Look to the Training *Annual* to find ways to improve a training session for ten to 1,000 people and anything else that falls in the human resource development category:

- Specific experiential learning activities that can be built into a training program;

- Techniques to improve training: debriefing exercises, conducting role plays, managing time;

- Topical lecturettes;

- Ideas to improve a boring training program;

- Icebreakers and energizers for a training session;

- Surveys that can be used in a classroom;

- Ideas for moving an organization from training to performance; and

- Ways to improve your skills as a trainer.

The Consulting *Annual*

The materials in the Consulting volume focus on intervention techniques and organizational systems as well as on the professional development of consultants. They generally focus on "tools" that you can have available just in case: concepts about organizations and their development (or demise) and about more global situations. Look to the Consulting *Annual* to find ways to improve consulting activities from team building and executive coaching to organization development and strategic planning:

- Skills for working with executives;

- Techniques for solving problems, effecting change, and gathering data;

- Team-building tools, techniques, and tactics;

- Facilitation ideas and methods;

- Processes to examine for improving an organization's effectiveness;

- Surveys that can be used organizationally; and

- Ways to improve your effectiveness as a consultant.

Summary

Even though the professions and the work are closely related and at times interchangeable, there is a difference. Use the following table to help you determine which *Annual* you should scan first for help. Remember, however, there is some blending of the two and either *Annual* may have your answer. It depends . . .

Element	Training	Consulting
Topics	Teams, Communication, Problem Solving	Teams, Communication, Problem Solving
Topic Focus	Individual, Department	Corporate, Global
Purpose	Skill Building, Knowledge Transfer	Coaching, Strategic Planning, Building Teams
Recipient	Individuals, Departments	Usually More Organizational
Organizational Level	All Workforce Members	Usually Closer to the Top
Delivery Profile	Workshops, Presentations	Intervention, Implementation
Atmosphere	Structured	Unstructured
Time Frame	Defined	Undefined
Organizational Cost	Moderate	High
Change Effort	Low to Moderate	Moderate to High
Setting	Usually a Classroom	Anywhere
Professional Experience	Entry Level, Novice	Proficient, Master Level
Risk Level	Low	High
Professional Needs	Activities, Resources	Tools, Theory
Application	Individual Skills	Usually Organizational System

When you get right down to it, we are all trainers and consultants. The skills may cross over. A great trainer is also a skilled consultant. And a great consultant is also a skilled trainer. The topics may be the same, but how you implement them may be vastly different. Which *Annual* to use? Remember to think about your purpose in terms of the big picture: consulting or training.

As you can see, we have both covered.

Introduction

to *The 2006 Pfeiffer Annual: Training*

Getting the Most from This Resource

The 2006 Pfeiffer Annual: Training is the latest addition to a series that has been in print since 1972. The *Annual* offers a collection of practical and useful materials for professionals in the broad area of human resource development (HRD). The materials are written by and for professionals, including trainers, organization-development and organization-effectiveness consultants, performance-improvement technologists, facilitators, educators, instructional designers, and others.

Each *Annual* has three main sections: Experiential Learning Activities; Inventories, Questionnaires, and Surveys; and Articles and Discussion Resources. A fourth section, Editor's Choice, has been reserved for those unique contributions that do not fit neatly into one of the three main sections, but are valuable as identified by the editorial staff. Each published submission is classified in one of the following categories: Individual Development, Communication, Problem Solving, Groups, Teams, Consulting, Facilitating, Leadership, and Organizations. Within each category, pieces are further classified into logical subcategories, which are identified in the introductions to the three sections.

"Cutting edge" topics are identified in each *Annual*. This designation highlights topics that present information, concepts, tools, or perspectives that may be recent additions to the profession or that have not previously appeared in the *Annual* or are currently "hot topics."

The series continues to provide an opportunity for HRD professionals who wish to share their experiences, their viewpoints, and their processes with their colleagues.

To that end, Pfeiffer publishes guidelines for potential authors. These guidelines are available from the Pfeiffer Editorial Department at Jossey-Bass, Inc., in San Francisco, California.

Materials are selected for the *Annuals* based on the quality of the ideas, applicability to real-world concerns, relevance to current HRD issues, clarity of presentation, and ability to enhance our readers' professional development. In addition, we choose experiential learning activities that will create a high degree of enthusiasm among the participants and add enjoyment to the learning process. As in the past several years, the contents of each *Annual* span a wide range of subject matter, reflecting the range of interests of our readers.

Our contributor list includes a wide selection of experts in the field: in-house practitioners, consultants, and academically based professionals. A list of contributors to the *Annual* can be found at the end of the volume, including their names, affiliations, addresses, telephone numbers, facsimile numbers, and email addresses. Readers will find this list useful if they wish to locate the authors of specific pieces for feedback, comments, or questions. Further information on each contributor is presented in a brief biographical sketch that appears at the conclusion of each article. We publish this information to encourage "networking," which continues to be a valuable mainstay in the field of human resource development.

We are pleased with the high quality of material that is submitted for publication each year and often regret that we have page limitations. In addition, just as we cannot publish every manuscript we receive, you may find that not all published works are equally useful to you. Therefore, we encourage and invite ideas, materials, and suggestions that will help us to make subsequent *Annuals* as useful as possible to all of our readers.

Introduction
to the Experiential Learning Activities Section

Experiential learning activities ensure that lasting learning occurs. They should be selected with a specific learning objective in mind. These objectives are based on the participants' needs and the facilitator's skills. Although the experiential learning activities presented here all vary in goals, group size, time required, and process, they all incorporate one important element: questions that ensure learning has occurred. This discussion, led by the facilitator, assists participants to process the activity, to internalize the learning, and to relate it to their day-to-day situations. It is this element that creates the unique learning experience and learning opportunity that only an experiential learning activity can bring to the group process.

Readers have used the *Annuals'* experiential learning activities for years to enhance their training and consulting events. Each learning experience is complete and includes all lecturettes, handout content, and other written material necessary to facilitate the activity. In addition, many include variations of the design that the facilitator might find useful. If the activity does not fit perfectly with your objective, within your time frame, or to your group size, we encourage you to adapt the activity by adding your own variations. You will find additional experiential learning activities listed in the "Experiential Learning Activities Categories" chart that immediately follows this introduction.

The 2006 Pfeiffer Annual: Training includes fourteen activities, in the following categories:

Individual Development: Diversity

Do Differences Divide Us? Learning About Diversity, by M.K. Key

Communication: Awareness

Opposite Chair: Learning to Ask Questions, by Chai M. Voris

To further assist you in selecting appropriate ELAs, we provide the following grid that summarizes category, time required, group size, and risk factor for each ELA.

Category	ELA Title	Page	Time Required	Group Size	Risk Factor
Individual Development: Diversity	Do Differences Divide Us? Learning About Diversity	11	30 minutes	5 to 50	Moderate
Communication: Awareness	Opposite Chair: Learning to Ask Questions	15	30 minutes	Any number	Moderate
Communication: Feedback	Pygmalion: Using the Power of Expectations for Developing Subordinates	19	2 hours	10 to 25	Moderate
Problem Solving: Generating Alternatives	Self-Powered Vehicles: Learning to Work as a Group	31	75 minutes	Any number of groups of 4 to 6 participants	Moderate
Teams: How Groups Work	Soda Can Carry: Building a Team	39	40 minutes	Several groups of 4 to 8 people	Moderate
Consulting, Training, and Facilitating: Facilitating: Opening	Picture This: Introducing Participants	43	25 to 60 minutes	10 to 25	Low
Consulting, Training, and Facilitating: Facilitating: Blocks to Learning	Word Cards: Reinforcing Learning	47	20 to 30 minutes	15 to 50	Low
Consulting, Training, and Facilitating: Facilitating: Blocks to Learning	Lyrical Look: Finding Insight in Songs	51	10 to 20 minutes	Any number, in groups of 2 to 5	Low
Consulting, Training, and Facilitating: Facilitating: Skills	Critical Reflection Relay: Reviewing What Was Learned	55	60 to 90 minutes	8 to 24	Low
Consulting, Training, and Facilitating: Facilitating: Closing	Rolling for Review: Reviewing Key Learning Points	61	Approximately 15 minutes	20 to 500 people in audience; 3 to 6 representatives	Moderate

(table continued on the next page)

Category	ELA Title	Page	Time Required	Group Size	Risk Factor
Consulting, Training, and Facilitating: Facilitating: Closing	Keynote Closer: Polishing the Gems	63	60 to 120 minutes	Up to 20	Moderate to High
Leadership: Ethics	What Is Moral Character? Defining Character	69	60 to 75 minutes	Any number of groups of 3 to 5	Moderate
Leadership: Motivation	How Do I Acknowledge Thee? Giving Praise When Due	75	2 to 2½ hours	1 to 100	Low
Leadership: Styles and Skills	Board Meeting Simulation: Establishing Leadership Perspective	85	2 to 2½ hours	20 to 30 in groups of 3 or 4	Low

Experiential Learning Activities Categories

Do Differences Divide Us?
Learning About Diversity

Activity Summary

A quick activity to learn about the value of diversity within organizations.

Goals

- To experience how differences divide us.

- To provide an energetic diversity training experience within an organization.

Group Size

5 to 50 participants from the same organization or as many as the room will allow to stand and move around at the same time.

Time Required

30 minutes.

Materials

None.

Physical Setting

Tables and chairs for initial seating. A room large enough for circulation of all participants from wall to wall.

Facilitating Risk Rating

Moderate.

Process

1. Explain to participants that they are going to look together at some ways in which they are different.

2. If people are seated, ask them to stand and put down purses, drinks, and papers.

3. Explain that you will be calling out a series of categories and asking them to sort themselves by moving to the certain section of the room (opposite sides, corners) that you designate.

4. Begin calling out categories, allowing enough time for participants to settle into groups and look at the others in their groups, and then calling out the next category:

   - Men on one side, women on the other.

   - Single, married.

   - Have children, no children.

   - Republican, Democrat, Independent, no affiliation.

   - Hair has been altered versus all-natural hair.

   - Feel you are overweight, underweight, or just right.

   - Have committed a crime (could be speeding) or not.

   - You or someone close to you has been in rehab.

   - You or someone close to you has been a victim of abuse.

   - You or someone close to you has financial problems.

   - Have worked at this organization longer than [some period of years] or less than [some period of years] or is brand new.

   - Believe in a higher power or do not.

   - Want to love and be loved or do not.

   - Want to find joy and meaning in work or do not.
   (10 minutes.)

5. The room should be tilted in one direction at the end of the exercise with the last category. Ask participants to be seated and to quietly reflect on what just happened.

6. Then in pairs or as a whole group, discuss these questions:

- Did some of these differences ever make you feel uncomfortable or even embarrassed?

- Did you ever feel like the outsider?

- Did you ever feel inferior—that your status was less than the others?

- Did you ever change places, that is, not move to the appropriate category, in order to avoid others' judgments?

- Imagine coming to work feeling the weight of a label and a judgment that goes with it. Do we want this kind of discomfort in our workplace?

- Are we more alike or are we really very different?
  (10 minutes.)

7. Conclude with these comments:

"We steered away from questions of race, ethnicity, religion, culture, or family background, but the conclusions that we could draw are the same.

"All around the world, people want the same things: to have a place, to be connected to something more important than themselves, to be loved, to have peace and stability in their communities, to see their children prosper, and to maintain a respect for life and a sense of fairness.

"It is not the differences that divide us; it is our judgments about others that do. Consider this experience the next time you are tempted to stereotype others.

"In our organization, we are seeking to build 'cultural competence'—the ability to understand and capitalize on our differences while we recognize and celebrate our commonalities."

Variation

Individuals can raise their hands rather than vote with their feet—or stand in a large circle, stepping in or backing out in response to questions.

Submitted by M.K. Key.

A licensed clinical-community psychologist, **M.K. Key, Ph.D.,** *is a writer, teacher, and consultant who has published extensively. Her most recent books include* Managing Change: Innovative Solutions for People-Based Organizations *(1999) and* Corporate Celebration: Play, Purpose and Profit at Work *(1998). Prior to forming Key Associates in 1997, she was vice president of the Center for Continuous Improvement with Quorum Health Resources, Inc.*

Opposite Chair
Learning to Ask Questions

Activity Summary

A change activity that emphasizes the importance of and need for two-way communication when giving messages and directions.

Goals

- To understand the importance of asking questions during change initiatives.

- To experience the different ways each person can interpret messages and directions.

- To discuss the responsibility each individual has for doing things the right way.

Group Size

Any number.

Time Required

30 minutes.

Materials

None.

Physical Setting

A room with tables and chairs with enough room for seating everyone and for movement in the room.

Facilitating Risk Rating

Moderate.

Process

1. Use this activity to motivate participants before a break or lunch or at the end of the day. Introduce it as "just a quick activity before we go."

2. Tell the participants, "I would like you to quickly move to the *opposite* seat from where you are now. Now, *GO*" and let everyone begin to reshuffle. Give no further instructions.

3. Keep telling participants to hurry up. Remind them that they cannot leave until the activity is over, so please hurry.
   (5 minutes.)

4. Possible outcomes. The majority of people will do one of two things: go to the opposite seat at or near their own table or go all the way across the room to a new seat. Whichever the majority does, claim your instructions meant the other!

5. Once everyone is seated, ask the group:

   - Do you know the meaning of "opposite"? If so, how did you do the task?

   - How did you decide where the "opposite" was?

   - Did all of you interpret "opposite" the same? Did anyone else sit in the seat you thought was *your* "opposite" seat?

   - Who thinks you did the task correctly?

   - What if I told you that none of you did it right? How would you feel?

   - How can such a simple message be received differently from how I intended it?

   - If something this basic can be misinterpreted, what does this tell you about how detailed our communications need to be? In addition, the heightened stress we experience during change initiatives may cause us to judge the actions of others harshly when they interpret things differently. What happens in this case?

   - On what do you make assumptions and interpret things? How do your experiences and perceptions affect your assumptions?
   (10 minutes.)

6. At this point, ask all the participants to close their eyes for a minute and picture a *chair*. Ask them to visualize the color, feel, pattern, use, place it sits, etc.

7. Ask them to keep their eyes closed and ask someone in the room to describe the chair. Ask a couple more people to describe their chairs.

8. Ask everyone to open their eyes. Ask the following questions:

   - Why don't all of you picture the same chair in your minds?

   - How does this activity apply to your communication during meetings?

   - How can you understand the meaning if you have no idea what "their chairs" look like?

   - Whose job is it to understand what is intended in a conversation?

   - How can you make sure you have the right understanding of the message as you go through a change initiative?

   - As you think about this issue, what will you do differently back on the job when communicating with others?

   (15 minutes.)

Submitted by Chai M. Voris.

Chai M. Voris, M.Ed., *is a dynamic and inspiring presenter, trainer, and consultant, with over twenty years of experience in helping good organizations find ways to create positive change results. She received her bachelor's in management from Franklin University, where she is currently an adjunct in the MBA program, and her M.Ed. in executive HRD from Xavier University. Ms. Chai is president of Dynamic Change Solutions, Inc., an inspirational change and leadership consulting and training company.*

Pygmalion
Using the Power of Expectations for Developing Subordinates

Activity Summary

An activity that allows participants to gain a deeper appreciation of the power of expectations and how to use it to make others set high goals and achieve them.

Goals

- To enable the participants to understand the Pygmalion effect and power of expectations.
- To help participants evolve various ways of using the learnings back on the job.

Group Size

10 to 25 participants.

Time Required

About 2 hours.

Materials

- One copy of the Pygmalion Introduction for each participant.
- One copy of The Pygmalion Case for each participant.
- Paper and a pen or pencil for each participant.
- Flip chart and markers.

Physical Setting

A room large enough to use a U-shape seating arrangement.

Facilitating Risk Rating

Moderate.

Process

1. Have participants sit in a U-shape arrangement. After initial briefing about the goals of the program and timeframe, ask them if they know what they want to become in their lifetimes. Hand out paper and pens or pencils and have them write down their responses. Once everyone has completed the task, ask them how they felt responding to this question. Obtain responses from a few volunteers. State that this activity is not easy for some of us because we seldom think about our own aims in life.

2. Ask, "For those of you who have a lifetime goal, whose expectations are you fulfilling?" Invite a few volunteers to share their responses. Conclude by saying that some of us strive to fulfill the expectations of others, while some of us form our own expectations and strive for fulfillment.
    (15 minutes.)

3. Distribute the Pygmalion Introduction and ask everyone to read it in silence.
    (10 minutes.)

4. After everyone has finished, ask what questions they have. Clarify the information and answer any questions. Summarize by presenting the expectation cycle (Figure 1) described briefly in the Pygmalion Introduction.
    (15 minutes.)

5. Divide the participants into small groups of 5 and ask them to sit in small circles. Ask them if they have experienced a Pygmalion in their lives or been a Galatea? In other words, ask them whether anyone has ever set an expectation for them and they worked for the fulfillment. For example, "My father set an expectation that I should top the list in the District Scholarship Examination for seventh-grade students. I made the effort, topped the list, and fulfilled his expectation." Ask participants to recall such experience(s) and share them in the small groups. Ask them to share their feelings of having such an experience and the benefits they derived.
    (15 minutes.)

6. Reconvene the large group. Invite a few volunteers to share with the large group what they shared in the small group. You may write the main points on a flip chart.

7. Synthesize the list and summarize the common points. Indicate how one person's (Pygmalion) expectations motivated another person (Galatea) to work for the fulfillment of the expectation and how the expectations were fulfilled.

8. Give a copy of The Pygmalion Case to each participant. Ask them to read the case, and then ask for short answers for the following questions as you post them on the flip chart:

   • What were the main behaviors (actions) of Dr. Dutt (the Pygmalion) that helped Amit and Sunil become confident and feel motivated to complete the task?

   • What were the behaviors of Sunil and Amit that indicate that they were influenced by the Pygmalion effect?

   (30 minutes.)

9. Divide participants into small groups again and ask them to share their answers and prepare a group response.
   (20 minutes.)

10. Reconvene the large group once again. Ask them to share the thoughts, feelings, and insights they had during the activity.

11. Invite the representative of any one group to make a brief presentation on what they prepared. When the presentation of that group is over, ask a representative of another group to come and make a presentation. Ask the participants to give their comments on the presentations. Keep going until all groups have presented.
    (15 minutes.)

12. After presentation by all groups, summarize and clarify any missing points. Concentrate especially on how participants will behave differently back on the job.

Variations

   • Close the activity by asking the participants to recall their own experiences of being a Pygmalion, for example, if they have set an expectation on a person who worked sincerely and fulfilled the expectation. Ask volunteers to share.

- Include one or more of the following questions in Step 8 also:

  ○ How did Dr. Dutt set a conducive climate for the two engineers?

  ○ How supportive was he?

  ○ How important did the assignments feel to the two engineers?

  ○ How did Dr. Dutt make the two engineers feel competent and important?

  ○ Did he create the climate only by verbal means or through nonverbal behavior also?

  ○ Did Dr. Dutt provide some inputs and teach useful information and resources (etc.) to the two engineers?

  ○ What was its impact?

  ○ What opportunities to learn and perform were provided by Dr. Dutt?

  ○ Did Dr. Dutt provide feedback on the efforts and performance of the engineers? What was some of the good feedback given by Dr. Dutt?

- Show the short film "Pygmalion Effect" (22 minutes) by CRM Learning (available by calling 800–421–0833).

- Before coming to the program, participants can be asked to read "Pygmalion in Management" by J. Sterling Livingston. Send them copies in advance. Ask participants to share the main learning points of the article as an opening discussion.

References

Livingston, J.S. (1969/2003). Pygmalion in management. *Harvard Business Review.*
McNatt, B. *The Pygmalion effect: Managing the power of expectations.* Carlsbad, CA: CRM Learning.
The Pygmalion effect (video). Carlsbad, CA: CRM Learning.

Submitted by Parth Sarathi.

Parth Sarathi *is a general manager (HRD) with Human Resource Development Institute of Bharat Heavy Electricals Ltd., a large engineering company in India. He holds post-graduate qualifications in engineering and management. He has over thirty-three years of managerial experience, including over twenty-two years in HR/HRD and OD. An accredited T-group trainer, MBTI trainer, Thomas Profile licensee, and competency assessor, he has authored five books and contributed over seventy-five papers to professional journals.*

Pygmalion Introduction

In ancient times there was a king named Pygmalion in Cyprus. He was a great sculptor. He started carving out the statue of an ideal woman and developed a passion for the lady, whose figure started emerging out of the marble stone during his sculpting. Gradually this passion transformed into an expectation that the statue should become alive. His tremendous concentration, hard work, dedication, and strong will made him create the statue of the most beautiful woman in the universe and, as the story goes, on completion of the statue, with the assistance of the goddess Venus and his own efforts, the statue became alive and he named her Galatea.

This phenomenon was explained as exhibiting power of expectation, which later became the basis of George Bernard Shaw's play "Pygmalion" and still later the musical movie *My Fair Lady,* wherein Professor Henry Higgins helps Eliza Doolittle, a flower girl, transform into a refined and elegant lady. This has been called "The Pygmalion Effect," and the person who sets higher expectations on a person who in turn fulfills that expectation is called Pygmalion. The person who responds to the expectation of Pygmalion and fulfills it is called Galatea. When a high self-expectation of a person results in great personal achievement, it is the result of the person being one's own Pygmalion, and the phenomenon is called "The Galatea Effect."

Merton was the first social scientist to note that our expectations have a powerful influence on the future, even though in many cases one may not be aware of those expectations. He stressed that people's behaviors and actions caused outcomes, not merely their beliefs or expectations. Later on, behavioral scientists worked and demonstrated that, besides influencing the outcome of events, our expectations influence other people also. In the following paragraphs the process has been briefly described, illustrated by Figure 1 and a case example.

The following are the stages.

I. Boss Forms an Expectation

A young industrial engineer having ten years of experience joined the corporate HR department of a large multi-unit engineering organization after transferring from the management services division. In fact, the engineer had not been getting along well with his boss, who had requested the chief of HR to counsel this fellow to improve his behavior. The HR chief called the man and, after a brief discussion, advised him to join the HR department, as he saw good potential. OD activities were going on in one of the major units, and the HR boss had a dream of having the company's own OD consultants. At the time the company had engaged a couple of reputed OD consultants. The boss after a few days formed an expectation of one the subordinates that

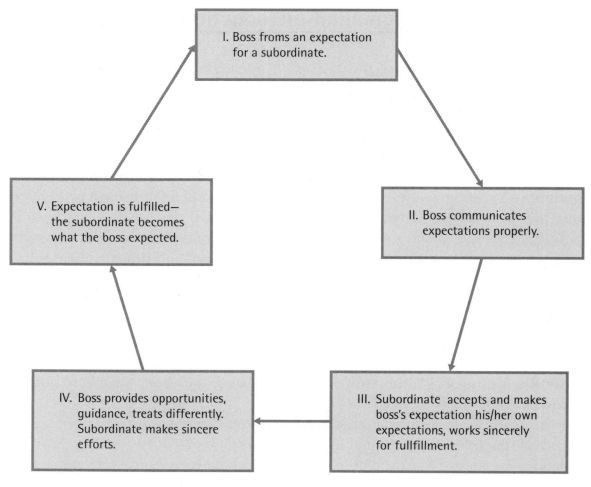

Figure 1.   Expectation Cycle

he should become an accredited T-group trainer/behavior process facilitator. He was visualizing tremendous process-based HR/HRD interventions in the company in the coming years and was feeling a strong need for developing internal facilitators.

II. Boss Communicates His Expectations

One day during the course of interactions on HRD-related matters, the boss expressed that he wanted to see the transferred worker as an accredited T-group trainer/process facilitator, which he considered essential for becoming an effective OD consultant. The subordinate did not even know what a T-group trainer/process facilitator was. The boss explained in brief and gave examples by naming a few leading T-group trainers who were well-known OD consultants. The subordinate knew a few of them in some other context. The boss also conveyed that it was a difficult task and said that to date there were not more that fifty such trainers in the country. He also mentioned that, for OD work, T-group trainers are in great demand. He added that he (the subordinate) appeared to possess the necessary aptitude and traits.

Success lies in the ability of the boss to gradually infuse the dream of success in the subordinate. What will be the scenario? How will others behave? How will he perform? What recognition will he receive? Will he rise professionally?

These are a few of the issues that should be addressed by the boss while conveying his expectations.

III. The Subordinate Listens, Accepts the Idea, and Starts Working Sincerely for Fulfillment of the Expectation

The subordinate listened and visualized being a T-group trainer by looking into the status, style, and images of the known trainers. He asked a few probing questions. By the words and nonverbal behavior of the boss, he became assured, excited, and more confident with the idea, felt important, and became motivated to succeed. He compared this vision with his dreams of a career; the new dream appeared attractive and meaningful; and with the encouraging words and positive gestures of the boss, he felt largely encouraged and ultimately agreed. The expectation of the boss became his own expectation!

IV. Boss Provides Opportunities, Treats the Subordinate Differently; Subordinate Responds and Makes Sincere Efforts

The boss briefed the employee about the professional development program of the Indian Society for Applied Behavioral Science and nominated the subordinate for the basic laboratory class. The subordinate became even more motivated after the first lab. He was promoted to higher levels of the professional development program.

The boss treated the subordinate differently, giving him more time, asking about his work and learning, giving feedback, advice, and relevant tasks and projects during the period, talking positively about the subordinate's programs and activities. The boss also kept sponsoring the subordinate for various stages of the PDP or other contact programs (labs), T-group training, or allied activities. He helped the subordinate become involved in a functional manner in many OD activities, including induction into the internal resource persons team (OD) being developed in one of the units. He was also given the responsibility to coordinate with OD consultants.

V. Expectation Is Fulfilled

Stage by stage, the subordinate fulfilled all the requirements of the PDP and earned his accreditation as a T-group trainer/behavioral process facilitator. The expectation, thus, was fulfilled.

The Pygmalion effect, thus, is based on a self-fulfilling prophecy. In this context a condition indicating a manager's expectation for an employee will cause the manager to treat the employee differently, and the employee will respond in a way that helps the expectation to be fulfilled.

VI. Boss Sets Another Expectation

Encouraged by the success of the subordinate, the boss's confidence in his own abilities was reinforced and he became more clear and confident about his own ability to become a Pygmalion. He set another expectation for the same subordinate and for another subordinate and followed the cycle shown in Figure 1. This becomes a continuous practice for many bosses, and such bosses become Pygmalions.

A few factors are essential for the success of Pygmalion effect:

1. *The image of the person who is setting expectations (Pygmalion).* The success largely depends on the image of the Pygmalion (the boss in the above example). The boss should be perceived as a caring, open, empathic, and trusting person by the subordinate. It is essential that the expectations be seen as genuine, not a manipulative way for either pleasing the subordinate or for achieving higher output. The perceived credibility of the boss, therefore, is critical for the acceptance of the expectation by the subordinate.

2. *The self-esteem and motivators of the subordinate.* A prior appreciation of the background of the person for whom the expectations are set is very useful. Knowledge of his or her intra-personal and interpersonal needs, aptitudes, and motivators helps in setting expectations. Positive self-esteem of the subordinate is highly helpful; therefore, expectations should be set after knowing the level of self-esteem and making planned efforts for its enhancement.

3. *The nature/level of expectations.* The expectations, as far as possible, should be aligned to the personal mission or goals of the subordinate. He or she should see the personal gains, along with the organizational gains. If the expectation is perceived as too high, the subordinate may become frightened and may not accept the expectation as willingly. He or she may not feel motivated to achieve, and therefore chances are that he or she will not make sincere efforts to reach the goal.

    If the expectation is too low, the subordinate's self-esteem may be hurt or he or she will find the task too easy, may not feel highly motivated, and may not give optimal attention and effort. The expectation should be moderately high, keeping in view some benchmark above the perceived current capability of the subordinate.

4. *The climate and style of conveying expectations.* The climate in which the expectations are communicated has to be conducive, friendly, courteous, and supportive. The recipient has to be given full freedom to seek clarification and accept or reject the proposition fearlessly. Thus, the boss's language, tone, and body language all should be appropriate and congruent.

5. *Input by the Pygmalion.* The person setting expectations should be ready to provide conceptual and/or professional inputs, clarification, or information to the subordinate whenever required, especially at the time of conveying the expectation. If the boss is not confident and comfortable in doing so, he or she should give references, either from literature or another resource person. He or she should be willing to invest time and resources.

6. *Performance of the recipient or subordinate.* The subordinate has to systematically perform with full sincerity. According to an ancient Indian scripture, whatever is done with Vidya, Shradha, and Upanishada alone becomes effective. Vidya, Shradha, and Upanishada are Sanskrit words. *Vidya* means knowledge and skills; *shradha* means totality of positive attitudes; and *upanishada* means deep and meditative thinking on the concerned subject. Success will come when the subordinate is learning and using his or her knowledge and skills with Shradha and Upanishada.

   A true Pygmalion, therefore, focuses not only on the behavior or actions of a subordinate, but also on the person's becoming a good human being.

7. *Feedback.* Subordinates should receive periodic feedback from the boss. The feedback should be aimed at improving the subordinate, specific, and descriptive. The subordinate should be appreciated for good performance and behavior and criticized constructively for any slippage, failures, and poor quality. The boss should be careful in all interactions, as expectations are conveyed in every interaction.

The Pygmalion Case

It was 1973. Amit and Sunil joined CEH Ltd., Ranchi (India), as engineer probationers two months ago, after the All India Recruitment Test and an interview. Both were metallurgical engineering graduates with about one year of experience in private companies. They were posted in the steel foundry. CEH was one of the most prestigious PSUs, having around 24,000 employees and excellent infrastructure and facilities, both in the factory and in the township.

One morning, the boss called and handed over to them a transfer letter. With that both were transferred to Corporate Management Services Division immediately. They had to report to Dr. P. Dutt, chief of Management Services.

Posting in the corporate office was considered to be very prestigious. When they worked in the foundry, the two men used to envy those smart guys. They had been disappointed because, as metallurgists, they had to work inside the factory only. This transfer, therefore, excited them, and they also started dreaming.

When they reached the corporate office, the P.A. went inside. A door opened and a smiling face welcomed and invited them into the room. This was Dr. Dutt. His very pleasant demeanor dispelled their many fears and apprehensions. He said, "Young men, I have brought you here for a very important assignment, not for training. Our systems people have developed an integrated computerized materials management system for the entire company, and this system is being implemented beginning tomorrow only in HMBP. You have to ensure its smooth implementation."

Hearing this, both were dumbfounded! When Dr. Dutt asked, "Is it okay?" they gathered courage. Amit said, "But, sir, we both are metallurgists. We neither know materials management nor systems." Sunil added, "In this type of company, computerization will invite a lot of resistance." He enumerated the examples of L.I.C. and other companies, where employees had gone on strike on this account.

Dr. Dutt listened attentively and, still smiling, asked, "Have you studied any papers on management in your institute?" Sunil stated that there was one subject but very little on materials management. Dr. Dutt asked, "Do you remember any topics or words?"

They replied, "ABC analysis, minimum level, maximum level. . . ." Dr. Dutt quipped, "That's what materials management is. I know I have chosen the right people. You need not know the entire scope of materials management. Nobody does!" This gave them their breath back.

Sunil said, "But sir, we know nothing about the system." Dr. Dutt took out a folding blackboard from his drawer, hung it on the wall, and explained, "You're smart, intelligent young men. You can pick it up fast. I could orient you within half an hour." With the help of simple questions, he explained all stages, documents, and flow of documents in the materials management system within 30 or 40 minutes. In between he also explained a few conceptual issues.

Just as they were to leave, somewhat comforted, the telephone rang. It was a call from Mr. Deewan, head of Materials Management of HMBP. He was requesting Dr. Dutt to postpone the implementation by about a month. "First, let us train all our people—and then implement," he said.

Dr. Dutt replied, "Deewan, you need not worry. I am sending two of my experts tomorrow. They will stay in your plant and solve all the problems on the spot."

Amit and Sunil did not expect such an elevated designation from the boss. They felt encouraged and turned back to leave. As they were leaving, Dr. Dutt stopped them and said, "I wish you all the best, young men! But I don't want to see you within the boundary of the corporate office for the next week."

Back in their room, they exchanged heated words, "Why didn't we refuse this transfer?!"

Soon they were on the task. They went to the system analyst, asked for blank copies of formats, and requested that he explain them. He clarified for them. They went back to their rooms again, did a lot of practice, borrowing books from the library, studying the whole night, and briefing each other. Another round of practice, some doubts—and they went to the system analyst's home at 6 in the morning, riding on a single bicycle. Again, they asked for some clarification.

On their reaching HMBP that morning, the head of materials management gave a lukewarm welcome and guided them to his people, who were to use the new system. They found two chairs and sat down. They were met with suspicion; some people were not asking anything from them, and some were willing to take anything from them. Some were dumping all their reports and papers on Amit and Sunil to do the work for them. They were not accustomed to documenting the process nor to a discipline where each bit of data was to be filled in on a form at exactly the appropriate places with the desired number of characters and decimal points. It was not an easy task. Amit and Sunil had to use a variety of strategies—instructing, demonstrating, explaining, teaching, and, of course, sometimes doing a process themselves. The next day, Amit and Sunil started working independently with different small groups to teach them the process.

On occasion, they ran into problems for which they didn't know the precise solutions. When this happened, they would call each other and discuss the problems and find the answers. On a few critical occasions, one of them would sneak into a corner and make a call to the system analyst and ask for the solution. Since they were not allowed to enter the corporate office, they had no other option. It was a difficult task, considering that they were new to corporate management systems and could not learn everything they needed to learn from the systems people in one day. Every evening, they met to share the problems they had experienced and how they had solved them. They also studied books and journals to develop a conceptual background.

They succeeded in expediting the task to the best of their ability and felt quite satisfied. By the last day, all the materials management people—storekeepers, clerks, supervisors, and officers—had gained respect for them. They all gathered to wish them well, gave their compliments, and assured them that they would do their best to get the system running per the new guidelines; a bond had developed that lasted over many years. It was a great achievement and provided a great sense of fulfillment. Amit and Sunil started feeling the difference immediately.

After one week, they went back to Dr. Dutt. The room opened again with Dutt's smile: "Congratulations!" He called a meeting and gave his heartiest appreciation to them.

Later on, when Amit read about the Pygmalion Effect, he realized that Dr. Dutt was Pygmalion.

Self-Powered Vehicles
Learning to Work as a Group

Activity Summary

A hands-on innovation task that allows groups to develop better communication strategies to improve their problem-solving ability.

Goals

- To develop means of identifying issues as a group.

- To develop ways to innovate to reach solutions.

- To appreciate creativity as a necessary component to business problem solving.

Group Size

Any number of groups of 4 to 6.

Time Required

75 minutes.

Materials

For Each Subgroup

- One box to contain items.

- Two 12-inch rulers.

- One modified traditional snapping mousetrap.

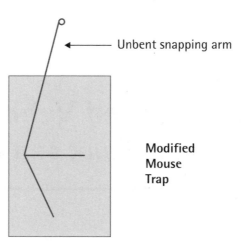

← Unbent snapping arm

Modified Mouse Trap

- One Self-Powered Vehicles Observer Sheet.

- One finishing nail (small).

- Two small rulers (6 inches) with holes.

- One 12-inch piece of string.

- Two unsharpened *round* pencils (the pencils must fit into the holes on the 6-inch rulers).

- Four pencil eraser tops.

- Four used CDs.

On a Separate Table

- X-acto® knife.

- Hot glue gun.

- Small, lightweight hammer.

- Extra modified mousetraps and other items from the list above.

For the Facilitator

- Self-Powered Vehicles: Hints for Building, cut into strips, one set of strips per team.

- Envelope for holding strips and a way to separate the strips by team.

- Flip chart and markers.

- Masking tape.

- A tape measure.

Physical Setting

A room large enough for each group to work at a separate table and a small table labeled "Spare Parts." An outlet will be needed near the spare parts table. A flat surface on which the vehicles may race (an uncarpeted hallway works well).

Facilitating Risk Rating

Moderate.

Preparation

1. Prepare a box for each group containing the parts listed above. Modify the mousetraps by sliding one side of the snapping arm off the base and unbending the arm so that it stretches out behind the mousetrap (see figure).

2. Copy the Self-Powered Vehicles: Hints for Building, cut the sheets into strips, and place them in small envelopes (one per group) you can easily carry around with you. Be sure the groups are identified in some way when you begin the activity.

3. Prepare a flip chart with the objective of the task: "Create a self-powered vehicle able to travel, under its own power, at least 5 feet." Do not reveal the objective just yet.

4. Set extra parts on the table and plug in the hot glue gun.

Process

1. Establish the groups and designate them in some way (green, blue, red; one, two, three) and assign an observer in each group. Give the observers each a Self-Powered Vehicles Observer Sheet. Provide each group with a box containing parts.

2. Display the objective of the task. Explain to the groups that the only requirement is contained in the objective, but if there is more than one group, the one whose vehicle goes the longest distance will be considered the "winner." Explain to the groups that the spare parts table is there for their use. Remind them that the hot glue gun is plugged in and is hot.

3. Explain that they will have about 40 minutes to complete the task. Answer any questions and then tell the participants they may begin.

4. Meander around the room and check in with every observer to answer any questions. Let the groups work through some basic group dynamics, then hand out one slip containing the most relevant hint for each of the groups. Place the hint next to the person acting in a leadership context in each group.
   (15 minutes.)

5. After 10 more minutes, hand out another relevant hint. Place the second hint next to the person most frustrated, yet engaged, in each group. Be sure every team receives a hint at approximately the same time. Additional hints should be placed in the center of a group as you feel they could be helpful.
   (30 minutes.)

6. When a team completes a vehicle, start the applause if they have not done so. Encourage the other teams to go ahead and finish. Allow the groups to test their completed vehicles.
   (20 minutes.)

7. When all teams are finished, establish a start line with masking tape and test all vehicles, one at a time, marking their end points. Measure distance covered, not speed.

8. Bring the full group back together. Ask the observers to comment on what they have observed, responding to each question on the sheet. After the observers have finished, ask the participants what turning points they felt in their groups.

   • What issues or challenges did you face?

   • How did you innovate in order to reach a solution?

   • Creativity is often described as seeing common things in unusual ways and in different relationships to each other. Where was creativity a component in your problem solving?
   (10 minutes.)

Variations

• Group the technically minded or the analytics together and observe and compare their process to that of the creative-leaning minds in the room.

• Have the groups select leaders prior to the start of the task, after they know the objective. Observe the leadership qualities displayed and discuss what was most effective about the style used.

Submitted by Pat Murphy.

Pat Murphy, Ph.D., *is the author of several articles on assessment and multimedia environments. Her work in leadership development and group dynamics has led her to the development of challenging, mind-engaging tasks to be used in the observation of human behavior. She holds a master's degree from Boston College and a doctorate from the University of Maryland.*

Self-Powered Vehicles Observer Sheet

Instructions: List behaviors you see and conversations you hear under each question that will provide you with examples from which to draw in a later discussion. Try to be as specific as possible.

How did the leader establish dominance (words, actions)?

Was the leader challenged? If so, what were the current dynamics at the time of challenge?

Did the group create barriers or boundaries to its success that were unnecessary (i.e., required four wheels)? What barriers were created? How were the barriers later broken?

When was innovation required?

What occurred to the energy level of the group when stumbling blocks were fully realized (remark on individuals' reactions)?

Did leadership ever change hands? If so, why and how?

Self-Powered Vehicles: Hints for Building

Instructions: Make one copy of this handout for each team. Cut the hints apart so that you can deliver one hint at a time to a team.

The "chassis" sits in the middle.

Nail's an anchor.

Potential energy in a string catapulting the vehicle forward.

With this in your house, mice are no longer free, but pulling back and winding will set things in motion.

Soda Can Carry
Building a Team

Activity Summary

A fun, energizing exercise to demonstrate the importance of teamwork.

Goals

- To demonstrate team dynamics in a fun, upbeat activity.

- To enable the participants to recognize supportive as well as dysfunctional behaviors on teams.

- To create a safe space to discuss potential team dynamics and how they can help or hinder the team's work.

Group Size

Several groups of 4 to 8 people.

Time Required

40 minutes.

Materials

- One full soda can for each team.

- Four pencils for each team.

- Two thick rubber bands (strong enough to go around a can and lift it) for each team.

- Fifteen-inch piece of string for each person.

- Prepared easel paper or whiteboard to "score" the activity.

- Masking tape.

Physical Setting

A space large enough to break the team into smaller groups as well as long enough to carry the soda can from one side of the room to another. Clearly mark Point A and Point B (with masking tape) on the floor (see Step 3).

Facilitating Risk Rating

Moderate.

Process

1. Introduce this activity as a way to demonstrate the importance of teamwork.

2. Divide the group into teams of 4 to 8 people. Hand out the materials for each team and give them the task: To carry their soda cans from one side of the room to the other side under the following conditions (which you may wish to post on a flip chart or whiteboard):

   - The soda can is "contaminated"; therefore no one can come within six inches of the can. If someone does, then the team will be fined 10 points for each violation.

   - You cannot upset or turn the can upside down at any time during the exercise. If this happens, then the team will be fined 20 points for each violation.

   - You cannot use any other materials than those provided to complete the task. If you do, then the team will be fined 30 points for each violation.

   - Finally, every member of the team must be involved in the carry.

   - Each team that successfully carries its soda can from one side of the room to the other side earns 200 points.

3. Provide a "starting" line (Point A) and "finish" line (Point B) by putting tape on the floor.

4. Ask if there are any questions and clarify if necessary. Let them know this is not a timed task (no extra points for speed), but that you will stop the activity in 20 minutes.

5. Allow the participants to complete the activity. Circulate and observe the team dynamics so you can comment during the debriefing.

6. After all have successfully carried their soda cans to the finish line, debrief the activity:

   - What did you like most about this activity?

   - What made your team successful?

   - How did individual team members help each other?

   - How did you make decisions?

   - What could you have done differently?

   - What did you learn from this activity that you can use in the workplace?

7. Summarize the learnings and ask:

   - How might you apply these lessons to your own team's work?

Variation

Perform this activity in two rounds:

- *Round 1:* Identify one person per group as the "team leader" and the rest as "team members." Have the team leader "direct" all the activities. (Even more fun, blindfold all the team members!)

- *Round 2:* Allow the team to fully participate in solving the problem.

Submitted by Kristin J. Arnold.

Kristin J. Arnold, CPF, CMC, CSP, *helps corporations, government, and non-profit organizations build high performance teams. She specializes in facilitating for executives and their teams, as well as training others to facilitate teams to higher levels of performance. An accomplished author, as well as a featured columnist in the* Daily Press, *Arnold is regarded as an expert in process and team development. She graduated with high honors from the U.S. Coast Guard Academy and earned her MBA with an emphasis on marketing strategy from St. Mary's College in California.*

Picture This
Introducing Participants

Activity Summary

An easy, effective, and non-intimidating icebreaker to encourage group participation during introductions.

Goals

- To provide a creative way for participants to introduce themselves to a group.

- To provide a way to learn more in-depth information about one another during introductions.

Group Size

10 to 25 participants.

Time

25 to 60 minutes, depending on the number of participants.

Materials

Three to five decks of "Expression" cards (available from www.ettq.ou.edu) or 75 to 100 pictures or drawings of random items. Create cards by cutting out photos from magazine articles, greeting cards, and postcards that show people of all ages in a variety of different settings. Paste these to index cards.

Physical Setting

Any place large enough for all members of the group to sit. A table is needed to display the cards in a manner for the group to see all of them at the beginning.

Facilitating Risk Rating

Low.

Process

1. Have participants sit around a table (if there are more than 10 participants, form several groups). Spread the Expression cards out on a table so that everyone can see them. Invite participants to choose three cards each (and also take three yourself). They should take one card each to:

    *   Represent their personality;

    *   Represent how they feel about the training topic; and

    *   Represent a memorable experience they have had.

    You may want to change the categories, depending on your goals for the program, and also may wish to post the three categories for the participants.

2. Once all participants have selected their cards, invite participants to show their cards to the other group members, sharing their reasons for selecting each card. After everyone has shared his or her cards, share your three cards with the large group.

3. If you wish, you may process this activity further by using these questions, either in small groups or with the total group:

    *   How did you decide what information about yourself to share?

    *   How much risk was involved in sharing your information?

    *   How did the group respond to what you said?

    *   Were there any surprises, either in how others reacted to your information or in what you learned about others?

    *   How can you take what we discovered in this activity and use it during this training session?

    *   What would you do differently if you did this activity again?

Trainer's Note

This simple activity can invite participants to introduce themselves in a way that you (and the group) will find out more in-depth information—beyond the typical short answers. The cards give participants a reason to talk about a scuba diving trip they took to Aruba or other memorable experiences. From a facilitator's mindset, the participants' answers give a better picture of who's in the group and how better to relate to the group as a whole.

Variations

You may use variations of the activity with the following goals in mind also:

- *Splitting teams into small groups:* Select cards with certain similar characteristics that the participants will have to decide how they fit together. An example might be to pick out all the animal cards or all of the cards with buildings on them or something similar. Then ask the participants as a group to find the appropriate cards and explain why they fit.

- *Check-in:* To find out how participants are feeling about a particular issue, ask them to choose two cards that represent their thoughts or feelings at that moment. Allow time for discussion in the group.

- *Closing activity:* Ask each participant to choose a card that gives his or her perspective of what occurred during a certain activity. Allow time for discussion and feedback.

- *Appreciation activity:* Ask each participant to think about the person sitting on his or her right and to pick a card that represent something that he or she has appreciated about that person during the program.

Submitted by Carrie Reilly and Mark Rose.

Carrie Reilly *is a training specialist for Executive Training ~ Team Quest at The University of Oklahoma. She has worked as a facilitator in a series of training videos,* Trainer Games in Action, *which show how trainers can use activities to help the retention of information for their learners.*

Mark Rose *is a training coordinator for Enogex, a natural gas processing company. He has worked as a facilitator in a series of training videos,* Trainer Games in Action, *which show how trainers can use activities to help the retention of information for their learners.*

Word Cards
Reinforcing Learning

Activity Summary

A series of short training exercises that energize participants while reinforcing curriculum concepts.

Goals

- To reinforce concepts learned in the training through group involvement.

- To provide a change of pace and raise group energy during training.

- To provide a useful transition between modules in a training curriculum.

Group Size

15 to 50 participants.

Time Required

20 to 30 minutes.

Materials

- Flip chart and paper.

- Felt-tipped markers.

- Masking tape.

- 4-inch by 6-inch index cards, one per person.

- Blank paper and pens for participants.

Physical Setting

Participants should be seated in table groups of 4 to 8 people.

Facilitating Risk Rating

Low.

Trainer's Note

This activity can be used after lunch or another break, after completing a discrete module of training, or any time the group energy is low.

Process

1. Distribute index cards, blank sheets of paper, and pens to each group, one each per person. Ask participants to take a moment to think of words that describe the training they have just experienced. These can be words from the actual content of the curriculum or words that describe their experience of it. Have each participant pick one word and write it on an index card.

2. Ask each group to collect the word cards at their table and pass them to the next table. Each group of word cards should rotate one table, so that Group A gives their cards to Group B, Group B gives their cards to Group C, Group C gives their cards to Group D, and so on.

3. Instruct each group to work together to creatively form a sentence using the words given to them by the neighboring table. They can add more words to fill out the sentence, but they should not delete any of the words they were given (a rare exception would be if someone writes a word that is inappropriate or offensive). For example, the list of words might be:

   - Communication.

   - Listening.

   - Experience.

   - Leadership.

   - Respect.

   The resulting sentence might read:

   "The *Leadership* can *Experience* better *Communication* by *Listening* with *Respect.*"
   (10 minutes.)

4. Give each group a marker and a piece of flip-chart paper and ask them to write their group's sentence in large letters.

5. One at a time, have groups present their sentences to the whole group and tape their flip-chart paper to the wall.

6. Relate the themes from the sentences back to the curriculum material or use them to transition into the next module of the training.

Variations

- *Charades Variation.* Repeat Steps 1 and 2 (to the point where each group has received a set of word cards from another table). Add the instruction that each group must talk quietly so that people at other tables won't know what their words are. Tell each group to select *one word* from the cards that they will act out in silent pantomime. Give them 1 minute to plan their charade and then have each group in turn act out their charade in front of the whole group, which tries to guess the word. The group that passed the word being acted out is, of course, disqualified from guessing during that round.

- *Pictionary® Variation.* Repeat Steps 1 and 2 (to the point where each group has a set of word cards from another table). Add the instruction that each group must talk quietly so that others won't know what their words are. Tell each table group to select *one word* from the cards. Explain that one of the groups will depict the word using pictures but no letters or symbols (like the board game Pictionary). Give them a minute to discuss ideas and select a designated "artist." In turn, each group's artist will draw a picture in front of the whole group, which tries to guess the word. The group that passed the word being drawn is, of course, disqualified from guessing during that round.

- *Play-Doh® Variation.* This variation is played simultaneously at each table instead of between groups. It also requires extra materials: several small cans of Play-Doh or pieces of modeling clay. Repeat Steps 1 and 2 above (to the point at which each group has a set of word cards from another table). Add the instruction that the cards must be passed *face down* so no one sees them. Before anyone looks at the cards, each group must select one person to be the designated "artist." The artist then looks at all the cards, without showing them to his or her tablemates, and selects *one word* to depict using the Play-Doh or modeling clay. As the artist works, tablemates try to guess what the word is. When all groups have finished, each artist can share his or her sculpture with the large group.

Submitted by Steve Sphar.

Steve Sphar, J.D., *is an internal organization development consultant for the California State Teachers' Retirement System. He has counseled managers and employees in both the private and public sectors for twenty years. He is a frequent contributor to professional publications, including the* Annuals *and the McGraw-Hill* Training and Performance Sourcebooks.

Lyrical Look
Finding Insight in Songs

Activity Summary

Trainees analyze song lyrics to gain topical insights.

Goals

- To visualize metaphors for the training topic.

- To create a multidimensional view of the training topic.

Group Size

Any number, in groups of 2 to 5.

Time Required

10 to 20 minutes.

Materials

- CD or audio tape player.

- CDs with the selected songs (check copyright restrictions).

- Song lyrics sheets (one per trainee group).

Physical Setting

Any training environment in which music can be played and heard by all the participants.

Facilitating Risk Rating

Low.

Trainer's Note

Every song has a message. Song lyrics, when matched with an appropriate training topic, are wonderful tools for fostering discussion, but be sure to obtain proper approvals. Music, just like real estate, is owned. Where real estate is tangible, music is considered "intellectual" property, providing the owner of the copyright with all the rights and considerations that any owner can claim, including the right to sell or rent the property. Copyright law is complicated and, if you have any doubts about the legality of your usage, seek the advice of legal counsel.

Fortunately, obtaining copyright approval is fairly simple. Song owners register their songs with organizations that collect royalties for them, including the two most common North America organizations: ASCAP and BMI. These organizations sell "site licenses" and song list approvals to businesses and individuals who "rent" the rights to specific songs. If the location you will train in already has a site license, your usage might be covered. If not, ASCAP and BMI will gladly help you purchase a license for a reasonable fee. The organizations can be reached at the addresses listed below:

The American Society of Composers, Authors, and Publishers (ASCAP); One Lincoln Plaza; New York, NY 10023; (212) 621-6000; www.ascap.com

Broadcast Music Inc. (BMI); 320 West 57th Street; New York, NY 10019-3790; (212) 586-2000; www.bmi.com

Preparation

Prior to the session, select pop songs that relate to the training topic. For example, "Respect" by Aretha Franklin, "True Colors" by Cyndi Lauper, "A Matter of Trust" by Billy Joel, and "Respect Yourself" by Madonna could all be used for a discussion about gender equality. Make copies of the song lyrics to use as handouts.

Process

1. Divide the participants into subgroups and assign a song to each. Distribute the appropriate lyric sheets to each subgroup.

2. Ask the subgroups to determine how their songs relate to the training topic. *(5 minutes.)*

3. Bring the participants back together. Ask each subgroup, in turn, to share ways in which their song relates to the training topic. When there is a break in the discussion, play the song (or a portion if time is limited). Ask the following questions:

    •   How did your song relate to the training topic?

    •   How do all the songs we have heard relate to the topic?

    •   How are the songs similar? Different?

    •   How do the relationships among the songs add to your knowledge of the subject?

    •   What conclusions can you draw from what's in the songs?

    •   What are you going to do differently as a result of what you have learned?

4. Continue the training while periodically referring to the trainees' discussion observations.

5. Play the songs again at appropriate moments during the training to reinforce the activity.

Variations

•   Use the activity to enhance discussion or conclude the topic.

•   Assign the exercise as homework and instruct the participants to find songs relating to the topic and bring them to the next session.

Submitted by Lenn Millbower.

Lenn Millbower, BM, MA, *the Learnertainment® Trainer, is an expert in the use of show biz techniques to enhance learning. He is the author of* Show Biz Training, Cartoons for Trainers, Training with a Beat, *the* ASTD InfoLine: Music as a Training Tool *and* Game Show Themes for Trainers; *an instructional designer and facilitator; a musical composer; a magician and comedian; a professional speaker; and the president of Offbeat Training®, where he helps organizations reinvent their training through show biz techniques that increase retention and decrease expense.*

Critical Reflection Relay
Reviewing What Was Learned

Activity Summary

Using critical reflection to review content.

Goals

- To reflect on a learning experience and solidify the learning objectives.

- To actively engage with other learners in a critical reflection process.

Group Size

8 to 24 participants.

Time Required

60 to 90 minutes, depending on group size.

Materials

- One copy of the Critical Reflection Relay Worksheet for each participant.

- Two large flip-chart sheets made by the facilitator in advance of the training session. Each sheet should be identified as belonging to one of the teams and be numbered from 1 to 12.

- Two easels or a wall space large enough to post the Critical Reflection Relay Team flip-chart sheets.

- Pens or pencils for participants.

- Extra paper for teams.

The 2006 Pfeiffer Annual: Training

- A marking pen for each team.

- Masking tape.

- Pencils or pens.

Physical Setting

A room large enough for participant seating in a U shape with enough space inside the U for two teams to line up side-by-side.

Facilitating Risk Rating

Low.

Preparation

1. List, for your own use, the twelve most critical learning points from the training just completed. You will use this to "grade" the results.

2. Post two relay team sheets, numbered 1 to 12 in front of the room.

Process

1. Introduce the learning activity by reviewing the adult learning principle of Critical Reflection, explaining how the principle enhances the learning process. State that Critical Reflection is a major principle of the theory of adult learning. Adults learn when they reflect on their learning experiences and are able to internalize the meaning of the knowledge, skills, behaviors, or attitudes that are being taught. Say to participants: "This activity will allow you to actively reflect on your learning experience."

2. Give Critical Reflection Relay Worksheets and pens or pencils to participants and instruct them to think of three learning points that were taught previously and to write the three learning points on their worksheets. *(6 minutes.)*

3. Now divide the group into two teams, give them extra paper, and have them meet where they cannot be overheard and agree on the twelve most critical learning points based on what they wrote on their individual worksheets. *(20 minutes.)*

4. Ask the participants in each team to stand up and form a single line according to the dates of their birth. They should take their worksheets along.

5. Ask each team to line up in front of one of the flip-chart sheets in front of the room and hand the person first in each line a marking pen. Explain that they will be filling out the posted sheets as relay teams. Each person will, in turn, write one of his or her team's learning points on the sheet, hand the marker to the next person in line, and go to the end of the line.

6. Start the relay. Each team (like a relay) tries to be the first to fill in all twelve learning points on the team sheet.
    (15 minutes.)

7. When everyone has had a turn (if groups are small, people may repeat) or when one group has all twelve learning points you have listed yourself, ask participants to take their seats. Choose one of the participants to come forward and to circle one of the learning points on the team relay sheet and to spend 1 minute describing why that learning point is important or meaningful to him or her.

8. Ask the presenter to choose another participant to come forward, circle a learning concept, and explain its meaning to the group. Continue this process until all participants have had the opportunity to share in front of the group.
    (30 minutes.)

9. Conclude the activity by asking the following questions:

    *   What are your reactions to this activity?

    *   What connections can you make between critical reflection and learning?

    *   What major points or principles summarize this activity?

    *   How will you use critical reflection in future training opportunities?
    (10 minutes.)

Variations

*   Prizes may be awarded to the team that wins the relay race.

*   Pairs can come up with a role play to illustrate some of the learning points, and other participants can guess which learning points are being demonstrated in the role play.

*   For larger groups, more than two teams can participate.

Submitted by Bonnie Jameson.

Bonnie Jameson, M.S., *is a designer, trainer, and facilitator in all areas of human resource development and organization development. She is an associate professor at California State University at Hayward, California, where she designs and teaches courses in the Nonprofit Management Certificate Program. She co-designed and facilitates the Training for Trainers Certificate Program. Ms. Jameson's structured experiences have been published in the* Pfeiffer Annuals. *She co-authored* Inspiring Fabled Service *(Jossey-Bass, 1996) with Betsy Sanders.*

Critical Reflection Relay Worksheet

Instructions: Think about what you have learned so far in the workshop. In the space below, write three important learning points you have experienced so far in this training.

1.

2.

3.

Keep these learning points in mind. You will share this information to help your team win a relay race.

Rolling for Review
Reviewing Key Learning Points

Activity Summary

A game-show-style activity to review key learning points.

Goals

- To start participants thinking about what they have learned during the training session and to review and revisit the key learning points.

- To end the day on a high note with friendly competition, laughter, and an enthusiastic way to review major points.

Group Size

20 to 500 people in audience, represented by 3 to 6 players who roll the dice.

Time Required

Approximately 15 minutes.

Materials

- A list of thirteen numbered questions of key learning points created by the facilitator in advance for his or her own use.

- Pens or pencils for participants.

- Large fuzzy dice or a pair of square boxes with black dots drawn on them to resemble dice for each group (the size is proportional to the audience size for easy viewing).

- Flip chart and markers for keeping score.

The 2006 Pfeiffer Annual: Training

Physical Setting

Conference room or any space large enough to throw the dice and have 6 to 12 people stand in front or on the stage at once.

Facilitating Risk Rating

Moderate.

Process

1. Select thirteen questions from the training materials for review at the end of the session. Do not hand these out or post them, as you want everyone to hear the questions at the same time.

2. Divide the group in half where they are seated and ask for either 3 or 6 representatives from each group to come to the front.

3. Alternate giving the dice to team representatives to roll on the floor. In each case, ask what number came up on the dice and ask the review question with the corresponding number. If the number has already been selected, then choose the next closest number or have the person roll again.

4. Ask someone from the audience to keep score of each team's correct answers on the flip chart so everyone can see.

5. The person who rolls the dice is responsible for answering the question. He or she may ask a fellow team representative or anyone in the audience from his or her team to help find the answer to the question that comes up.

6. If one team cannot answer the question, give the other team a chance to answer it before that team rolls the dice and answers a question.

7. Ask the first twelve questions. In case there is a tie, ask Question 13 as a tie breaker and allow everyone an opportunity to yell out the correct answer. The first person who answers correctly represents the winning team.

Submitted by Gail Hahn.

Gail Hahn, MA, CSP, CPRP, CLL, *is the CEO (chief energizing officer) of Fun*cilitators and author of* Hit Any Key to Energize Your Life, *as well as contributing author to over seventeen other books. She is an international keynote speaker, corporate trainer, and an award-winning team-building facilitator who is the only person in the world holding all four authentic certifications of Speaking Professional, Parks and Recreation Professional, Laugh Leader, and Strength Deployment Inventory® Facilitator.*

Keynote Closer
Polishing the Gems

Activity Summary

An integration activity designed to process learnings and provide closure at the end of a training experience.

Goals

- To provide participants an opportunity to review and summarize their learnings ("the Gems") from a training experience.

- To teach a quick and effective way to deliver a "polished" speech.

- To allow each person to share his or her key learnings with the rest of the group.

Group Size

Up to 20 participants who have just completed a training session.

Time Required

60 to 120 minutes, depending on the group size.

Materials

- Chairs and writing surfaces for all participants.

- Pens and/or pencils and paper for all participants.

- One Keynote Closer Handout for each participant.

- Timer or stopwatch.

Physical Setting

A room set up classroom style with space for individuals to speak to the group from the front.

Facilitating Risk Rating

Moderate to High.

Process

1. Remind the group that the workshop will be ending soon, and say that they will have an opportunity to process their overall learnings.

2. Explain to the group that they are going to prepare and deliver 3-minute keynote speeches that summarize their learnings from the training experience.

3. Give each participant a Keynote Closer Handout, extra paper, and a pen or pencil and ask that they follow the instructions on the handout.

4. Inform the group they will have 30 minutes to complete the handout and prepare to give their 3-minute keynote speeches.
   (30 minutes.)

5. After the 30 minutes, say to the group, "We have a number of featured guests today who will honor us with keynote addresses; let's welcome each one as he or she comes up with a standing ovation."

6. Solicit an initial volunteer from the group to come to the front of the room. Ask the group to give the person a standing ovation.

7. At the end of the first 3-minute keynote, have that person select the next speaker. Continue until all have given their speeches.

8. End with a group standing ovation for all of the speakers.

9. Debrief the experience with the following questions:

   • What did you notice when you heard other participants' learnings?

   • What were the similarities? Differences?

   • What was it like having to articulate (that is, "polish") the significance of your learnings?

- How could you use your "keynote" after this training?

- What will you do differently during your next training session or back on the job as a result of this experience?

Variations

- Use this as an opening activity and ask participants to reflect on learnings from past training experiences.

- Have participants pair up and practice their keynotes with partners prior to delivering them to the group.

_____

Submitted by Frank A. Prince

Frank A. Prince *is president and founder of Unleash Your Mind LLC, a consulting firm focused on applied innovation within corporations. He is the author of* C & the Box: A Paradigm Parable, *published by Pfeiffer. He is also the voice of and inventor of "Speed Sleep," an innovative audio CD that accelerates sleep and creativity at a subconscious level.*

Keynote Closer Handout

This handout is designed to help you organize your learnings from the training session into a 3-minute keynote address. Your keynote will be made up of three parts:

- The Introduction.

- The Key Learnings—"The Gems."

- The Summary.

Remember to keep your keynote address simple and to the point.

STEP ONE: Reflect on the training experience from the beginning until now. Create a list below of as many learnings, insights, discoveries, and surprises as you can.

STEP TWO: Circle three key learnings from the list above—ones that you would like to share with the group.

STEP THREE: Write a brief description of each of your top three learnings below and briefly explain why each is significant.

Learning 1:

Learning 2:

Learning 3:

STEP FOUR: Write your introduction. The introduction will headline the three learnings you plan to talk about and generate interest, e.g., "Hi, I'm here to . . ." or "Have you ever. . . ?" or "How many of you have. . .?"

STEP FIVE: Write your closing. The closing will summarize your three key learnings and what they will do for you back on the job or in your life, e.g., "In summary, ..."

STEP SIX: Put it all together into your 3-minute keynote. On a blank piece of paper, rewrite your introduction, your three key learnings, and your summary.

STEP SEVEN: Prepare to deliver your keynote to the group. After reviewing it a few times in your head, say it softly out loud without your notes.

STEP EIGHT: Volunteer to go first and do it!

What Is Moral Character?
Defining Character

Activity Summary

An experiential activity that allows participants to determine the major traits of moral character and to rate themselves on a questionnaire developed to measure six common traits of moral character.

Goals

- To determine, as individuals and groups, the basic traits of moral character.

- To discuss the importance of moral character in how people interact and who they choose as leaders.

- To rate oneself on six common traits of moral character.

Group Size

Any number of groups of 3 to 5.

Time Required

60 to 75 minutes.

Materials

- One copy of the What Is Moral Character? Questionnaire for each participant.

- Paper and a pencil for each participant.

- A flip chart and marker for each small group.

- Masking tape.

Physical Setting

A room large enough for several groups to work without disturbing one another. Writing surfaces should be provided. Wall space is required for posting flip-chart sheets.

Facilitating Risk Rating

Moderate.

Process

1. Introduce the session by talking about the importance of moral character when choosing business leaders, political leaders, team members, friends, and even organizations to join:

    "A key criterion in selecting political and business leaders is their 'character.' One of the worst things you can say about a person is that he or she 'lacks character' or 'lacks moral character.' Apparently, moral character is of utmost important in judging others and in picking leaders, but what do we mean by moral character? What is moral character?"

2. Have participants form groups of 3 to 5 members each. Hand out paper and pencils. Ask the participants, "When you think of moral character, what are the traits that come to mind? More specifically, what are the five or six primary traits of moral character?" Ask each of the participants individually to list not more than five or six traits on a piece of paper. Allow approximately 5 minutes for the task, giving the participants a 1-minute warning before calling time.
    (10 minutes.)

3. Ask each small group to reach a consensus on four or six primary traits of moral character using the lists each person has created. Have each group member explain his or her individual list to the other group members. Once everyone has shared his or her list and rationale, the group is to arrive at a consensus of the five or six most critical traits of moral character. Tell them that they will have 10 to 15 minutes to complete their lists. While they are working, give each group a sheet of flip-chart paper and a marker.
    (10 to 15 minutes.)

4. After about 15 minutes of group discussion, ask the groups to write their final lists of traits on the flip-chart pages and tape them to the wall.

5. After all lists are posted, ask a spokesperson from each group to explain the traits on their list.
   (10 minutes.)

6. Once the spokespersons are finished, ask the participants how the lists from each group are similar or different. (Typically, the lists are very similar.) Ask why the lists are so similar.
   (10 to 15 minutes.)

7. Facilitate a discussion regarding similarities across the lists. State that if one would ask people in other countries to list the basic traits of moral character their lists would probably be very similar to those posted by the groups in the room. The traits generated by the groups would probably also be very similar to lists generated by teenagers, by religious groups, by elementary school teachers, and by government workers. Ask:

   • What does that mean?

   • Are there universal traits of moral character recognized by almost everyone? If so, why?

   • Why are these traits so very critical as to how we interact (and lead) across the world?
   (10 minutes.)

8. Hand out the What Is Moral Character? Questionnaire. The six traits on the list are those traits most often cited by groups who have completed this exercise. Ask participants to answer the questions on the questionnaire. When they finish, ask them to compute their scores.
   (10 minutes.)

9. Discuss the six traits of moral character evaluated on the questionnaire, either in small groups or in the large group. Summarize points on the flip chart.

Variations

• Participants could review their scores on the questionnaire and note their areas of strength and areas (or specific behaviors) that need improvement. Each person could then develop an action plan to improve his or her performance in one behavior.

• If participants are members of the same organization, the exercise could continue by having the participants discuss which of the behaviors on the questionnaire are practiced fully in the organization and on which behaviors the organization sometimes fall short. Discuss how the organization could improve its performance on those behaviors that need improvement.

Submitted by Homer H. Johnson.

Homer H. Johnson, Ph.D., *is a professor in the School of Business Administration at Loyola University in Chicago, where he teaches courses in values-based leadership and organization development. He is the author of numerous articles and several books, the most recent being* Essentials of Consulting, *co-authored with Linda Stroh.*

What Is Moral Character? Questionnaire

Instructions: Below are several statements. For each statement, determine the extent to which it describes your behavior by putting a number on the line in front of the statement. Use the following scoring key:

1 = This is something I try to do, although I often find it difficult to do it consistently.

2 = I am pretty consistent about doing this, although I sometimes slip.

3 = This is something I am very aware of and always do.

I . . .

_____ 1. Treat everyone with respect and dignity.

_____ 2. Accept responsibility for my actions and do not blame others.

_____ 3. Am willing to stand up for ideas, even if they are unpopular.

_____ 4. Am honest and truthful.

_____ 5. Treat everyone fairly and consistently.

_____ 6. Can be counted on; my word is good and I keep promises.

_____ 7. Am tolerant of differences and embrace diversity.

_____ 8. Am considerate of the feelings of others.

_____ 9. Do not give in to pressure or to others' opinions in order to avoid confrontation.

_____ 10. Make sure everyone is given an equal opportunity.

_____ 11. Am not afraid to stand up for what is right.

_____ 12. Genuinely care for others and act in their best interests.

_____ 13. Accept responsibility for important tasks and step forward when there is a need.

_____ 14. Do not play favorites. Do not give special consideration to a few.

_____ 15. Use respectful and appropriate language and behavior.

_____ 16. Do what is morally and ethically right.

1 = This is something I try to do, although I often find it difficult to do it consistently.

2 = I am pretty consistent about doing this, although I sometimes slip.

3 = This is something I am very aware of and always do.

I . . .

_____ 17. Take others' interests and concerns into account when making a decision.

_____ 18. Am someone you can count on when something important needs to be done.

Scoring

A. Respect and Dignity

Add responses to questions 1, 7, and 15 =   _____

B. Trust and Integrity

Add responses to questions 4, 6, and 16 =   _____

C. Fairness

Add responses to questions 5, 10, and 14 =   _____

D. Compassion and Caring

Add responses to questions 8, 12, and 17 =   _____

E. Courage

Add responses to questions 3, 9, and 11 =   _____

F. Responsibility and Accountability

Add responses to questions 2, 13, and 18 =   _____

Please note: This questionnaire is to be used for discussion purposes only, and the scores are not implied to be an accurate and valid assessment of the traits they represent.

How Do I Acknowledge Thee?
Giving Praise When Due

Activity Summary

Drawing on neurolinguistic programming theory, this activity heightens participants' awareness of the importance of appropriate acknowledgment in the workplace, specifically how to determine employees' preferences and then deliver acknowledgment in a way people prefer to receive it.

Goals

- To explore the importance of the role of acknowledgment in selecting and retaining employees.

- To discover how participants like to be acknowledged.

- To practice acknowledging others.

Group Size

1 to 100.

Time Required

2 to 2½ hours.

Materials

- One How Do I Acknowledge Thee? Handout for each participant.

- How Do I Acknowledge Thee? Lecturette for the facilitator.

- The "Meaningful Recognition" figure prepared ahead of time on flip-chart paper (see sample).

Meaningful Recognition

	Symbolic	Tangible
Public	Acknowledgment by the department head in an all-employee meeting, with a call up on stage	A plaque displayed in the lobby, with engraving of name and stellar accomplishments
Private	A sincere thank-you verbalized in a supervisory meeting for an *above and beyond* effort	A handwritten and hand-delivered letter on the manager's notepaper. with a copy to the file

- Writing paper and pens or pencils for participants.
- Flip chart and markers.
- Masking tape.

Physical Setting

Extremely flexible, anything from auditorium seating or tables to couches and pillows.

Facilitating Risk Rating

Low.

Process

1. Explain the goals of the activity, that is, learning to give appropriate recognition. Be sure to tie this to the business context for the session. Conclude by remarking on the importance of acknowledgement for *both* employer and employee.
   (5 minutes.)

2. Give copies of How Do I Acknowledge Thee? Handout to all participants and give them 5 minutes to read it in silence.
   (5 minutes.)

3. Ask participants to reflect on the following questions as you lead a brief discussion on the importance of recognition in the workplace and bring it home to participants that it is their issue, *whether on the giving or receiving end:*

   - If you supervise others, do you value their work?

   - How frequently do you tell or show your employees that you do value their work?

   - Do you think they *feel* that you appreciate their work?

   - When was the last time you expressed a "thank you" to each of your subordinates?

   - Do you believe that *your* work is valued by your supervisor?

   - What indications do you have that your work is valued or is not valued?

   - When was the last time your boss expressed appreciation for your efforts and the results you accomplish?

   - How did that expression of thanks meet your expectations?

   - Do you prefer public or private praise?

   - When have you been recognized in a way that was very meaningful to you?
   (15 minutes.)

4. Now say to participants:

   "We know that a little thanks goes a long way. Many managers, however, miss that it would have a greater impact if acknowledgments were expressed in a way that best suits the receiver. When it comes to gratitude and praise, one size does not fit all."

5. Tell this story, the theme of which may be familiar to participants:

   "A client hired a coach to map out a strategy for changing jobs. She loved her work as a lawyer, yet she did not think she was a good fit for her firm. Quite disgruntled, she described the long hours she put in, how hard she worked, and how unappreciated she felt. In the next breath she reported that she had just received a large bonus that would make many people drool. What is wrong with this picture?"

Wait for responses. Then say:

> "The answer is that she was not appreciated in a way that fit her mode. Her efforts had been written up in the firm's newsletter; an elegant and obviously expensive achievement plaque adorned the space above her desk. Even though she was the recipient of multiple forms of visual praise and monetary symbols of recognition, she still felt unappreciated.
>
> "Her boss, colleagues, and staff did not know that she craved verbal feedback. 'If only my boss would praise me,' she bemoaned. 'Just a miniscule utterance of appreciation from my staff! I don't go in for the big deals, just the daily stuff,' she explained. Anything verbal would have made her very happy.
>
> "The above situation is common in business and could have been avoided with proper training of managers in how to identify and deliver appropriate acknowledgment.
>
> "Two more considerations regarding acknowledgment are whether employees expect or respond best to private or public praise and whether they like to receive symbolic or tangible expressions of gratitude."

6. Present the "Meaningful Recognition" visual on the flip-chart pad. Ask participants for examples of other recognition that fit in the public and private, symbolic and tangible categories. Next, ask participants to examine each of the examples. Which might be best suited to people whose preferred mode of interpreting the world is visual? Auditory? Kinesthetic? Write the results on a flip chart.
   (20 minutes.)

7. Summarize the discussion and state that, while any form of acknowledgment is better than none at all, managers can learn how to praise in a way that ensures that employees recognize and value the message that is intended.

8. Now introduce the concepts of neurolinguistic programming by giving the How Do I Acknowledge Thee? Lecturette, being sure to emphasize the following information:

   - People have greater comfort in their preferred mode and feel stronger rapport with others who have the same mode or intentionally use their modes.

   - It is possible (and quite easy) to determine someone's preferred modes by watching their eye movements, which reveal the part of the brain where visual, auditory, and kinesthetic information is being accessed.

   - Eyes go up and to the right or left when a person accesses visual information.

- Eyes go to the side (toward the ears) to the right or left when a person accesses auditory information.

- Eyes go down and to the right when a person accesses kinesthetic information.

(10 minutes.)

9. Ask participants to spend time identifying their own and others' preferred modes. Have participants find partners. Have them spend about 15 minutes with their partners. Tell them to ask their partners a question that requires an answer other than yes or no. For example, Where did you go on your last vacation? Where would you like to travel and why? or What was the best surprise or gift you ever received or gave? While their partners speak, have them notice where their eyes go during the reply. Do they go up, to the side, or down and right most of the time? (*Note:* Look for the most frequent place. Our imagination and memory do demand several types of information, and the challenge is to identify the most frequent.)

    (15 minutes.)

10. Have participants tell their partners what they observed and what mode they think is dominant. Ask whether this rings true.

11. Have pairs switch and repeat the questions to identify the other's preferred mode and confirm the accuracy of the observation.

    (10 minutes.)

12. Continue by having each person repeat the process with two additional partners, again switching roles to obtain validation on their own modes and to provide confirmation for partners on their modes.

    (10 minutes per pairing.)

13. Answer any questions participants may have. Remind participants that dominant modes do not change and that, under stress, people fall back on their dominant modes. Non-dominant modes can be learned, as evidenced by professional speakers, masterful salespeople, and competent therapists, who weave all three into their communication to maintain rapport.

14. Divide participants into groups based on their styles according to the feedback—all visually dominant people in one group, all with auditory dominance in another, and all kinesthetic dominance in a third group. Hand out paper and pencils. Ask each group to select a spokesperson. Have the groups identify different ways they would like to be acknowledged on the job.

    (10 minutes.)

15. Ask the spokesperson for each group to share ways the group members would like to be acknowledged. Write these on the flip chart.
(10 to 20 minutes.)

16. If no one mentions the information on the visual you have posted, remind them, or give the following examples:

    - Visual—discovering an article in the company newsletter.

    - Auditory—announcing accomplishments at a staff meeting.

    - Kinesthetic—a pat on the back.

17. Have participants roam around the room or turn to people they have not yet partnered with. Tell them to converse with each person until they have determined that person's mode and then to acknowledge the person in his or her mode.
(10 minutes.)

18. Answer any questions.

19. Ask participants to acknowledge themselves for learning something new.

20. Ask them what they will do differently the next time they are at work. Remind them to create a list of people whom they can tell about the way they prefer to be acknowledged.

21. Summarize these teaching points:

    - People have greater comfort in their preferred modes and feel stronger rapport with others who have the same modes or intentionally use their modes.

    - It is possible (and easy) to determine preferred modes by watching eye movements to see where visual, auditory, and kinesthetic information is accessed. Eyes go up to the right or left when a person accesses visual information. Eyes go to the side (toward the ears) to the right or left when a person accesses auditory information. Eyes go down to the right when a person accesses kinesthetic information.

    - People can expand the ways in which they acknowledge others.

    - While any form of acknowledgment is better than none at all, managers can help ensure that employees recognize and value the message that is intended.

Submitted by Teri-E Belf and M. Sheila Collins.

Teri-E Belf, M.A., C.A.G.S., M.C.C., *is a purposeful, inspired coaching leader, trainer and coach, author, and speaker, cited in the* International Who's Who of Entrepreneurs. *Her passions include sharing her 37,000 hours of coaching experience and eighteen years of HRD and T&D management experience through presentations, articles, and books. She is the founder and director of Success Unlimited Network®, L.L.C., an international coaching community and an ICF-accredited coach training program.*

M. Sheila Collins, MA, MS, *brings over twenty-five years of professional experience to coaching and organization development consulting. President of MSC Consulting, Inc., she coaches executive teams to work together with greater purpose, power, and productivity. With graduate degrees in spirituality and applied behavioral science and an affiliation with Success Unlimited Network®, L.L.C., she shares a passion for learning with individuals seeking greater fulfillment and satisfaction in their work and/or personal lives.*

How Do I Acknowledge Thee? Handout

In a survey conducted by CareerBuilder.com, 43 percent of respondents reported that they do not feel valued by their employers. According to Bob Nelson, author of *1001 Ways to Reward Employees,* the award most valued by employees is *verbal appreciation or praise;* the second most valued award is *written appreciation or praise.* Nelson cites a survey suggesting that over half of employees feel their work goes unappreciated by their boss.

But unfortunately, firms (during the recruitment and selection process) and job seekers (while defining and seeking the job) pay very little attention to the topic of acknowledgment. Organizations are sometimes surprised when they find out they do not have a pulse on what employees want. Management erroneously assumes that money is the only form of acknowledgment and gives bonuses and salary increases when something else might have equal or greater value for staff satisfaction and retention. At a healthcare organization, Teri-E Belf and her co-workers polled the staff for what form of acknowledgment they most wanted. They responded, "If only the physicians would say please and thank you." Imagine the organization's surprise. Clearly, the bottom line is not always money.

Additionally, senior executives receive little acknowledgment. Who remembers to praise the boss? Belf caught these words almost inaudibly muttered under the breath of an executive vice president who had just finished praising a manager, "I wish I could receive some praise. It's lonely up here."

By matching acknowledgment to an employee's desires, organizations can save money, increase staff retention, and enhance their reputation as a good place to work. Meaningful recognition brings great benefits for both employer and employee.

References

Belf, T. (2002). *Coaching with spirit: Allowing success to emerge.* San Francisco, CA: Pfeiffer.

Belf, T., & Ward, C. (1997). *Simply live it UP: Brief solutions.* Bethesda, MD: Purposeful Press.

Careerbuilder.com survey, *Life at Work 2004,* conducted February 19, 2004, to February 29, 2004.

Nelson, B. (2005). *1001 ways to reward employees* (2nd ed.). New York: Workman.

How Do I Acknowledge Thee? Lecturette

The field of neurolinguistic programming (NLP) puts forth the presupposition that the map is not the territory. Consider consulting your map while driving to your favorite restaurant. You see the roads turn left and right.

Outside your window is a dog chasing after a Frisbee® and children swinging in the park. A jogger jogs in place waiting for the light to turn green. The dog, Frisbee, children, swings, and jogger are not on your map. Hence, the map is not the territory.

Everyone has a map, an internal map that interprets and makes sense out of the external territory. The territory itself does not change; the eyes, ears, and sense of the beholders do. NLP suggests that most people have one preferred mode of interpreting the world, visually, auditorially, or kinesthetically. Some people do have more than one dominant mode, although this is less common. It is through our map that we relate to, and make sense of, the territory.

In the example above, visually dominant people notice the dog, the color of the collar, view the children in the background, and the jogger's brightly colored orange T-shirt in the foreground. Those who have auditory dominance tune into the barking of the dog and the squeals of the children. The kinesthetics will sense the movement of the dog and children and feel the motion of the jogger jumping up and down. The territory has not changed. The maps are different.

Resource

O'Connor, J., & McDermott, I. (1996). *Thorson's principles of NLP.* San Francisco, CA: Harper-Collins.

Board Meeting Simulation
Establishing Leadership Perspective

Activity Summary

Provides an opportunity to experience other roles in a corporation.

Goals

- To develop participants' awareness of the perspectives of a chief executive officer and of a member of the board of directors.

- To experience a CEO's role when facing a board of directors.

- To experience a director's role, providing oversight and advice.

Group Size

20 to 30 participants, in groups of 3 or 4.

Time Required

2 to 2¹/₂ hours.

Materials

- One Board Meeting Simulation Agenda for each participant.

- One Board Meeting Simulation Director's Prompts handout for each participant.

- A pencil or pen and additional paper for each participant.

Physical Setting

Tables and chairs to comfortably seat groups of 3 or 4.

Facilitating Risk Rating

Low.

Process

1. Review the goals of this activity. Ask the group:

   - If you were a chief executive officer (CEO) of your company, how might that change your perspective?

   - If you were accountable to a board, would you procrastinate less on the job?

   - What would it be like to be on a board of directors?

   - How would being responsible to a board increase your ability to accomplish goals? Could it change the size and types of your goals?

2. Tell the group:

   "Boards have different functions. A *policy* board creates broad policies and goals for the organization. Other board functions are to keep the CEO accountable for his or her goals or to lend support and give advice. The board of directors also represents the shareholders' interests.

   "*Advisory* boards are another type of board used to guide companies and inject customer or clientele points of view. Growing businesses use advisory boards to give their expertise to CEOs."

3. Give each participant a Board Meeting Simulation Agenda, some extra paper, and a pen or pencil. Ask them to develop an agenda that would fit their own work-related goals (or personal goals, if appropriate).
   (15 to 20 minutes.)

4. When everyone has finished, divide participants into groups of 4. (Use groups of 3 to shorten the total meeting time.) Tell them that one person in each group will play the role of CEO first; the other three will play directors on the board. Distribute a Board Meeting Simulation Director's Prompts handout to each participant. Tell the groups to familiarize themselves with the handout.
   (5 minutes.)

5. After everyone has read the handout, answer any questions and then tell the groups to pick their CEOs for the first round (if any groups have difficulty choosing, designate one for them). Explain that the "director" seated clockwise from the CEO will begin with his or her agenda, read the first goal, and ask a question. After the CEO's response, the next "director" clockwise reads the next item. Following the CEO's response, the remaining director will repeat the process. Explain that the directors will use the prompts and questions on their own worksheets, along with any other questions or expertise of their own. Answer any questions, and then have them begin. Circulate among the groups to monitor and encourage participation and to remind them to take notes.
    (10 to 15 minutes.)

6. After 10 or 15 minutes, remind the groups that they are next to develop action items and recommendations. Each CEO should write down any action items and recommendations that were suggested. Directors should write any commitments they have made to support the CEO. Suggest that the group members share thoughts about the board meeting process. Allow approximately 10 minutes for this step.

7. Now tell them to hold a meeting for the next CEO in turn. Repeat the prompts from Steps 5 and 6, as necessary, reminding the groups to develop action steps and recommendations at the end of their meetings. Allow approximately 20 to 25 minutes per rotation.

8. Ask the groups to share any final observations or thoughts within their groups. Then discuss and debrief the exercise with the whole group, asking for thoughts, feelings, and ideas for application in the future. Ask what they have learned about their company from the CEO's point of view.
    (15 minutes.)

Variations

*   Invite directors of an actual board to speak to the group.

*   Arrange for the group to attend an actual board meeting.

*   Schedule a follow-up summary of accomplishments and learnings at a future session.

Submitted by W. Norman Gustafson.

W. Norman Gustafson, M.S., *is a consultant and educator, teaching business and technology at the college and secondary level for eighteen years. He directs a training project at Fresno Pacific University. Mr. Gustafson specializes in web-based training, performance improvement, and business model development. As a director, he is known for his board evaluation and development work. He has published a variety of consulting and training articles, including four in Pfeiffer's* Annuals.

Board Meeting Simulation Agenda

Instructions: This agenda is your chance to declare important goals for your company and to hear advice from the directors. Write legibly, as the "directors" will read this agenda.

Call to Order and Statement of Purpose

Goal 1

  Resources

  Barriers?

  Measurable Results

Goal 2

  Resources

  Barriers?

  Measurable Results

Goal 3

  Resources

  Barriers?

  Measurable Results

Future Commitments and Checkpoints

Board Meeting Simulation Director's Prompts

Instructions: In role playing as a director, you are responsible for general policy or goals. You should hold the CEO accountable for the execution of his or her stated goals or activities, and you should offer advice and encouragement. Use the following as an outline to keep your meeting on track.

Evaluation of the CEO's Agenda

- Does the CEO have clear, measurable goals?

- Does the CEO present a compelling and detailed vision of each goal's result?

- Do the goals work together with a clear purpose?

- Are the steps to attain his or her goals clear?

- What barriers separate the CEO from the goal?

- Are the required resources specified?

- Does the CEO have a support network or a partnership with others?

Action Items

- Suggest how the goals can be refined.

- Do you have suggestions to eliminate the barriers?

- What action should the CEO take next?

- What other advice do you have for the CEO?

- Can you promise to follow up with the CEO about an item?

Rules of Order

- Call to order and statement of purpose: Director 1.

- For each goal, the indicated director should lead the discussion.

- Statement of goal and how it is measured: Director 1.

- Explanation of resources to attain the goal: Director 2.

- Description of steps or barriers toward the goal: Director 3.

- Future Commitments and Checkpoints: Any director

Introduction
to the Editor's Choice Section

Unfortunately, in the past we have had to reject exceptional ideas that did not meet the criteria of one of the sections or did not fit into one of our categories. So we recently created an Editor's Choice Section that allows us to publish unique items that are useful to the profession, rather than turn them down. This collection of contributions simply does not fit in one of the other three sections: Experiential Learning Activities; Inventories, Questionnaires, and Surveys; or Articles and Discussion Resources.

Based on the reason for the existence of this section, it is difficult to predict what you may find. You may anticipate a potpourri of topics, a variety of formats, and an assortment of categories. Some may be directly related to the training and consulting fields, and others may be related tangentially. Some may be obvious additions, and others may not. What you are sure to find is something you may not have expected but that will contribute to your growth and stretch your thinking. Suffice it to say that this section will provide you with a variety of useful ideas, practical strategies, and creative ways to look at the world. The material will add innovation to your training and consulting knowledge and skills. The contributions will challenge you to think differently, consider a new perspective, and add information you may not have considered before. The section will stretch your view of training and consulting topics.

The 2006 Pfeiffer Annual: Training includes three editor's choice items. One is an activity and two are articles. All three have valuable information for the training professional, but do not fit in the topic categories. Keep in mind the purpose for this section—good ideas that don't fit in the other sections.

Activity

    El Quixote and the Quest for Management Skills, by Teresa Torres-Coronas

Articles

    Why Sales People Fail, by Jeffrey P. Bosworth

    How to Protect and Profit from Your Training Assets, by Diane M. Gayeski

El Quixote and the Quest for Management Skills*

Activity Summary

A reflective activity that allows participants to think about how to meet the challenge of being a skilled manager.

Goals

- To consider and evaluate key management skills.

- To focus attention on what makes a good manager.

- To allow participants to use deductive reasoning to discover a topic.

Group Size

Any large or small groups.

Time Required

90 minutes.

Materials

- One copy each of *El Quixote* Reading 1 and *El Quixote* Reading 2 for each participant, sent to participants in advance by the instructor.

- One *El Quixote* Synopsis for each participant.

- A flip chart and a variety of colored markers for each subgroup.

---

*This activity has been prepared to commemorate the Fourth Centenary of the first publication of *Don Quixote de la Mancha (El Quixote)*, a chivalrous book written by the Spanish author Miguel de Cervantes Saavedra, as an opportunity to popularize *El Quixote* as a management concept.

- Masking tape.

- Paper and pens or pencils for participants.

Physical Setting

Any training room in which participants can be seated comfortably without the subgroups disturbing one another and with enough wall space for participants to hang the flip-chart pages.

Facilitating Risk Rating

Low.

Preparation

Prior to the session (or at the beginning of the session if there is time), give participants copies of the two readings from *El Quixote* and ask them to read them through, thinking of Quixote as a manager or leader of men.

Process

1. At the beginning of the workshop, provide a brief synopsis of *El Quixote* to re-familiarize participants with the main characters of the book. (You can either hand out the *El Quixote* Synopsis or read it to participants.) *(5 minutes.)*

2. Divide participants into subgroups of 4 or 5. Vary the number and size of the subgroups based on the number of participants. Have each team sit at a separate table and give each a flip chart and markers. *(5 minutes.)*

3. Tell participants to draw one vertical line on a flip-chart sheet covering the entire length of the sheet from top to bottom, and tell them to use a different colored marker to write their thoughts and ideas on each part of the sheet so their own beliefs and ideas from *El Quixote* can be clearly differentiated. *(5 minutes.)*

4. Give everyone paper and a pen or pencil. Tell them to explore their beliefs about management skills by discussing in their groups the following open-ended questions:

- Which kinds of management skills would be useful for today's organizational environments?

- Which managerial skills are more essential to successful management?

Stimulate group discussion on management skills by pointing out that in order to perform the functions of management and to assume multiple roles, managers must be skilled, although being a good manager isn't necessarily linked to any innate management skills. The objective must be knowing how to become the boss everyone loves to praise, rather than the boss everyone loves to hate.
(15 minutes.)

5. Tell participants to list at least twelve management skills they have come up with on the left side of their sheets.

6. Explore participants' insights from *El Quixote* by asking participants to list at least twelve ways Don Quixote advised Sancho Panza to conduct himself on the right side of their sheets.
(15 minutes.)

7. Call time and invite each team to present their ideas to the rest of the group. Tell them to tape their flip-chart pages on the wall near where they are sitting. The discrepancy between what participants write down in Step 5 and what they write down in Step 6 will provide good data for discussion about the positive characteristics of a good manager. Discuss each characteristic and why it is important. Ask:

- What similarities do you find between the two lists?

- What differences do you find between the two lists?

- What can you surmise from these comparisons?
(30 minutes.)

8. Summarize the learnings of the session at this point. Use a flip chart to list participants' learnings.
(10 minutes.)

9. Thank the participants for sharing their knowledge and encourage them to continuously work on developing their management skills and, of course, encourage them to read the whole book.

Submitted by Teresa Torres-Coronas.

Teresa Torres-Coronas, Ph.D., *has a bachelor's degree in economics (Barcelona University) and a Ph.D. in management (Rovira i Virgili University). She won first prize in the 2000 edition of EADA-related management research. She is the author of the book* Valuing Brands *(Ediciones Gestión, 2000), co-author or the book* Retrieve Your Creativity *(Septem Ediciones), co-editor of the book* Changing the Way You Teach: Creative Tools for Management Education *(Septem Ediciones, in press), and co-editor of the book* e-HRM: Managing Knowledge People. *She is management professor at the Universitat Rovira i Virgili and an active member of the Management Education and Development Division (Academy of Management) and the Information Resources Management Association.*

El Quixote Reading 1*

Part II, Chapter XLII

*Of the counsels which don Quixote gave Sancho Panza before he set
out to govern the island, together with other well-considered matters.*

Here Don Quixote joined them; and learning what passed, and how soon Sancho was to go to his government, he with the duke's permission took him by the hand, and retired to his room with him for the purpose of giving him advice as to how he was to demean himself in his office. As soon as they had entered the chamber he closed the door after him, and almost by force made Sancho sit down beside him, and in a quiet tone thus addressed him: "I give infinite thanks to heaven, friend Sancho, that, before I have met with any good luck, fortune has come forward to meet thee. I who counted upon my good fortune to discharge the recompense of thy services, find myself still waiting for advancement, while thou, before the time, and contrary to all reasonable expectation, seest thyself blessed in the fulfillment of thy desires. Some will bribe, beg, solicit, rise early, entreat, persist, without attaining the object of their suit; while another comes, and without knowing why or wherefore, finds himself invested with the place or office so many have sued for; and here it is that the common saying, 'There is good luck as well as bad luck in suits,' applies. Thou, who, to my thinking, art beyond all doubt a dullard, without early rising or night watching or taking any trouble, with the mere breath of knight-errantry that has breathed upon thee, seest thyself without more ado governor of an island, as though it were a mere matter of course. This I say, Sancho, that thou attribute not the favour thou hast received to thine own merits, but give thanks to heaven that disposes matters beneficently, and secondly, thanks to the great power the profession of knight-errantry contains in itself. With a heart, then, inclined to believe what I have said to thee, attend, my son, to thy Cato here who would counsel thee and be thy polestar and guide to direct and pilot thee to a safe haven out of this stormy sea wherein thou art about to engulf thyself; for offices and great trusts are nothing else but a mighty gulf of troubles.

"First of all, my son, thou must fear God, for in the fear of him is wisdom, and being wise thou canst not err in aught.

"Secondly, thou must keep in view what thou art, striving to know thyself, the most difficult thing to know that the mind can imagine. If thou knowest thyself, it will follow thou wilt not puff thyself up like the frog that strove to make himself as large as the ox; if thou dost, the recollection of having kept pigs in thine own country will serve as the ugly feet for the wheel of thy folly."

---

*Reading is from *Don Quixote* (1605, 1615) by Miguel de Cervantes Saavedra, translated by John Ormsby, 1885.

The 2006 Pfeiffer Annual: Training

"That's the truth," said Sancho, "but that was when I was a boy; afterwards when I was something more of a man it was geese I kept, not pigs. But to my thinking that has nothing to do with it; for all who are governors don't come of a kingly stock."

"True," said Don Quixote, "and for that reason those who are not of noble origin should take care that the dignity of the office they hold be accompanied by a gentle suavity, which wisely managed will save them from the sneers of malice that no station escapes.

"Glory in thy humble birth, Sancho, and be not ashamed of saying thou art peasant-born; for when it is seen thou art not ashamed, no one will set himself to put thee to the blush; and pride thyself rather upon being one of lowly virtue than a lofty sinner. Countless are they who, born of mean parentage, have risen to the highest dignities, pontifical and imperial, and of the truth of this I could give thee instances enough to weary thee.

"Remember, Sancho, if thou make virtue thy aim, and take a pride in doing virtuous actions, thou wilt have no cause to envy those who have princely and lordly ones, for blood is an inheritance, but virtue an acquisition, and virtue has in itself alone a worth that blood does not possess.

"This being so, if perchance anyone of thy kinsfolk should come to see thee when thou art in thine island, thou art not to repel or slight him, but on the contrary to welcome him, entertain him, and make much of him; for in so doing thou wilt be approved of heaven (which is not pleased that any should despise what it hath made), and wilt comply with the laws of well-ordered nature.

"If thou carriest thy wife with thee (and it is not well for those that administer governments to be long without their wives), teach and instruct her, and strive to smooth down her natural roughness; for all that may be gained by a wise governor may be lost and wasted by a boorish stupid wife.

"If perchance thou art left a widower—a thing which may happen—and in virtue of thy office seekest a consort of higher degree, choose not one to serve thee for a hook, or for a fishing rod, or for the hood of thy 'won't have it'; for verily, I tell thee, for all the judge's wife receives, the husband will be held accountable at the general calling to account; where he will have repay in death fourfold, items that in life he regarded as naught.

"Never go by arbitrary law, which is so much favoured by ignorant men who plume themselves on cleverness.

"Let the tears of the poor man find with thee more compassion, but not more justice, than the pleadings of the rich.

"Strive to lay bare the truth, as well amid the promises and presents of the rich man, as amid the sobs and entreaties of the poor.

"When equity may and should be brought into play, press not the utmost rigour of the law against the guilty; for the reputation of the stern judge stands not higher than that of the compassionate.

"If perchance thou permittest the staff of justice to swerve, let it be not by the weight of a gift, but by that of mercy.

"If it should happen thee to give judgment in the cause of one who is thine enemy, turn thy thoughts away from thy injury and fix them on the justice of the case.

"Let not thine own passion blind thee in another man's cause; for the errors thou wilt thus commit will be most frequently irremediable; or if not, only to be remedied at the expense of thy good name and even of thy fortune.

"If any handsome woman come to seek justice of thee, turn away thine eyes from her tears and thine ears from her lamentations, and consider deliberately the merits of her demand, if thou wouldst not have thy reason swept away by her weeping, and thy rectitude by her sighs.

"Abuse not by word him whom thou hast to punish in deed, for the pain of punishment is enough for the unfortunate without the addition of thine objurgations.

"Bear in mind that the culprit who comes under thy jurisdiction is but a miserable man subject to all the propensities of our depraved nature, and so far as may be in thy power show thyself lenient and forbearing; for though the attributes of God are all equal, to our eyes that of mercy is brighter and loftier than that of justice.

"If thou followest these precepts and rules, Sancho, thy days will be long, thy fame eternal, thy reward abundant, thy felicity unutterable; thou wilt marry thy children as thou wouldst; they and thy grandchildren will bear titles; thou wilt live in peace and concord with all men; and, when life draws to a close, death will come to thee in calm and ripe old age, and the light and loving hands of thy great-grandchildren will close thine eyes.

"What I have thus far addressed to thee are instructions for the adornment of thy mind; listen now to those which tend to that of the body."

El Quixote Reading 2*

Part II, Chapter LI

Of the progress of Sancho's government, and other such entertaining matters.

Don Quixote of La Mancha's Letter to Sancho Panza,
Governor of the Island of Barataria

"When I was expecting to hear of thy stupidities and blunders, friend Sancho, I have received intelligence of thy displays of good sense, for which I give special thanks to heaven that can raise the poor from the dunghill and of fools to make wise men. They tell me thou dost govern as if thou wert a man, and art a man as if thou wert a beast, so great is the humility wherewith thou dost comport thyself. But I would have thee bear in mind, Sancho, that very often it is fitting and necessary for the authority of office to resist the humility of the heart; for the seemly array of one who is invested with grave duties should be such as they require and not measured by what his own humble tastes may lead him to prefer. Dress well; a stick dressed up does not look like a stick; I do not say thou shouldst wear trinkets or fine raiment, or that being a judge thou shouldst dress like a soldier, but that thou shouldst array thyself in the apparel thy office requires, and that at the same time it be neat and handsome. To win the good-will of the people thou governest there are two things, among others, that thou must do; one is to be civil to all (this, however, I told thee before), and the other to take care that food be abundant, for there is nothing that vexes the heart of the poor more than hunger and high prices. Make not many proclamations; but those thou makest take care that they be good ones, and above all that they be observed and carried out; for proclamations that are not observed are the same as if they did not exist; nay, they encourage the idea that the prince who had the wisdom and authority to make them had not the power to enforce them; and laws that threaten and are not enforced come to he like the log, the king of the frogs, that frightened them at first, but that in time they despised and mounted upon. Be a father to virtue and a stepfather to vice. Be not always strict, nor yet always lenient, but observe a mean between these two extremes, for in that is the aim of wisdom. Visit the gaols [jails], the slaughter-houses, and the market-places; for the presence of the governor is of great importance in such places; it comforts the prisoners who are in hopes of a speedy release, it is the bugbear of the butchers who have then to give just weight, and it is the terror of the market-women for the same reason. Let it not be seen that thou art (even if perchance thou art, which I do not believe) covetous, a follower of women, or a glutton; for when the people and those that have dealings with thee become aware of thy

---

*Reading is from *Don Quixote* (1605, 1615) by Miguel de Cervantes Saavedra, translated by John Ormsby, 1885.

special weakness they will bring their batteries to bear upon thee in that quarter, till they have brought thee down to the depths of perdition. Consider and reconsider, con and con over again the advices and the instructions I gave thee before thy departure hence to thy government, and thou wilt see that in them, if thou dost follow them, thou hast a help at hand that will lighten for thee the troubles and difficulties that beset governors at every step. Write to thy lord and lady and show thyself grateful to them, for ingratitude is the daughter of pride, and one of the greatest sins we know of; and he who is grateful to those who have been good to him shows that he will be so to God also who has bestowed and still bestows so many blessings upon him. My lady the duchess sent off a messenger with thy suit and another present to thy wife Teresa Panza; we expect the answer every moment. I have been a little indisposed through a certain scratching I came in for, not very much to the benefit of my nose; but it was nothing; for if there are enchanters who maltreat me, there are also some who defend me. Let me know if the majordomo who is with thee had any share in the Trifaldi performance, as thou didst suspect; and keep me informed of everything that happens thee, as the distance is so short; all the more as I am thinking of giving over very shortly this idle life I am now leading, for I was not born for it. A thing has occurred to me which I am inclined to think will put me out of favor with the duke and duchess; but though I am sorry for it I do not care, for after all I must obey my calling rather than their pleasure, in accordance with the common saying, amicus Plato, sed magis amica veritas. I quote this Latin to thee because I conclude that since thou hast been a governor thou wilt have learned it. Adieu; God keep thee from being an object of pity to anyone.

Thy friend,
Don Quixote of La Mancha"

El Quixote Synopsis

Don Quixote is a middle-aged man from La Mancha who is obsessed with books on chivalry and decides to become a knight. He builds a not-so-sturdy helmet, polishes an extremely old suit of armor, meets a peasant named Sancho Panza and convinces him to be his squire, and then he is off to right all the wrongs in the world in the name of his lady-love, Dulcinea. Against the better wishes of his friends, Don Quixote and Sancho travel across the land, encountering many ill-fated adventures. He reunites old loves, helps those in harm's way, mistakes strangers and inanimate objects as his foes, and is beaten to near death many times. Most of his misfortunes are blamed on the evil work of an enchanter set out to stop Don Quixote.

Don Quixote mistakes many of his commonday encounters for the legendary. He often confuses buildings for castles, windmills for giants, and prostitutes for princesses. These inanities are what make him the target of other people's humility. People everywhere he goes play elaborate tricks on him. Sancho and his friends often try to fool him for his own good. However, just as often, Don Quixote's vision of the world inserts itself into the lives of those around him.

Don Quixote travels all over Spain, stopping at countless inns and villages along the way. He sits around many campfires, becoming the centerpiece for entertainment on several nights. The knight is sometimes victorious—as he is with the Knight of Mirrors—and sometimes not so victorious—as he is trampled by herds of animals and thrown by windmills. In every instance he remains true to his fantastic beliefs. Finally, on his deathbed he renounces chivalry, but he has already touched the hearts of many others, and Sancho Panza, who longs to return to their adventures, along with other once-skeptical friends, beg him to reconsider. His babbling and talking of nonsense convince everyone there that his madness has finally overwhelmed him.

Why Sales People Fail

Jeffrey P. Bosworth

Summary

Effective selling techniques are something many of us don't consider educating ourselves on, even though we're tasked to sell ourselves as consultants every day to make a living. In this short synopsis, which has been written for all types of sales people, I hope you will find at least the basics of what to concentrate on if you are going to work harder at selling yourself and your skill set to others. "Sales" is an art and, like any art, it must be practiced over and over again. You'll find that if you truly work at the art of sales, you will be very effective at generating recurring revenue on a continual basis for your consultancy.

After nearly twenty years in direct sales, I think I've finally isolated the top five reasons why sales people fail to achieve a return on their investment for the companies they are employed by and, most importantly, for themselves.

In my humble opinion (hmmm. . .), I truly feel *sales is an art.* The mechanics of taking a potential prospect to a closed sale can be a cumbersome one. We all know that! It's the art of devising a game plan for a prospect and carrying that plan out on the field (with sheer intensity), where you see so many competent sales people fail.

In no necessary order, here are the top five reasons why I believe potentially great sales people fail:

Poor Sales Management

Top sales managers know how to motivate, inspire, and truly go out of their way to help their team members by building a relationship with them. They know the personalities of their players. They know what's important to each one of them and they know how to earn their respect/support. Many of the sales managers I meet in business have developed an "ego-centric mantra" that filters down to their staff, blowing the wind right out of their sails every day. A great sales manager *helps his or her team define its market, offers the team the tools, training, and technique*s to give team members what they need to present the company in its best possible light, and *trains them to ask for the business.* Sales people are supposed to look up to their managers with ultimate respect and want to "play hard on the field" every day for their team. Sales managers generally do not have *"building a relationship with their staff"* as one of their ongoing objectives, a mistake that literally costs tens of thousands of dollars in lost recurring revenue to many companies every month.

Lack of Self-Training

It never ceases to amaze me that there are sales people out there who consider themselves consummate sales professionals who have never studied the art of being one. I can ask ten sales people what the five steps to effective sales are, and I'll get 9.5 who won't even know what I'm talking about. It's very simply something we learned in Sales 101 in our first year of college: *Prospect, Qualify, Present, Close,* and *Service (Substantiate)*. The most consummate sales professionals live, eat, and breathe this every day, and they do it seamlessly. They know their products/services, they know their target demographic, they know how to find that target demographic, and they present their case in the most professional, organized manner that they can. They're willing to fill their pipeline every day with qualified prospects by playing the numbers game, and they do this by consistently *touching* new prospects every day with a combination of communication mechanisms (telephone, voice mail, email, fax, postal [thank you cards], personal visits, and so forth). They win business by training themselves to be great sales people first, and then they educate themselves about their products/services, more than enough to be considered a professional at what they do in their respective industries.

Lack of Research

Too many times I see sales people run out to meet with a client completely unprepared as to what their prospect does and how their products/services can *help* that prospect achieve their objectives. One of Central Florida's finest sales trainers, Dave Rothfeld of Creative Sales and Management, Inc., calls this selling from a *"features and benefits"* standpoint. Think about how effective a sales person could be if he or she took the time to do some research on the company and matched up the company's needs to the products/services the sales person's company provides. Whoa! What a concept! Those sales people who effectively learn about their potential clients and have their best interests at heart are the most successful. That is the bottom line.

Poor Time Management

There is an old adage that says, "Plan your work and work your plan." How many sales people do you know who have no idea what they are going to be doing tomorrow? I was lucky enough to experience the working atmosphere of about fifty-five sales people on the floor of a major organization here in Central Florida recently. Maybe it's the 80/20 rule taking over, but 20 percent of those sales people were making 80 percent of the money, and vice versa, simply because they planned their work and they worked their plan. *Sales* is a lifestyle, not a job, and as a sales person you have to feed off the intensity of getting a deal. I truly believe that innate nature or the Type A personality is something that cannot be taught; it's inbred. With email, voice mail, reporting, internal meetings, and so forth nipping away at your precious "face-to-face" time with clients, you'll lose on making your quota if you don't plan well. Those sales people who have adopted the best system for themselves to work productively every day to produce their numbers are the ones making 80 percent of the money. You can see it in their eyes at both 8 a.m., when they start their day, and at 7 p.m., when they are finishing their day. And they know what they are going to be doing tomorrow, and the day after, and the day after.

Salaries/Draws

I know a consummate sales professional who has never taken a salary and/or a draw in over fifteen years of direct selling. In fact, he's turned down positions that offered him that revenue in turn for higher percentages on the deals he closes. The company gets its share and he gets his, and he moves on to the next sale. He earns 35 to 50 percent more in annual salary by putting himself in the position of *having* to close deals to eat every month. Therefore, he works that much harder and feeds off the challenge. Consummate sales professionals thrive off their ability to hunt in an open forest and come back with dinner, every day.

Companies that offer base salaries and draws need to "spell out" their costs for "carrying" someone and see whether they can achieve a return for each other. I see the base salary/draw as an easy way to make the rent/mortgage payment and not perform to someone's ultimate ability. If things go bad, and a sales person is dumped within three to six months (sometimes less), he or she simply moves on to another position that offers enough to make his or her bill payments. If sales people need more, they'll work for it (if they deem it necessary that month). Not a good mantra to have. Surely sales people need to make a living, but I find too often that companies give this salary/draw up-front and then do not task that sales person to return that each and every month *before* he or she is paid another dime. With proper, ongoing, professional sales training, the salary/draw idea should not even be a consideration for consummate sales people who feed off the challenge of making as much as they possibly can.

Conclusion

To employ top-shelf, consummate sales professionals, companies need to work hard at building relationships with their teams by motivating, inspiring, and, most importantly, *training* them—not only with in-depth product knowledge, but also with the mechanics of how to be a great sales person.

To be employed by a company where he or she has earned ultimate respect from the management staff, a sales person needs to understand "elbow grease" and how to make something happen on the field. Although everyone plays the numbers game, it's playing the *consistent* numbers game that matters.

Bringing the two together is what creates successful businesses and great, manageable careers for sales people. It's really not all that hard, if you think about it.

Jeffrey P. Bosworth *is the president of Sales Growth Group, based out of Longwood, Florida, which specializes in helping small- to medium-size businesses capitalize on their sales, marketing, and operational efforts. Mr. Bosworth is a twenty-year sales management veteran, a graduate of the University of Massachusetts at Dartmouth in marketing/management, and is a seasoned sales trainer/motivational speaker with continual engagements across the United States.*

How to Protect and Profit from Your Training Assets

Diane M. Gayeski

Summary

Training and performance improvement departments are increasingly under pressure to demonstrate a return on investment. One way to bolster your department's budget is to create new revenue streams from existing materials, services, and facilities. This article presents ideas and examples to help training managers examine their current assets and determine whether or not to become a profit center. Additionally, issues and techniques surrounding the protection of a company's intellectual assets are discussed.

Whether you're an internal training and performance professional or a vendor, you should know how to protect and create new revenue streams from your existing materials, tools, and facilities. With increasing pressure on training departments to show a return on investment, and with heightened competition in the training vendor marketplace, it's important to leverage every possible asset (Gayeski, 2005). According to Bob Zeinstra, the associate dean for the School of Retail Professional Development at University of Toyota, the vast majority of corporate universities recover less than 5 percent of their costs through profit-making initiatives. However, his corporate university aims to recover more than two-thirds of its total costs (Zeinstra, 2004). Such goals are not uncommon among training departments—yet they are not simple to achieve.

Several strategies are being used to protect and/or generate revenue from training investments:

1. Ensure that materials and proprietary knowledge are protected so that they are not shared or copied improperly.

2. Require employees or their departments to pay the full or partial costs of training courses and performance aids.

3. Repackage and market materials and processes to a wider audience.

4. Turn an in-house training and performance department into a profit center, taking on outside clients for consulting or services.

Every income-producing strategy has its potential benefits and drawbacks, and it's important to carefully explore whether any of these are a good fit for your organization.

Protecting Your Assets

Unfortunately, it's common for training materials and performance aids to somehow find their way out of the hands of their intended audiences. Most people feel that training provided to them was "free," and so it's fine to share in-house training materials with other colleagues or to "borrow" them for other purposes.

For example, one of my graduate students raved about the extensive and effective training provided to her as a waitress for a little local restaurant. When she told me about some of the materials, it became obvious that the manual had been lifted from the restaurant owner's previous employer, a large chain restaurant. I've shown up to deliver training at a client site only to find them setting up a video camera to tape my presentation so that they could show it to other groups. While it may not seem that these infractions impact a training department's or vendor's income stream, they do. Moreover, they can leak out important strategic knowledge and strategies.

Inform Others

The first strategy for protecting your assets is to clearly indicate that the material is proprietary. Many in-house HR and training departments require employees to sign a form acknowledging that what they are receiving is proprietary information and that the company is prepared to prosecute anyone who copies or distributes materials or content outside the company. You may want to mark materials clearly as "confidential." The same goes for working with outside vendors; you should have a nondisclosure clause in all your contracts so that vendors can't take some of your unique in-house information and use it in training that they develop for other companies.

Clarify Ownership

A second strategy is to be clear about ownership and contracts. If you're a vendor, by default if a client pays you for work, they own it as "work for hire." This can create a number of problems. Let's say that I develop training materials on facilitation skills based on my own research and experience. I offer courses based on this to various companies and tailor the courses to each client. Unless I specify in my contract that my company owns the rights to the materials, I give up my rights to those materials when I am paid to customize and deliver the training. That means two things:

- My client has the right to reproduce, edit, and re-use my materials for other in-house clients—or even to market it to others.

- I lose my rights to use my own materials!

Obviously, it's hard to imagine that a client would come after me and tell me that I could no longer offer my facilitation skills workshops to other clients. However, it is legally possible. There could be misunderstandings about whether the client paid me to research and develop the materials for him—or whether he was just paying for my one-time delivery of the workshop.

How do I get around this? In my contracts, I make it clear that the client is paying for *delivery* of a workshop, not for the materials or the course—and that my company retains all rights to the materials. I offer a *license* to reproduce the materials only for the number of trainees in the actual course for which I'm being paid. I may even offer the option of licensing the right to make additional copies of the materials—or for me to conduct a train-the-trainer workshop and grant the license to have her own in-house trainers offer future sessions of the same course. In many instances, the clients are happy to pay for the ability to offer more sessions or reproduce the materials.

Register a Copyright

There are legal strategies to protect various intellectual assets. The most common is copyright; this protects a particular manifestation of ideas as expressed in writing or some other medium. Although you may want to file for copyright, it's not necessary to do so to protect your work. As soon as you put something in a tangible form (handout, book, video, or audio recording), you can put a copyright notice on it, as long as you are the author and nobody else is paying you to develop it. The rule is that the company that is paying for the development (your client or employer) owns the rights to the work, unless otherwise specified. You cannot copyright an idea, a slogan, a procedure, or a concept; copyright pertains only to a specific manifestation of your creation.

Register a Trademark

If you have a particular name or slogan that you want to protect, you can explore trademarking. You might want to trademark the name of a course or a particular performance tool that you've developed. If you have developed a process or computer routine, you can explore obtaining a patent for it. Most people think of patents as something that protects a formula or a particular design for some object. However, let's say that your company has developed a unique process for preventive maintenance or for screening applicants applying for jobs. If you can defend the uniqueness and specificity of your process and want to go through the time and money necessary to patent it, you can protect it by law.

This opens the opportunity for you to license this to others (see the following section on repackaging and marketing materials). The downside of patenting a process is that you must make the formula or process public—anyone can read your patent. They are, however, prohibited from using the exact process without licensing or buying the rights from you.

Individual or Departmental Payback

Many training departments work as cost centers; this means they are given an annual budget from corporate funds, and with it they develop and offer training for free to any in-house clients who request it. While this is attractive to clients, it creates considerable problems for training departments, which then have little flexibility to expand or contract their services, depending on demand.

There is a trend for training departments to adopt a full or partial charge-back funding model; they charge their in-house clients for the complete or partial costs of actually developing and offering the training. Although this internal exchange of money may sound like "funny money" because it's all eventually coming from the same corporate funds, it does allow the training department to account for its expenditures.

In a full charge-back model, training departments figure in their entire costs of developing and offering training, including staff time, overhead, materials, and other out-of-pocket expenses. They charge their clients either by the project or for each trainee seat in courses. In a partial charge-back model, the training department usually does not charge for aspects such as research and development time, consultation, overhead, and so on. It merely recovers its out-of-pocket costs for developing and delivering training and other projects. In either approach, the training department can show that clients are willing to pay for its services, and it can expand or contract its offerings and staff, depending on demand.

Many organizations complain that after they spend considerable time and money training employees, the employees leave and the company never really gets to recoup its investment. Some organizations have actually come up with policies that mandate that trainees pay back expenses for training if they voluntarily leave the organization soon after their training ends. For example, the U.S. government has a policy that states:

> "An employee selected for training for more than a minimum period prescribed by the head of the agency shall agree in writing with the Government before assignment to training that he will

(1) continue in the service of his agency after the end of the training period for a period at least equal to three times the length of the training period unless he is involuntarily separated from the service of his agency; and

(2) pay to the Government the amount of the additional expenses incurred by the Government in connection with his training if he is voluntarily separated from the service of his agency before the end of the period for which he has agreed to continue in the service of his agency. (US Code Collection, 2004)"

There is a lot of controversy about this strategy. Many people feel that it is only fair for employees to pay for extensive training if they don't really use it to benefit the organization that offered it. On the other hand, many HR departments feel that such a policy is a turnoff to potential applicants for positions that are difficult to fill, for example, in information technologies.

Repackage and Market

Many in-house training departments and vendors have developed products, such as courses, videos, or performance aids, that could be more widely marketed. In the same way, it's common for independent instructional designers and training companies to be asked to develop courses and materials that are quite generic and might be marketed to a wider audience. To take advantage of this, you can develop strategies for repackaging and marketing materials.

If you're an in-house department, you have two challenges:

- Ensure that you're not distributing proprietary knowledge or processes outside your own company. In order to "sanitize" materials, you may need to remove any specific company material, such as examples or proprietary procedures.

- Develop some mechanism for marketing. You first must determine whether there is a good market for your materials. Once you make them generic, you need to find other organizations that may need similar training.

One good approach is to find smaller companies in your industry or locale who may not be able to afford to pay for the development or delivery of classes on their own. You can either license materials or offer courses with open enrollment to such companies. Marketing is no easy job, and it takes considerable time, expertise, and resources, so think carefully about this approach.

Retaining Your Rights

If you're a training consultant or vendor, you may want to explore contracts that allow you to retain rights to materials you develop for a client. For example, one of my clients asked me to develop a course on supervisory communication, but he had a limited budget. I had a lot of my own research material to provide, and the client was not going to provide any extensive material from his own sources. I developed a contract that allowed me to license the course to the client while retaining the rights to distribute and sell the course to other clients. It was a win-win situation; the client got a great course at a great fee, and I have the rights to re-sell the content to other clients, creating a continuing revenue stream.

Converting Materials to e-Learning

One possibility for marketing and distributing courses is to convert them to e-learning and work with a partner who distributes such courses. One organization that used this strategy is (ISC)^2, a non-profit association dedicated to training and certifying information security professionals worldwide. The association had developed extensive classroom training programs to help information systems security professionals and practitioners further their education and achieve or maintain certification by earning continuing professional education (CPE) credits. To extend its reach, (ISC)^2 partnered with VCampus, a vendor of online learning, who worked with (ISC)^2 to develop online training courses for certification exams. With no up-front investment, (ISC)^2 launched a private-labeled learning portal, and the online courses helped (ISC)^2 tap a new audience for its courses that generates revenues along with its traditional classroom program (VCampus, 2005).

Publishing Materials

Another way to market your materials is to publish them. There are a number of book publishers who distribute short training manuals and supporting materials, such as electronic slides and handouts. You can take out any company-specific references or proprietary information and develop trainer and trainee materials for generic topics, such as quality methods, diversity training, troubleshooting, or various kinds of workplace literacy training in language or mathematics. Look at trends in training, and examine what's available in the marketplace. Then contact some publishers and see whether they're interested in publishing your materials in print or web-based forms.

Even if an entire course is not marketable, there may be parts of it that are. For example, you may have shot still photographs or video that are usable as stock resources. There are companies that will buy the rights to such assets and then sell them as stock photos/footage to others. Or perhaps you've developed computer programming routines for courseware or expert systems that can be reused for other content. Again, you can license these routines to other organizations that may want to develop similar kinds of courseware routines or job aids.

Taking On Outside Clients

"They're asking for our advice. We're spending all this time answering questions anyway. Why don't we package what we know and sell it?" Questions such as these are exactly what have led firms (whose primary business isn't HR or consulting) such as The Walt Disney Co., Xerox, Deere & Co., IBM, AMR Corp., and Pacific Bell to sell their HR expertise to companies outside their own (Kotch, 1995).

The most dramatic shift from being a free in-house training department to becoming a revenue generator is to split off as a separate consulting or training entity. The primary adopters of this strategy were in-house media production centers that, in the 1990s, found themselves to be targets for downsizing because of the large overhead that they generated. Many of them came up with strategies to take on outside clients—some even spinning themselves off as separate companies. For example, the in-house video production department of Reliance Electric spun itself off as a separate company, Avid Productions, that was partly owned by its employees and partly by Reliance. Employees continued to be housed at a Reliance location and offered their services to Reliance at a reduced rate and on a priority basis. But they also offered their services and extensive production facilities to outside companies, generating a nice profit.

Other organizations, such as The Walt Disney Company, have found that their colleagues from other corporations were frequently asking them for advice and benchmarking information. After they were featured in a PBS special, these requests got out of control so they decided to start Disney University Seminars, a training arm for their own company and a provider of courses to the public.

In 1986, Disney University in Florida—which is part of Disney's combined HR and community relations departments—packaged and started selling what it had been giving away informally before. The goal was partially to help offset the costs of answering questions informally. The first seminar HR managers developed was called "The Disney Approach to People Management," a three-and-a-half-day seminar. They subsequently have added "The Disney Approach to Quality Service," "The Disney Approach to Creative Leadership," and "The Disney Approach to Orientation." Disney has seen the demand for these programs grow dramatically. Although the company declines to discuss exact attendance figures, last year alone, hundreds of individuals from more than forty different industries and thirty different countries attended Disney University's training seminars (Kotch, 1995).

Caveats

Although these profit-making ideas may sound enticing, they are not without their drawbacks. For in-house training departments, becoming a profit center has a number of challenges. Your in-house clients may not be happy about paying for your services or for standing in line while you serve outside customers. It's necessary to get buy-in and understanding from your own executives and sponsors before launching any such undertaking. A useful case study and commentary to read is Kirby's (2002) "The Cost Center That Paid Its Way," published in *Harvard Business Review.*

Your staff may also not be organized, selected, or incentivized properly to function as an effective entrepreneurial entity. It takes time, perseverance, and a certain mix of personality and skill to effectively sell products outside your own organization. Don't underestimate the time and resources necessary to promote your products and to woo and actually win clients.

If you're already a training vendor, it may not be a big step to convert some of your materials into a format that can be sold more widely. But developing these new versions and partnerships also costs time and money that could otherwise be spent working on other billable projects.

References

Gayeski, D. (2005). *Managing learning and communication systems as business assets.* Englewood Cliffs, NJ: Prentice-Hall.

Kirby, J. (2002, April). The cost center that paid its way. *Harvard Business Review,* pp. 31–38.

Kotch, J. (1995, May). HR for profit: Selling expertise. *Personnel Journal,* pp. 84–92.

US Code Collection. (2004). *Employee agreements' service after training.* Retrieved from http://assembler.law.cornell.edu/uscode/html/uscode05/usc_sec_05_00004108——000-.html (last accessed January 6, 2005).

VCampus (2005). *VCampus empowers associations to generate non-dues revenue and enhance member services.* Retrieved from http://www2.vcampus.com/verticals/index.cfm?page=51 (last accessed January 6, 2005).

Zeinstra, B. (2004, December). Converting from a training department to a profit center. *Chief Learning Officer.* Retrieved from www.clomedia.com/content/templates/clo_feature.asp?articleid=734&zoneid=31 (last accessed January 6, 2005).

Diane M. Gayeski, Ph.D., *is CEO of Gayeski Analytics, an Ithaca, New York, based consultancy that helps clients to develop new management strategies for training and corporate communication. She maintains academic affiliations as professor of organizational communication, learning, and design at Ithaca College and adjunct professor at Boise State University's program in instructional and performance technology. Dr. Gayeski is the author of thirteen books and a frequent presenter at conferences and executive briefings.*

Introduction

to the Inventories, Questionnaires, and Surveys Section

Inventories, questionnaires, and surveys are valuable tools for the HRD professional. These feedback tools help respondents take an objective look at themselves and at their organizations. These tools also help to explain how a particular theory applies to them or to their situations.

Inventories, questionnaires, and surveys are useful in a number of training and consulting situations: privately for self-diagnosis; one-on-one to plan individual development; in a small group to open discussion; in a work team to help the team to focus on its highest priorities; or in an organization to gather data to achieve progress. You will find that the use of inventories, questionnaires, and surveys enriches, personalizes, and deepens training, development, and intervention designs. Many can be combined with other experiential learning activities or articles in this or other *Annuals* to design an exciting, involving, practical, and well-rounded intervention. Each instrument includes the background necessary for understanding, presenting, and using it. Interpretive information, scales, and scoring sheets are also provided. In addition, we include the reliability and validity data contributed by the authors. If you wish additional information on any of these instruments, contact the authors directly. You will find their addresses and telephone numbers in the "Contributors" listing near the end of this volume.

The 2006 Pfeiffer Annual: Training includes two assessment tools in the following categories:

Individual Development

Assessing One's Own Facilitation Skills, by Lois B. Hart

Problem Solving

Measuring Employee Resilience, by Jeffrey Russell and Linda Russell

Assessing One's Own Facilitation Skills

Lois B. Hart

Summary

This paper presents the rationale and background for conducting an assessment (1) for participants who will attend a facilitation training program or (2) for individuals who need coaching on these skills. The two surveys presented here help the respondents value what they already know as well as decide what they will need to learn more about. The trainer can use the information to create a program design that will meet these needs. The coach can use the information to focus on what should be covered in coaching sessions. Detailed instructions are provided for a 50- to 60-minute module.

Rationale and Background

Everywhere today, the talk is about teams! The names for teams are diverse, and their purposes are multifaceted. There are site, functional, and work teams, plus self-managed teams formed around similar functions in the organization. There are special teams formed to solve problems and improve processes; these may be called ad hoc teams, task forces, quality action teams, value engineering teams, or process management teams, among other labels. Traditional groups formed to provide advice and oversight, such as councils and steering committees, are now often called teams also. The one common element across all these teams is that facilitation skills are critical.

There are three possible ways in which facilitators are used in teams:

1. In many teams, there is a *designated team leader* who must use appropriate facilitation skills and methods to help the team work well together and accomplish its goals efficiently.

2. In some other situations, the *facilitator is neither the team leader nor a member of the team.* The facilitator remains neutral and objective while conducting the meeting so that the organizational leader can be a "participant." Consultants, for example, often serve as neutral facilitators when their clients want to have a management retreat, work through interpersonal conflicts, or learn how to function better as a staff or department.

3. In the third case, *the team leader and facilitator share the duties* of conducting team meetings.

People in various roles can serve as facilitators. For example, internal consultants help teams form, facilitate their initial meetings, then coach the team leader until the team is functioning smoothly.

Consultants and trainers with experience using facilitation skills are in the best position to train others how to be facilitators. But how can they teach people to be effective facilitators?

The key is for them to (1) identify the skills needed; (2) assess participants' strengths and needs; (3) design a comprehensive program around those needs; (4) provide extensive opportunities for practice; and (5) schedule follow-up. The two surveys presented here can help with the assessment stage, prior to designing a training program.

The respondents to the two surveys focus on both their needs and their strengths. Both surveys are intended as self-assessments, and the results can be used for discussion purposes as well as for planning a training program on facilitation skills.

Survey 1, General Self-Assessment of Facilitation Skills, requires respondents to give narrative answers. The questions cover respondents' experiences using facilitation skills.

Survey 2, Facilitation Skills Self-Assessment, asks respondents to rank their abilities to help clarify exactly what skills they need to work on in order to be effective facilitators. The results help the trainer identify the skills that definitely need to be taught in a facilitation skills workshop. At the end of a training program, the second survey can be re-administered to give participants a picture of how much they have learned and what other skills still must be acquired.

Administration of the Surveys

The surveys are designed to be administered during a one-hour pre-training module. The objectives for the module are

- To review participants' past experiences as facilitators;

- To identify their strengths and skills as facilitators;

- To identify the skills they need to develop; and

- To gain their commitment to becoming better facilitators.

An outline of the session, along with suggested wording for the trainer, are provided below. It is assumed that this will be only the opening for a later workshop on facilitation skills with the same group of participants. The actual workshop could follow later the same day, but may take at least some overnight preparation.

Session Outline and Script

To begin the program, the participants should be in groups of three to five at round tables, in their actual work groups, if feasible. First, introduce the theory to participants, which will take five to ten minutes. Engage them immediately by asking them to raise their hands if any of the following are true for them:

- Do you frequently facilitate meetings and teams?

- Are you a team leader who isn't sure which facilitation skills are needed to help the team work better together and achieve their goals?

- Do you conduct strategic planning retreats?

- Are you an internal consultant required to coach others on their facilitation skills?

Say: "As you could see by the show of hands, there are others here who fit your role descriptions. All of us can benefit from some additional skills in facilitation and could use some additional self-confidence. In our brief time together, you will be taking a couple of self-assessment instruments to determine the types of facilitation experiences you have had and to find out what skills could benefit you in the future as you facilitate other groups. We will come together again to practice the skills we need, as determined by some self-assessments we will do today."

Additional background information about the rationale for assessment (as explained at the beginning of this paper) could be given, especially if participants are not familiar with the use of assessments. To broach the topic, ask participants what other assessments or feedback surveys they have completed in the past, including whether the assessment was self-administered, 360-degree feedback, or observation only.

Say: "The first leg of this journey to learn how to become a faultless facilitator is to identify what you already know and what you need to develop further. Today you will assess the past experiences you have had with groups and teams and your motivation to learn more, and we will plan some future opportunities to put what you've learned into practice.

"Part of this process includes rating yourself on a list of skills and methods that experienced facilitators utilize.

"You will complete two surveys and then discuss the results in small groups. Later, I will poll the total group on some of your strengths and needs for certain skills. Finally, I will collect the assessments and use them to design a future workshop on training skills designed just for you. At that workshop, you will receive your self-assessments back and be able to refer to them as needed."

Give the following information to everyone: "The first survey asks you to write your past experiences as a facilitator, your motivation to learn more about facilitation, and what you expect to learn from this workshop.

"The second survey uses a rating scale to help you assess your level of competence and confidence in facilitation. Note that the rating scale has a range from '1,' which indicates that you have no knowledge or experience in this area, to '5,' which indicates that you feel confident and competent enough to teach someone else that facilitation skill.

"Please complete these two surveys. You can do either one first. Do this silently. When you finish your surveys, do not disturb others while they are working."

Hand out the two surveys and pencils. Stay available to answer questions and maintain silence. Give respondents ten to fifteen minutes to complete both surveys, then bring them back to attention. Present the following to the large group:

"By filling out the first survey, you assessed your past experiences as a facilitator, opportunities you have for using facilitation skills, and how you will benefit from participating in this facilitation training program. In the second survey, you rated your level of confidence and competence on many facilitation skills.

"There is an irony to self-assessment that often is hard to understand. It is that we often rate ourselves harder than if others rated us based on observation. So look over your self-ratings for Survey 2 and see whether, in retrospect, you were especially hard on yourself."

After two or three minutes, continue by saying:

"You may be wondering why you were asked to consider your *competence* as well as your *confidence* scores. Well, sometimes we know *how* to do something (our competence) but don't necessarily feel confident about it. Therefore, the goal is to feel both competent and confident."

Ask participants to comment on their scores if they wish and lead a short discussion, but keep it brief. Then ask them to select one person in each group to facilitate the discussion and a second person to be a timekeeper. (This establishes the precedent for practice that will be integral in the facilitation program design.)

Give copies of the Instructions for Small Group Facilitators to the "facilitators," who will then give the instructions to their own teams. Also hand out blank paper for notes. Say:

"You will be the facilitator for your group for the next fifteen to twenty minutes. Read the instructions I have given you and then explain them to your work team."

Be available to answer questions as the teams work. After about twenty minutes, call the participants to attention. Explain the process, as follows:

"Next, I will be asking each team facilitator to share a sample of some of his or her team's strengths. We will post these on the flip chart."

Help facilitators, in turn, list the strengths they have noted. Ask someone else to record them on the flip chart, if desired. When you have collected all the strengths, say:

"Next, I want each team facilitator to share a sample of some of their team members' needs. We will also post these on the flip chart."

Put these needs on a second flip-chart sheet. After discussing the results, explain what the next step will entail.

Explain how you will use the information from both surveys to design the next workshop session. Point out how the workshop design will in fact teach the skills they need. Reassure them that you will provide additional resource materials and individual coaching on needs that may not be covered in the workshop and explain that you will draw on individual strengths, as identified from their surveys.

Say: "I am collecting your assessments so that I can learn more about your facilitation skills and needs and address those needs in this training program. I may also call on some of you to share your knowledge later in the program. I will return the surveys to you later. You will need them to measure the progress you have made as a result of the training program."

Collect the surveys, and then have the group practice giving feedback to one another.

Explain: "Since feedback is essential for our learning, I'm asking the members of each small group to provide feedback to their facilitators. Throughout the facilitation program, we will do this after every practice session."

Ask the small groups to reflect on their facilitator behaviors and methods and to discuss the following questions, which you should post on the flip chart:

- What did the facilitator do that helped your team accomplish its task?

- What suggestions can you give the facilitator to try another time?

After giving them about ten minutes to consider and provide feedback to one another, wrap up the session.

References

Hart, L.B. (1996). *Faultless facilitation: A complete resource guide for facilitators and team leaders* (2nd ed.). Amherst, MA: HRD Press.

Hart, L.B. (1996). *Faultless facilitation: Instructor's manual for facilitation training* (2nd ed.). Amherst, MA: HRD Press.

Lois B. Hart, Ed.D., *is executive director of both the Courageous Leadership Consortium and the Women's Leadership Institute. Dr. Hart has over thirty years of experience as a consultant, facilitator, and trainer, presenting programs on leadership, facilitation, teams, gender relationships, and conflict. She has written twenty-three books, including* Faultless Facilitation (Instructors Manual and Resource Guide); 50 Activities for Developing Leaders (Volumes I and II); Learning from Conflict; *and* Training Methods That Work.

Survey 1: General Self-Assessment of Facilitation Skills

Lois B. Hart

Instructions: Please answer the following questions about your facilitation experiences.

Experiences as a Facilitator and Team Leader

List below any experiences you have had facilitating or leading a group or team, both at work and in your community.

Go back and put a star on the ones that were most satisfactory to you and indicate why.

Motivation

Categorize why you want to learn about facilitation and team leadership skills.

How will you *benefit* from learning these skills?

Do you currently have any *responsibility* for facilitating or leading a group or team?

If not, do you plan to facilitate any groups or teams in the future?

Survey 2: Facilitation Skills Self–Assessment

Lois B. Hart

Instructions: The following skills and methods are used by experienced facilitators. Read over this list and rate your current level of competence and confidence on each skill listed using the following scale:

1 = I have no knowledge or experience in this area.

2 = I have some knowledge or experience in this area.

3 = I can do this at an average level of competency.

4 = I am confident in this area.

5 = I feel competent and confident enough to teach and/or coach others on this skill.

_____ Knowing the difference between a group and a team

_____ Identifying the characteristics of a high-performance team

_____ Knowing the differences among leading, training, and facilitating

_____ Recognizing the phases a group goes through to become a team

_____ Identifying behaviors people display in groups

_____ Handling problem people

_____ Knowing the role of the facilitator

_____ Knowing the role of the team leader

_____ Knowing the role of the recorder

_____ Knowing the role of a process observer

_____ Using outside resource people

_____ Setting up arrangements for a group meeting

_____ Gaining management's commitment

_____ Building and using an agenda

_____ Setting up arrangements for a group meeting

_____ Knowing how to warm up and get your group started

_____ Developing team guidelines

_____ Facilitating a team through its phases

_____ Developing vision and mission statements

_____ Observing nonverbal signals

_____ Listening and paraphrasing

_____ Asking questions

_____ Mastering your timing

_____ Building commitment and synergy

_____ Identifying causes of conflict

_____ Working with the conflict phases

_____ Mediating conflicts between people

_____ Keeping energy flowing

_____ Regrouping creatively

_____ Using multi-voting

_____ Reaching consensus

_____ Guiding your team through the problem-solving cycle

_____ Using brainstorming

_____ Using the nominal group technique

_____ Setting a goal

_____ Using fishbone and cause-and-effect diagrams

_____ Knowing the value of collecting data

_____ Understanding survey techniques

_____ Using Pareto charts and histograms

_____ Using force field analysis

_____ Knowing when and how to use process improvement

_____ Knowing how to use a flip chart

_____ Knowing how to use a videotape and VCR

_____ Knowing how to prepare a presentation

_____ Knowing how to write summary and status reports

_____ Evaluating your team's progress

_____ Knowing how to end the team's experience and celebrate

Instructions for Small Group Facilitators

Ask each of your group members to first identify and then share one or two of their strengths, experiences, and knowledge as facilitators. Make a list of their strengths, including your own. Take no more than ten minutes for this step.

Next, ask your team members to identify one or two areas from Survey 2 for which they want to increase their confidence and competence (items rated 1 to 3). Make a list of these needs, including your own. Take no more than ten minutes.

Measuring Employee Resilience

Jeffrey Russell and Linda Russell

Summary

Resilience—the capacity of a body to "spring back" to its original shape in the face of adversity or stress—is a key factor contributing to an individual's effectiveness in life and at work. This paper explores the growing importance of this concept in understanding personal and organizational effectiveness, summarizes the research behind resilience, and describes the development and use of the Resilience Quotient™ (RQ), an assessment tool that individuals and organizations can use to measure their resilience capacities. The authors conclude by inviting organization development professionals and researchers to help further develop the RQ.

As we enter the 21st Century, it is clear that the rapid pace of change in society and in our workplaces has a profound effect on those who are asked to undergo these changes. Some people seem to thrive on change—they seek out changing environments and often initiate change when things seem too stable. Others run in the opposite direction of the change. Instead of embracing change, these change-averse individuals may drag their feet, pray for a reprieve, or actively work to undercut the change initiative. Still others put on a brave face and muddle their way through the confusion, uncertainty, and anxiety of a change—neither embracing it nor fleeing from it, but doing nothing overtly to either move it forward or block its progress.

What factors might explain an individual's response to either embrace, muddle through, or flee from and resist a given change? Researchers and practitioners have identified such factors as (1) the level of trust in those who are leading the change; (2) the degree of perceived opportunity or loss resulting from the change; (3) the individual's past history with change efforts; (4) the degree of influence or control over the impact and future course of the change; and/or (5) disagreement over the need for the change or in the solutions offered to "solve" the problem driving the change (Bridges, 1991;

Conner, 1992; Dunham, 1984; Russell, 1998, 2003, & 2005). Based on the authors' research and practice in the field of organizational change, an additional factor that stands alone as a force, and one that contributes to most of the others, is *employee resilience.* An individual's internal resilience capacities, we believe, powerfully influence the response behaviors of those who are affected by a change. Our practice, grounded in more than twenty years of work with diverse organizations, suggests that people who are resilient tend to face change more proactively, making it work *for* them, while those who lack resilience tend to, at best, *endure* the change and, at worst, actively avoid or resist it.

What Is Resilience?

The root of the word resilience is *resile,* which in the original French and Latin means to "jump back or recoil." This root translates into the modern concept of resilience as the ability of a body to recover from or adjust to misfortune or change. Within this context, resilience is also the capability of a strained body to recover its size and shape after being subjected to adversity or stress.

Contemporary applications of this concept to the human experience date from landmark research conducted by two developmental psychologists, Emmy Werner and Ruth Smith (2001). Werner and Smith tracked the progress of 698 children from birth to beyond their thirtieth birthdays, seeking to identify why some children thrived, while others withered when faced with significant familial and social hurdles. Their findings on resilience are echoed in comparable studies on youth under stress done by Bernard (1991), Rutter (1977), and Garmezy (1991).

Fortunately, the resilience of adults in work and non-work settings has also been the focus of research. Psychologists and researchers Reivich and Shatté (2002) and Brooks and Goldstein (2004) have examined resilience in adults dealing with stressful situations, each identifying the characteristics that enable someone to bounce back in the face of adversity and stress. Within the context of organizational change, Conner (1991) and Russell (1998, 2003) have built on the work of Reivich and Shatté by identifying and developing an inventory of characteristics of resilient people that can be used by change leaders and HRD/OD professionals to help guide the strengthening of employee resilience (through training, mentoring, coaching, etc.) and help shape the design and implementation of change initiatives to maximize employee commitment.

Our work in the field of change resilience, grounded in the research of Werner and Smith, Bernard, Rutter, Garmezy, and the others referenced above has led to several key conclusions:

1. *Resilience is a mindset, a way of thinking, versus a hard-wired and innate quality.* It is less about who we are and more about how we *think* about ourselves and how we *interpret* the world around us. This "mental model" of how we view ourselves and the world directly influences how we experience threats and challenges—viewing them as either devastating setbacks or as hidden opportunities, or something in between. This mindset, in turn, influences the set of behaviors we use—which can run the gamut from fight or flight, to passive acquiescence, to proactive engagement that attempts to take direct control of the change.

2. *Resilience is not a static quantity that you either have or not.* It is a dynamic quality that changes in response to the environment. A person may be resilient at certain times and not at others, due to the variable quality of his or her own resilience capacities and the degree and intensity of the stress or change that he or she is facing. Because the resilient mindset is a *moving* target, even people who tend to be highly resilient have their good days and their bad days.

3. *Resilience can be developed and strengthened.* Since we are dealing with a mindset, versus genetic characteristics or even one's core personality, someone's resilience can be enhanced and strengthened. While increasing one's resilience capacities is largely a personal effort by individuals, organizations can and should facilitate its growth through training, coaching, and mentoring.

4. *Resilience has a number of facets or dimensions.* Resilience is not a monolithic concept, but instead is comprised of eight interdependent and highly correlated cognitive dimensions. By assessing the relative strength of each of these eight dimensions, individuals acting alone or with the assistance of HRD/OD professionals can develop more targeted efforts to strengthen their personal resilience.

The Characteristics of Resilient People

We have identified eight dimensions of individual resilience. These facets evolve from our extensive practice in change management efforts and are reinforced in the research cited earlier. The core dimensions of resilience are

1. *Self-Assurance.* This dimension involves a high level of self-confidence and a belief that one can meet any challenge with hope and realistic optimism. Self-assurance also includes the understanding that, while the world is complex

and challenging, one has the ability to find the opportunity and to succeed despite these challenges.

2. *Personal Vision.* Resilient people know what they believe in and have a clear idea of what they want to accomplish or create in their lives. With a larger life purpose pulling them forward, resilient people approach adversity and stress with a sense of opportunity and hope.

3. *Flexible and Adaptable.* The most resilient people are those who are keenly aware of and sensitive to the changes occurring in the world around them. With the help of this awareness, they are able to shift gears and direction if necessary to accommodate the new reality while remaining true to their life purpose/vision. Resilient people adapt to the environment as both a survival mechanism and also as a vehicle for enabling them to continue the pursuit of their personal goals.

4. *Organized.* In the face of chaos and uncertainty, resilient people find ways to create a level of order and structure that provides them the focus and stability they need. This can involve setting short-term goals, thinking through the situation before taking action, putting together "to-do" lists, and so forth.

5. *Problem Solver.* Resilient people have the ability to analyze problems, discover the root causes, and create lasting solutions. They are also effective at seeing the relationship of a problem to other problems within a larger system or network of deeply interdependent issues. This awareness of the bigger picture enables them to recognize the limits of their own influence and to expect (and not be blindsided by) the unexpected.

6. *Interpersonal Competence.* A key dimension of resilience is an individual's ability to understand and empathize with others. Resilient people demonstrate the competencies of emotional intelligence: a high level of self-awareness and social awareness and the ability to use this awareness to effectively manage themselves and their relationships with others (see Golman, 1997).

7. *Socially Connected.* Closely related to interpersonal competence, this resilience dimension involves the quality of a person's personal and professional network of relationships. Resilient people tend to have a strong relationship network within which they share ideas, problems, solutions, frustrations, hopes, and so forth. In the face of adversity and stress, resilient people call on this network for support, affirmation, and problem solving.

8. *Proactive.* Resilient people, rather than simply reacting to a change, actively engage it. They tend to have an internal locus of control (Rotter, 1966) where

they believe that they have the capacity and the *responsibility* to determine their own destiny, versus feeling powerless in a given situation. Resilient people, as a result, focus on *expanding* their influence over a change through assertive behaviors and actions. This proactivity enables them to preserve their self-efficacy in the face of any change—even a traumatic one. Viktor Frankl's moving testament of life in the Auschwitz Nazi concentration camp speaks to the power of being proactive in the face of adversity (see Frankl, 1963).

Description of the Resilience Quotient Assessment

The Resilience Quotient (RQ) Assessment consists of thirty-two statements to which the person responds using a 6-point scale. For each statement, the respondent is asked to identify his or her level of agreement on the scale. The thirty-two statements are organized within the RQ instrument according to the eight dimensions of the resilience model.

Administration of the RQ Assessment

The RQ Assessment can be administered individually or in a group setting. Respondents are asked to read each statement carefully and then to check the box that best reflects their level of agreement with the statement.

Scoring and Plotting the RQ Assessment

After completing the RQ Assessment, the respondent transfers his or her selections to the scoring worksheet to calculate the overall RQ score as well as the individual RQ dimension scores. Once the individual RQ dimension scores are determined, the respondent then plots the eight RQ dimension scores on the RQ Radar Chart to gain a graphical depiction of his or her resilience capacities.

Interpreting the RQ Assessment Scores and the RQ Radar Chart

The maximum possible overall RQ score is 192; the lowest possible RQ score is 32. The maximum and minimum possible RQ scores for each of the eight dimensions are 24 and 4, respectively. Interpreting the overall RQ Assessment score is aided within the instrument with a descriptive narrative that guides respondents in analyzing their RQ results and in developing a personal plan for strengthening their resilience capacities.

Interpreting the RQ Radar Chart involves examining the overall size of the "wheel" (a wider wheel suggests greater resilience) and the "balance" or proportionality of the wheel. A wheel out of balance, for example, would be evident if the respondent's scores indicated low levels of resilience in one or more dimensions (such as *personal vision* or *interpersonal competence*) as compared to other dimensions.

Action Planning Using the RQ Assessment

Based on the overall RQ value and the individual RQ dimension scores and an examination of the size and shape of the RQ "wheel," those who complete the RQ Assessment will be able to identify areas to target to strengthen their resilience capacities. If the overall RQ value is strong, but individual RQ dimensions suggest potential resilience vulnerabilities, the dimension scores and radar chart help point the individual toward the potential growth area.

When developing a personal resilience improvement plan, respondents can benefit most from the instrument by examining the individual statements that comprise each of the RQ dimensions. These statements can suggest areas for personal growth and development as strategies for enhancing resilience in the respective RQ dimension.

Facilitating the Growth of Resilience Capacities

Organization development and HRD professionals can use the RQ results to guide both individuals and the organization toward enhancing resilience. This effort will be especially useful in anticipation of future stress or planned change initiatives. While growing or strengthening resilience is a gradual process (there are no fast paths to being resilient), identifying potential vulnerabilities with the RQ Assessment is one important benefit of the tool. It can also be used to help people begin strengthening their resilience through focused attention and formal action planning.

For *personal* action planning, the OD/HRD professional can best facilitate the strengthening of employee resilience by integrating the RQ Assessment into existing workshops on change and personal effectiveness or designing stand-alone workshops on growing resilience. A half-day workshop on the RQ Assessment might include:

- An overview of resilience

- Administering and scoring the RQ Assessment

- Sharing and discussing the RQ results in dyads or small groups

- Identifying ideas for strengthening resilience using a small group process

- Personal action planning

Compiling the RQ Assessment scores from a group of people can also benefit individual teams or the larger organization. To facilitate team or *organizational* action planning based on the RQ results, the OD/HRD professional will need to gather individual RQ scores of the team or organizational members and analyze the overall level of resilience of the team/organization. Care must be taken to ensure anonymity of the data collected. We recommend that individuals completing the RQ Assessment be asked to complete two scoring worksheets and to forward one copy of the scoring worksheet to the OD/HRD professional.

By pooling and analyzing the data across multiple respondents for a team or the organization, OD/HRD professionals can gain insights into the resilience capacities of the group and also provide follow-along skill building, mentoring, coaching, and so forth to address potential group vulnerabilities.

Reliability of the RQ Assessment

The reliability of the RQ Assessment was calculated by analyzing the variance across variables for internal consistency. This generated a Cronbach alpha value of .90.

A Cronbach alpha value was also generated for each of the RQ dimensions. These values are: *self-assurance* (.77); *personal vision* (.70); *flexible and adaptable* (.74); *organized* (.69); *problem solver* (.73); *interpersonal competence* (.60); *socially connected* (.56); and *proactive* (.60).

Further tests concerning the reliability and validity (using factor analysis) of the instrument are continuing.

Invitation to Strengthen the RQ Assessment Instrument

We encourage OD/HRD professionals who are interested in improving the RQ instrument to use the RQ Assessment in their practice and then to share the RQ results with the authors. Contact the authors at RCI@RussellConsultingInc.com if you would like to contribute to this ongoing research.

References

Bernard, B. (1991). *Fostering resiliency in kids: Protective factors in the family, school, and community.* Portland, OR: Northwest Regional Education Laboratory.

Bridges, W. (1991). *Managing transitions.* Reading, MA: Addison-Wesley.

Brooks, R., & Goldstein, S. (2004). *The power of resilience: Achieving balance, confidence, and personal strength in your life.* New York: McGraw-Hill.

Connor, D.R. (1992). *Managing at the speed of change.* New York: Villard Books, Random House.

Dunham, R. (1984). *Organizational behavior.* Homewood, IL: Richard D. Irwin.

Frankl, V. (1963). *Man's search for meaning.* New York: Simon & Schuster.

Garmezy, N. (1991). Resiliency and vulnerability to adverse developmental outcomes associated with poverty. *American Behavioral Scientist, 34*(4), 416–430.

Goleman, D. (1995). *Emotional intelligence: Why it can matter more than IQ.* New York: Bantam Books.

Reivich, K., & Shatté, A. (2002). *The resilience factor: 7 essential skills for overcoming life's inevitable obstacles.* New York: Broadway Books, Random House.

Rotter, J.B. (1966). Generalized expectancies for internal versus external control of reinforcement. *Psychological Monographs, 80,* (1, Whole No. 609).

Russell, J., & Russell, L. (1998). *Managing change.* Dubuque, IA: Kendall/Hunt.

Russell, J., & Russell, L. (2003). *Leading change training.* Alexandria, VA: ASTD Press.

Russell, J., & Russell, L. (2005). An integrative model for leading change in organizations. In *The 2005 Pfeiffer annual: Consulting.* San Francisco, CA: Pfeiffer.

Rutter, M. (1977). Protective factors in children's responses to stress and disadvantage. In M.W. Kent & J.E. Rolf (Eds.), *Primary prevention in psychopathology. Vol. III: Social competence in children.* Hanover, NH: University Press of New England.

Werner, E., & Smith, R. (2001). *Journeys from childhood to midlife: Risk, resilience, and recovery.* Ithaca: NY: Cornell University Press.

Jeffrey Russell *and* **Linda Russell** *are co-directors of Russell Consulting, Inc., Madison, Wisconsin. They provide consulting and training services in such areas as leadership, strategic planning, change implementation, resilience, employee surveys, organization development, and performance coaching. Their clients include Fortune 500 companies, small businesses, non-profits, and government agencies. Their most recent books include* Leading Change Training *(ASTD Press, 2003) and* Strategic Planning and Problem Solving Training *(ASTD Press, 2005). They publish the journal* Workplace Enhancement Notes.

Resilience Quotient Assessment

Jeffrey Russell and Linda Russell

Instructions: The statements below list a variety of beliefs that deal with your perceptions of yourself and your interactions with the environment and others. Read each of the following statements and, using the 6-point scale, indicate the extent to which you agree or disagree that each statement accurately describes how you perceive yourself.

1 = strongly disagree	4 = slightly agree
2 = disagree	5 = agree
3 = slightly disagree	6 = strongly agree

In general . . .

_____   1.   I believe that I have the knowledge, skills, and abilities to deal with almost anything that happens to me.

_____   2.   I know what's important to me in my life.

_____   3.   I approach new situations with an open mind as to what needs to be done.

_____   4.   When faced with a major change, I usually find a way to create systems or structures that give me a degree of control that I find useful and helpful.

_____   5.   When I have a problem to solve or a decision to make, I usually spend time defining the problem or decision.

_____   6.   In social interactions at work and in my personal life, I am usually able to laugh at myself when appropriate.

_____   7.   I have a diverse group of people whom I consider good friends.

_____   8.   I view change—even difficult and challenging change—as an opportunity for me to learn and grow.

_____   9.   I think and speak positively about myself and my abilities when facing a challenge or stress.

_____   10.   When I look back on my life, I see a clear pattern in the choices and decisions that I have made.

1 = strongly disagree   4 = slightly agree

2 = disagree   5 = agree

3 = slightly disagree   6 = strongly agree

_____ 11. I am willing and able to make adjustments to my goals and plans when situations and expectations of me change.

_____ 12. I start each work day by thinking about what I need to accomplish during that day, and I end each day reviewing what I need to accomplish the next day.

_____ 13. I see the problems that I face in life and at work as challenges that I can solve.

_____ 14. I find it easy to empathize with others' frustrations, hurts, joys, misfortunes, and successes.

_____ 15. I find it easy to form lasting friendships.

_____ 16. When an unwelcome change is forced on me, I can usually find a way to either influence the course of the change or find a way to make the change work for me on my terms.

_____ 17. When I face difficult challenges, I am able to maintain confidence in my ability—one way or another—to overcome the challenge.

_____ 18. I have a pretty good idea of what I want to accomplish in my work and life.

_____ 19. I find that, most of the time, I am able to find a way to meet both my needs and the needs of others in a changing environment or during conflict.

_____ 20. I usually maintain some sort of a "to-do" list to help me focus on what I need to work on.

_____ 21. I usually try to get down to the root cause of a problem before I try to solve it.

_____ 22. In stressful or conflict situations, I am usually able to maintain effective relationships with others.

_____ 23. I frequently turn to my circle of friends when I am frustrated, confused, angry, or uncertain—and when I have great news to share.

1 = strongly disagree   4 = slightly agree

2 = disagree   5 = agree

3 = slightly disagree   6 = strongly agree

_____ 24. Rather than focusing on what others are doing to me, I tend to focus my energy on how I can make the best of a situation.

_____ 25. When I face great challenges, I look within myself for the answers about what to do and how to respond to the challenge.

_____ 26. I know what I need to do to achieve my personal and professional goals.

_____ 27. I can usually accommodate others' needs (adjust my behaviors) while remaining true to my personal goals.

_____ 28. When I am confused about what I need to do or the choices I need to make, I usually try to write out my thoughts.

_____ 29. When I solve problems or make decisions, I try to identify the relationships between the problem I am solving or decision I am making and other issues, problems, and challenges.

_____ 30. I value the diverse beliefs, approaches, and methods that people bring to their work and to their daily interactions with me.

_____ 31. I regularly participate in one or more non-work-related group activities with friends (e.g., church, sports, cultural, etc.), where I can let off steam, learn, grow, and have fun.

_____ 32. I believe that my own decisions and actions during a change will make the biggest difference in how the change affects me.

Resilience Quotient Scoring Worksheet

Instructions: Transfer the scores you gave to each item on the RQ Assessment to the appropriate box below (note the vertical listing of the numbers). Then add the numbers in each row to calculate the score for each RQ dimension and enter it in the right-hand column. To determine your *overall* RQ score, add the numbers for all eight RQ dimensions and enter your total RQ score in the box at the lower right of the grid.

RQ Dimension	Tally Box				RQ Scores
Self-Assurance	1:	9:	17:	25:	
Personal Vision	2:	10:	18:	26:	
Flexible and Adaptable	3:	11:	19:	27:	
Organized	4:	12:	20:	28:	
Problem Solver	5:	13:	21:	29:	
Interpersonal Competence	6:	14:	22:	30:	
Socially Connected	7:	15:	23:	31:	
Proactive	8:	16:	24:	32:	
				Overall RQ Score:	

Plotting Your Resilience Quotient

Instructions: Following the sample RQ Radar Chart provided below, transfer the eight RQ dimension scores to the RQ Radar Chart. Place a "dot" on the approximate location of each RQ dimension score on the numbered line asso-ciated with each RQ dimension.

Sample RQ Radar Chart

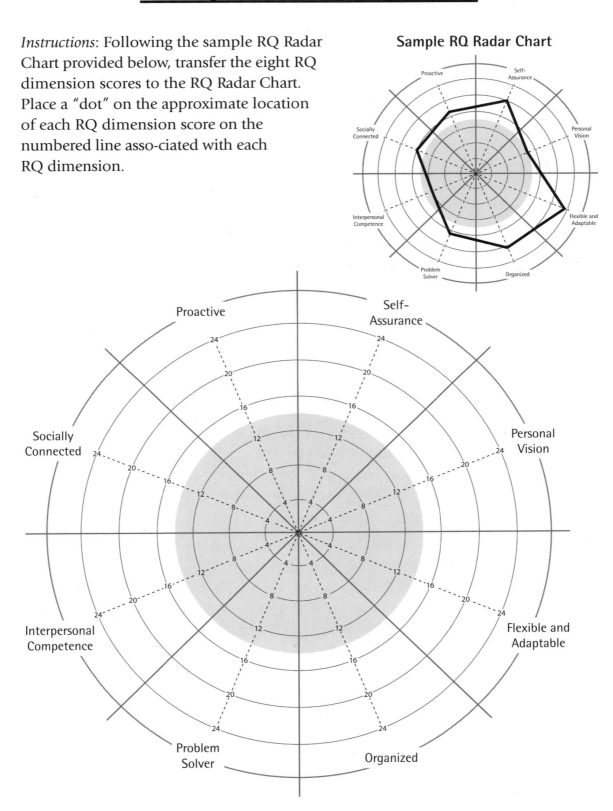

Interpreting Your RQ Scores

The maximum overall RQ score is 192. The lowest possible overall RQ score is 32. For individual RQ dimensions, the maximum possible score is 24, the lowest possible score is 4.

Instructions: Locate your overall RQ score in the range of RQ values below. Follow the suggestions offered in the explanations of each resilience level to begin developing and strengthening—or preserving—your personal resilience.

175 to 192   *Very Resilient*: You are consistently able to deal effectively with and even thrive on change. You have effective mechanisms in place that give you direction, structure, support, and self-confidence.

128 to 174   *Resilient*: Most of the time you are able to deal with change in a positive manner. You have a number of mechanisms in place that help you deal with the uncertainty of change. You could strengthen your RQ by further developing your skills in your lower-scoring RQ dimensions.

96 to 127   *Somewhat Resilient*: Change has a tendency to knock you off your best performance. You have some difficulty regaining your footing. While you have some stabilizing mechanisms in place, you could work at developing and exercising more of them. Look to your lowest-scoring dimensions as a place to start.

32 to 95   *Not Very Resilient*: Change creates major challenges for you. You are frequently unprepared for the uncertainty and lack of stability that change creates. While there are times when you are able to find stability and focus, you need to develop and enrich a broad range of resilience capacities. Look to your lowest-scoring dimensions as a place to start, and then develop your RQ development plan.

Interpreting Your RQ Radar Chart

Interpreting the meaning of your completed RQ Radar Chart involves examining the overall size of the "wheel" (a wider wheel suggests greater resilience) and the "balance" or proportionality of the wheel. A wheel out of balance, for example, would be evident if the your scores indicated low levels of resilience in one or more dimensions (such as *personal vision* or *interpersonal competence*) as compared to other dimensions. The gray area represents a low to moderate level of resilience.

To maintain or strengthen your resilience, you should focus on both expanding or growing the size of the wheel, as well as targeting for special emphasis any RQ dimension that is, in general, lower than the other dimensions—hence creating an imbalance. If one RQ dimension is significantly higher than the others, consider this an important asset that you can build on as you strive to grow or strengthen the other dimensions.

Introduction

to the Articles and Discussion Resources Section

The Articles and Discussion Resources Section is a collection of materials useful to every facilitator. The theories, background information, models, and methods will challenge facilitators' thinking, enrich their professional development, and assist their internal and external clients with productive change. These articles may be used as a basis for lecturettes, as handouts in training sessions, or as background reading material. This section will provide you with a variety of useful ideas, theoretical opinions, teachable models, practical strategies, and proven intervention methods. The articles will add richness and depth to your training and consulting knowledge and skills. They will challenge you to think differently, explore new concepts, and experiment with new interventions. The articles will continue to add a fresh perspective to your work.

The 2006 Pfeiffer Annual: Training includes eleven articles, in the following categories:

Individual Development: Developing Awareness and Understanding

Plan by Turning Time Around, by Stephen Randall

Individual Development: Life/Career Planning

Who Am I and Where Do I Fit Today, Tomorrow, and Beyond?
by Neil J. Simon and Fred Zimmer

Communication: Technology

Training Personnel to Use Speech Recognition Software, by Martha C. Yopp

Groups and Teams: Techniques to Use with Groups

Reluctance to Role Play, by Susan El-Shamy

As with previous *Annuals,* this volume covers a wide variety of topics. The range of articles presented encourages thought-provoking discussion about the present and future of HRD. We have done our best to categorize the articles for easy reference; however, many of the articles encompass a range of topics, disciplines, and applications. If you do not find what you are looking for under one category, check a related category. In some cases we may place an article in the "Training" *Annual* that also has implications for "Consulting" and vice versa. As the field of HRD continues to grow and develop, there is more and more crossover between training and consulting. Explore all the contents of both volumes of the *Annual* in order to realize the full potential for learning and development that each offers.

Plan by Turning Time Around

Stephen Randall

Summary

Linear time, the paradigm of time that is usually espoused by conventional time management and typically presumed when Westerners plan things, inaccurately presumes that time only flows uncontrollably through past, present, and future. This paradigm produces serious, yet usually unnoticed, side-effects: (1) our plans are strongly determined by the past; (2) the anxiety we feel about time passing becomes stronger; and (3) we confirm the perception that the time we have available is limited.

However, other examples of *personal time,* ways of experiencing time, are accessible. We can turn our habitual linear perspective of "going forward" around. Then instead of fighting within the confines and pressure of linear time, trying to get to our goals, we can, even while thinking about the future, *be here* instead of effortfully striving to *get there.* And our plans can be freed from past, deterministic influences.

How Do Westerners Usually Plan?

What's the typical way we plan things? We're in a kind of "room" in our experience called "the present," looking off toward another "room" called "the future," imagining some vague, yet desirable changes. From a present point of view, we look toward a distant future time when we would like to see something completed, and we visualize what the situation could be. When we're satisfied with the image visualized, i.e., when the image seems like it will fulfill our desires, needs, or aspirations, we inquire about the tasks necessary to complete the goal in the available time, then schedule the tasks, prioritize, and so forth.

So what's wrong with this picture? How could this produce side-effects? WYSIWYG. What You See Is—or helps determine—What You Get. This way of planning unnecessarily includes a paradigm of time called the *linear view, a perspective with built-in effort, confusion, and pressure.*

Three Types of Time

To discuss clearly what's happening with our typical planning, we can distinguish different facets of time. This is very helpful, but almost never done in time-management writings, causing us a lot of confusion, as well as limiting our productivity and sense of well-being. First, *event time* is the continual occurrence of physical and experiential events. The word *event* is used to describe something that happened, or is happening "now," like getting up in the morning, feeding a pet, or noticing that you're hungry.

A second facet of time uses different tools for *measuring* "event time." Most cultures use clocks and watches, and subtract a "start time" from a "stop time" to figure out how long something takes. "Telling time" is knowing how to measure time in your culture, knowing what measured "clock time" corresponds to the events that are happening "now."

The third facet of time is the one that is probably most important for our productivity and fulfillment, although it's probably also the facet that is least understood and most undervalued. Here we will call it *psychological time;* it might also be called *personal time.* Psychological time includes all the different ways we feel or experience time. Just as we have a personal space, we have a personal or psychological time. We may feel time move quickly when we're having a great time. During some of the best moments of our lives, things seem *timeless,* with little or no feeling of time passing. We feel time "drag" or pass slowly when we're bored or having a bad time. We feel anxious about time when we're reading an article like this, and it seems we don't have enough time. All these examples of psychological time are laid on top of, or based on, what can be called *linear time,* that fundamental aspect of psychological time common to many people in Western countries.

Linear Time—The Limiting Western View of Time

Linear time is the simple, yet foundational feeling of time passing from one moment to another, on which many other feelings—such as overwhelm, pressure, anxiety, hurry, time poverty, and boredom—are based. Most of us have learned to think that this feeling of time flowing is built into event time, but it's not: physical time doesn't have a "flow" feeling. Scientists have never discovered anything like a standard flow of time in nature. Psychiatrist Hartocollis says, "The experience or sense of time, and later the perception of time as an attribute of objective reality, is a function of consciousness" (1983, p. 6).

Anthropologist Edward Hall described our sense of linear time as "a horizontal conveyor belt that moves from past to present to future at the same unchangeable speed for all of us" (1983, pp. 78–79). We now know from anthropologists, psychologists, physicists, and meditation masters that *the flow of time*, along with the past, present, and future "rooms" in our experience, *develops within an individual's consciousness and results from trying to suppress or repress negative feelings and emotions*. (See "How Our Sense of Time Flow Is Created," www.manage-time.com/crttime.html.)

Although time's flow is a function of consciousness, Westerners teach each other that it is an external reality, independent of consciousness, beyond our control. *We come to think we can only adapt to this "reality."* And despite this view of event time as external and objective, we somehow learn to feel a flow of time within ourselves. This internal mirroring of the "real" external flow is considered normal. Then the attendant time pressure and anxiety, as well as the feeling that what we can accomplish in a given period of time is limited, are presumed to be "facts of life."

Description of Ordinary Work Experience

To clarify the effects of the linear view, we can look at four aspects of work done with this type of psychological time as a backdrop. Think about the qualities of your typical experience of working and compare them to the following, a distillation from thousands of participants in my workshops:

Experience of Time

Time is felt to flow among three rooms in experience, from past to present to future, at a constant and uncontrollable rate, no matter what you do or think. *There's anxiety and pressure as time constantly slips away.* You may struggle or race against time, but nothing that you do can slow time down. Occasionally you look toward a distant future time when you want to complete something. *Every time you plan or think about the future, especially if there's a deadline, there's anxiety and pressure,* because you "realistically" might not have enough time to get the work done on time.

Well-Being

There's dissatisfaction or a lack of fulfillment here as you work in the present. It might feel like you are being squeezed or confined or overwhelmed. Since the feelings are so unpleasant, there's a tendency to look forward to a better time after completing things.

Effort

The work feels stressful and seems to require effort. You might fear that it's gradually wearing you down to the point where you could get sick.

Clock Time Estimation

The dividers between the past, present, and future rooms have hazy windows in them. Even though we cannot go into the future room, we can look into it through its window. Planning an activity is similar to peering through the hazy window to see how the fuzzy future forms might shape up. We then get a vague idea of what's "coming down the pike" toward us on the conveyor.

The river of time seems to carry containers for our activities. These containers are all the same size, so in the present we can put only so many activities in a given container; then that time is used up, and the container moves into the past. Every box on the month's calendar is the same size; each day usually has the same size box; every hour on the to-do list has the same size space next to it. Since each container has the same size, *what we can accomplish in any time period appears to be limited by the structure of time itself.* Racing against the conveyor of time and trying to overfill containers can lead to overwhelm and burnout.

To estimate how much time we'll need to finish something, we guess how many of the conveyor's containers the activity will fill up. The inflexible aspect of this estimation process is related to the perceived fixed and "real" capacity of units of linear time. It's also determined by past experiences of how long it took to accomplish similar things. Thus, *your work capacity—how much you can accomplish in a given period of clock time—seems fixed.*

Clearly, working with the linear view in the background is stressful, and planning is the difficult guesswork we're familiar with. And the effects may be worse than we realize. Physician Larry Dossey says, "*Many illnesses—perhaps most—may be caused either wholly or in part by our misperception of time. . . .* I am convinced that we can destroy ourselves through the creation of illness by perceiving time in a linear, one-way flow" (1982, p. 21 [italics mine]).

Moving Beyond the Linear View for Optimal Work

Fortunately, we're not stuck with the linear view. With a little recollection, most of us confirm that the linear view is not our only available option for psychological time. Recall a few of those times in your life when your work was a peak experience. Think of some times when you were in what is now sometimes called "the zone." Not just when you were very productive, but also when most aspects of experience were best.

When at your best, how did you experience time/timelessness? How was your sense of well-being? Was there effort involved in the work?

Now see whether the following descriptions (from peak performance research) fit your recollection of optimal work:

Experience of Time

Only during breaks do you feel time flowing from past to present to future. During peak work performance you're so absorbed in what you're doing that there's no awareness of time flowing (80 percent of adults, according to surveys I've conducted with about two thousand people). If you had to describe your experience of time, most likely you'd say it was timeless. On the other hand, you might (20 percent of adults) say that time was going very quickly, yet it wasn't making you anxious with its passing. In either case, *time doesn't feel out of control, and you're not trying to race against it.*

In general you don't feel a lack of time—you just concentrate on what you're doing, which is going very well. You occasionally plan and might think about a deadline, but this thinking doesn't cause much anxiety or pressure.

Well-Being

There's very little sense of dissatisfaction; in fact, you probably feel invigorated, whole, and happy with the way things are going. As you work, you might occasionally think of the fact that the task isn't done, but this is very inconsequential. You're not worrying about not being done, nor are you looking forward to being done because that will be a better time than the present. The important thing is that you're really involved in what you're doing—*you're getting results and having a good time by being engrossed.*

Effort

The work may be requiring mental or physical energy, but it doesn't feel very stressful. *In a sense the work might even seem to be effortless,* flowing with a momentum of its own. You may not feel separate from the activity. Like being in the eye of a hurricane, there can be a sense of presence and peacefulness, even in the midst of quick or physically demanding activity.

Clock Time Estimation

Instead of flowing in a fixed and relentless way, with equal-sized containers, time seems very flexible and changeable, even unpredictable. Occasionally you check your progress and estimate whether you'll be able to finish on time. But you may not consider these estimates fixed in stone, partly because time feels very malleable during this peak experience, and partly because you know these estimates proved inaccurate so many times before. *There's a sense of ever-present opportunity and possibility*: any second, you might get some insight on how the work process can be improved.

Again, fortunately, we're not stuck with the limitations of the linear view. "It [our perception of linear time] has long been the dominant architecture in our lives. It has enabled us to create the walls and rooms of our existence. In our rush to build, however, we've forgotten that while we have the ability to construct these walls, we also have the power to tear them down" (Hunt & Hait, 1990, p. 13). Whenever we can, we should take the opportunity to move toward the "zone" of peak experience, where event time isn't accompanied by psychological pressure and planning isn't influenced by a relentless, anxiety-inducing flow of limited capacity containers.

How do we do this? We can consider future events and possibilities in a way that does not project them away from here, creating anxiety about time in the process. Many techniques are available—see www.manage-time.com for some of these. Following is one very powerful way of planning that isn't so influenced by linear time. And *Reversing Temporal Structure* doesn't reinforce the pressure and confusion we're so familiar with—in fact, it dissolves a measure of these by turning our typical linear perspective around.

Reversing Temporal Structure

We often feel a bit pressured and anxious when we plan or just think about a future time. This pressure and anxiety occur because over years we have developed a habitual way of looking at the future, a way that can be called the *pressure perspective*: we occupy a point in time we call "the present," and we look from this point to a somewhat distant segment of time called "the future," which contains the time that is relentlessly closing in on us here in the present, with a speed that seems unchangeable. In other words, "First we pick out a point situated 'up ahead' in time, then we measure the distance to that point, then we react to this situated point" (Tulku, 1994, p. 93).

What if we tried to loosen up this rigid way of looking forward to things by viewing from the future back? Would that relieve some of the pressure and anxiety? Try it and find out!

Setting Up the Exercise

First, set up your environment so you'll be undisturbed for twenty minutes. Then choose some future date by which you'd like to see some specific goal or goals completed. Or choose a specific future date you'd like to plan toward. Write this date at the top of a piece of paper.

Checking Emotional Momentum

Since we sometimes look forward to things largely to avoid what's here in the present, and since planning is a way of looking forward to things, there's a good chance that our planning will also partly be an attempt to avoid some feelings. Avoiding feelings will add to the intensity of the pressure and anxiety we feel with time's flow. (See "How Our Sense of Time Flow Is Created," www.manage-time.com/crttime.html.) *By becoming aware of our feelings we can free our plans from their fixed, determining directions.*

Make notes as you respond to the following questions: How do you feel? Are there one or more feelings that you're aware of? Why are you motivated? What feelings are involved? Would some of your feelings like to push things away or get rid of something? Is there some feeling that makes up some of the momentum that is moving you to plan now? How are these feelings moving you to plan? In which directions are these feelings moving you?

Looking Back

Now, don't just pretend, but as much as you can, get into the sense that it *is* that day. *Now from this date, look back over "the past" and make a few notes about what happened on the project up till this day.* Write your notes in the past tense, as if whatever comes to mind (no effort or special intuition is necessary) really did happen in the past, and you're just remembering it (Fanning & Fanning, 1979). Keep an open mind; don't expect, hope, fear, or assume anything. Don't be optimistic or pessimistic.

Just relax and see whether you can "remember" what happened to your goals during the period. You may not remember right away—but we don't always remember things immediately when we try, do we? Write whatever you remember was accomplished, as well as any insight you realized and any personal changes you see that you went through.

About Doing the Exercise

After you feel that the exercise is complete, take a few more minutes and write down how you experienced doing it. Did anything interesting happen? Did you get any insights or creative ideas? Did you enjoy doing the exercise? Did you get a sense of completion and satisfaction? How was it different from your typical way of planning or thinking about doing things?

Other Ways to Do the Exercise

Instead of making a daily "to-do list," you can effectively use this exercise to write a "done list" for the day. Assume that the workday is over and write down in past tense what happened.

How about a different approach to New Year's resolutions? Making resolutions is often a matter of will power and guilt, an exercise in strongly intending to do what we think we should. You can cut through hazards of wishful thinking by reviewing accomplishments from a future time. Assume the year is over, and it's the morning of January 1st! Then write down what happened during the "previous" year.

Explore a more creative and insightful alternative to consensus building and five-year plans for a group. You can effortlessly and intuitively plan projects by doing a presumé, reviewing accomplishments from a future time. Then compare individuals' views of the group's progress to determine alignment and get insight for new directions.

Rather than have to switch back and forth between writing and remembering what happened, you may prefer to use a tape recorder or dictate to a friend.

When doing the exercise, you may get images or scenes that can be sketched and included with your writing.

And finally, if after doing the exercise you do not achieve the results you want, you can do it again from a point of view farther in the future.

Conclusion: About Changing Perspective

During this exercise, you may get a sense of relief, peace, presence, or rest—even if the goal didn't appear to be completed. Why? A lot of our lives is spent trying to get to goals up ahead, in the future, "going forward," as business and news people often say these days. We often expect that we'll be happier later on, after we complete a goal. But the quality of our experience—the natural fulfillment that is available no matter what we're doing—is depreciated by a habitual perspective of looking forward to things.

When we turn our habitual perspective of "going forward" around, we break through this temporal structure of seeking happiness somewhere else. Then instead of fighting within the confines and pressure of linear time, trying to get to our goals, we can visualize and plan here in peace and presence. We can, even while thinking about the future, *be here* instead of trying to *get there.* And our plans can be freed from past, deterministic influences of linear time.

References

Dossey, L. (1982). *Space, time, and medicine.* Boston & London: Shambhala.

Fanning, T., & Fanning, R. (1979). *Get it all done and still be human.* New York: Ballantine Books.

Hall, E.T. (1983). *The dance of life.* Garden City, NY: Anchor Press/Doubleday.

Hartocollis, P. (1983). *Time and timelessness.* New York: International Universities Press.

Hunt, D., & Hait, P. (1990). *The tao of time.* New York: Henry Holt.

Tulku, T. (1994). *Dynamics of time and space.* Berkeley, CA: Dharma Publishing.

Stephen Randall *is a psychologist, time and stress management consultant, and peak performance researcher. He has published the most complete time management resources online, at www.manage.time.com. Dr. Randall wrote* Results in No Time, *which suggests that we can find the peaceful, yet most productive "zone" at the center of our whirlwind of activities. Since 1985, Dr. Randall has taught cutting-edge time mastery methods to thousands in ninety workshops in the United States and abroad.*

Who Am I and Where Do I Fit Today, Tomorrow, and Beyond?

Neil J. Simon and Fred Zimmer

Summary

Anxieties exist for today's workforce around the subject of vocational stability. As professional consultants and/or coaches, we see these stresses, particularly with the older generation of workers who grew up in a "thirty-years-and-out" environment, and also with those personality types who have desires for things to be constant. Human resource professionals are predicting that people now entering this economy will experience three significant vocational shifts and fifteen to nineteen jobs within their working careers. Based on this prediction, major questions become:

- What is my vocation? Who am I vocationally?

- Where do I fit today?

- Where will I fit tomorrow?

- Where might I fit beyond tomorrow?

This article will explore factors underlying today's shifting work world, help explore the changing, vocational future, and provide a template for planning one's own future direction.

Vocational stability is a paradigm from the past. In today's workforce, vocation itself is beset with many changing circumstances, and stability certainly seems to be part of a distant, utopian dream. Workers with traditional jobs constantly face threats that are based on the current economy. This intimidation includes job loss, reduced hours, reduced overtime, or the impacts of workforce reduction on workplace survivors. Those displaced workers have a different set of concerns. These concerns deal with such things as employability; the obsolescence of their knowledge, skills, and performance; age discrimination; short-term contracts without benefits; self-employment tax; and being home all the time. They come to doubt their vocation and its worth.

The authors define vocation as not only "the job," but also the "intended course in the world" (whether fate or choice can be debated!). How one perceives the non-materialistic aspects of "the job" shapes what this notion of vocation is. Vocation is addressed in this article as the basis of one's working life. If vocation is "the top job," then the course of action is determined in a particular way—the cut and thrust of politics in the office and all that it entails. If vocation is "service," then the course of action is very different (although it could even entail those politics). Vocation does determine fundamentally how satisfied one can be with one's working life.

A current human resources tenet is that people must sell themselves as commodities—specialists who go to the highest bidder. From this perspective, individuals seek to be recognized, in part, for their existing work skills. From the organization's perspective, their "use" to the company is in aiding the quest to become profitable or to maintain profitability while meeting stockholder—or owner or leadership—financial demands. The successful job seeker has convinced the employer of his or her economic value to the company and kept intact his or her vocation.

The New Normal

However, the major impact in today and tomorrow's environment is the effects of the "new normal" on the global economy. The new normal comprises, among other things, the changes in business assumptions, paradigms, and practices in a globalized world. Some globalization factors include changes in outsourcing of the workforce, use of contractual employees, threats of terrorism, the demands of more sophisticated customers, an overabundance of employees who are highly trained yet missing "today's skill sets," and independent domestics and internationals who are promoting their goods on a global scale. These all create an atmosphere in which worker uncertainty and anxiety thrive.

Changes in today's competitive corporate environment include:

- Globalization and increased competitiveness;

- Increased pressures to ensure profitability;

- Creation of "leaner and meaner" organizations; and

- Greater demands placed on organizations to meet and exceed their customer expectations.

At the same time, today's customers have changed as well. They have matured and become astute, demanding purchasers who are keen to meet their own organization's needs. They have increased their demands for product and service quality and reliability. This maturation has led to customers being better able to:

- Specify products and services in terms of their own needs and values;

- Discern competitive marketing schemes;

- Create new and unique "bedfellow" relationships;

- Engage in enhanced "deal making," limiting "vendor" profitability; and

- Effect change within vendor organizations so that their own customer needs are better met (co-location).

Organizations have responded to these changes by redefining the use of the employee. They have breached the old and outdated "patriarchal employee promise"— "work for me and I will take care of you forever." This breech has led to significant and fundamental changes in the employer/employee relationship. Employees had to become more responsible for themselves in the work world. They had to fundamentally change their views of the organizational "family" to one of being entrepreneurial and/or commodity based. All are orphaned now, trying to find new relations in the world, and so experience the anxieties of the displaced worker. This situation suggests acquiring or enhancing the skills in the following areas:

1. Gain specialized knowledge to increase personal and organizational worth.

    a. Offer the organization "intellectual" capital.

    b. Develop requisite technical mastery that includes:

    Development of content expertise.

    Development of process expertise.

    Keeping up with technological advances to ensure competitiveness within the business world.

2. Develop requisite and appropriate skill sets to ensure being "state of the art."

    a. Constant reassessment of personal skills, scanning for obsolescence and/or emergence of state-of-the-art technology.

b.   Socialization.

Develop new global social skills.

Compensate for lack of person-to-person communication skills.

Overcome breakdowns of social structures (that is, loss of "water cooler" discussions and after-work get-togethers).

Adapt to expanded roles of minorities and women in the workplace and their becoming the majority of the workforce.

Adapt to racial, cultural, and educational diversity that is now "de rigueur."

Work smart, which usually includes working in teams or with collaborative efforts.

c.   Communication skills.

Live with the pressure of real-time communication, 24/7 in many cases.

Develop global communication skills and abilities to be able to converse with the diverse cultures they may present.

Compensate for the lack of fundamental communication skills—writing, spelling, and speaking.

3. Develop as employees who have a special focus based on each individual's unique strengths and aptitudes.

a.   Blend personal preferences with the demands of the employing workforce so that the employee likes what he or she is doing.

b.   Create personal outlets for needs outside of the work environment.

c.   Enhance the self-image of employees as something more than merely a commodity.

d.   Create a different type of networking—the "good ol' boy network" is trying to hold on, but is being superceded by the cyber and superficial networking of the "Hail fellow, well met" variety.

e.   Enable one to live with constant risk.

f.   Work more for less.

g.   See that a shift in worker attitude in that work is only a means to an end—workers work for time off to recreate and spend time as they choose for themselves.

Employees are being required to think differently while taking on a different set of responsibilities. The role of the employee "in the old days" used to be perceived as the "hands and feet," with management as the "head." Based on the above-mentioned breech in that cozy "family," the work world then moved to a relationship of the accountability and responsibility of employees, the employees having to prove themselves in the work world just in order to maintain their jobs. Thus, employees had to work with constant innovation in order to keep business alive as well as create functional working environments. Finally, in this "developmental/evolutionary" training, employees went from an individual responsibility basis to one where they had to work with others in teams, work groups, and different "cultures" involved in the creation of organizational processes, innovations, constant changes, and ongoing problem solving. This shift required the development of a variety of interpersonal business skills. This change in worker responsibility and interpersonal relationships coincided with:

- Assumptive changes in business practices due to the creation of an instantaneous global environment;

- Import of an organizational culture when there was a takeover or buyout;

- Rapid turnover of executives and employees, based on desired performance or lack of performance;

- Executives becoming commodities with a 2.5-year lifespan;

- Employees being charged with managing the "evolution and revolution" of organizations (Greiner, 1998); and

- Ongoing "organizational turbulence."

Today's Employee

The foundations of today's "independent" employees are based on four key areas:

1. *Professional mastery*—having a thorough understanding of your discipline and its impact on the world of work.

2. *Personal style*—understanding your work style and personal growth needs and their impact on the organization with which you are working.

3. *Understanding others*—constructively engaging in interpersonal relationships within professional settings.

4. *Futuring*—prediction and self-positioning for the future.

These are the keys for surviving the next couple of work generations.

Professional Mastery

Professional mastery is the individual's ability to develop a knowledge base and rapidly apply it to the discipline of choice. This includes ongoing learning, mastery of supportive technologies, and integration of related processes. Today's and tomorrow's workers will require a fundamental knowledge of their own disciple and the ability to comprehend its present and future impact, and then an ability to synthesize new knowledge, and finally to apply the learning derived from that experiential feedback.

Today's environment often demands innovative solutions. Part of professional mastery is being able to think beyond one discipline and incorporate concepts from others. Blending professional concepts leads to vocational leadership and/or innovations.

However, workers are being "forced" down professional paths based on their experiential background, opportunities, and education. They are often "tracked" based on their past experiences and their own presentations of their *curriculum vitae.* Once a worker is tracked in this way, he or she continues on that path until the type of work he or she does expires or until the worker wants a change. A worker, to succeed today, needs to have flexibility and responsiveness to the environment in which he or she works or wants to work.

If a worker wants to change his or her professional activities, he or she needs to build a credible track record in that new direction. This could include gaining experience through other jobs, "re-framing" current jobs to meet new employer requirements, going to a learning institution (that is, schools, institutes, or long-distance learning), or creating some perception of mastery that an employer would "buy."

Personal Style

Personal style is understanding one's own work style and personal growth needs and how that style and those needs impact on the organization in which one works.

Each person has deep within a "preferential learning style." This style forms the foundation for our perceptions of the world. It pre-determines our natural thinking and learning patterns. It affects how we see the world. These patterns are then shaped by the social forces around us (from our early childhood to last week's encounters) and then finally forged by our personal psychology.

For example, our style influences whether we first look at things globally or at an individual level; whether we see things discretely as if they were photographs or panoramically as if it were a movie; whether we start with things and generalize or we start with the broad picture and then determine the specifics. Likewise, performance style is how we actualize what we want to do. It is the patterns we use to create these accomplishments. For example, some people are "plodders." They break things down into finite tasks and accomplish each one one at a time, and sometimes in infinite detail. Others may multi-task, addressing several chores simultaneously. These styles make us unique and allow us to be interested in certain specialties and to nurture specific vocations.

These "genetic dispositions," our social and psychological "training," and related influences develop our unique paradigms—the ways in which we have learned to perceive the world. Each paradigm is a "closed system"—we affirm what we believe by viewing and interpreting our environment through the paradigm so we can continue with our comfortable perceptions. We continue with this pattern until it can no longer be validated, which means we have to change.

Many have created a dynamic paradigm when it comes to continuous growth and development. They cultivate themselves as growing, lifelong learners who constantly grow and adapt to the ever-changing work environment. This paradigm of continuous growth allows one more easily to accept changes that affect what one is currently doing. Consequently one sees what one needs to do in order to stay continually employed.

Knowing personal style helps one create success within the world of work. One can improve on what is "natural" and learn to compensate for those things that are more difficult for each individually. Not only does style need to "fit" with the tasks at hand, but it also helps influence the fit within organizational culture in which one wants to work.

Another dynamic of personal style is one's ability to lead and to follow. Leadership may take the form of functional titles or may take the form of proactive behavior. These traits are currently required in the ever-dwindling workforce. Likewise, followership is critical as well. Followership takes the form of working with others to assist in accomplishing a "greater good." Both leadership and followership are critical to personal success that is limited by one's personal style.

An often-forgotten aspect of success in this arena is maintaining a balance between work and personal life. Knowledge of personal style allows one to fashion work and play in a manner that meets needs and assists in perpetual growth. Balance of personal and professional life allows people to be who they are and fulfill themselves on several levels of growth and development.

The overall "ideal" of personal style was captured by Maslow (1987), who described the concepts of "self actualization" and "meta-motivation," which imply being able to be who you are and fit fulfillingly within an organization.

Understanding Others

Unless one works in a vacuum, interpersonal relationships are critical to today's world of work. Understanding others' drives and constructively engaging interpersonal relationships within professional settings fills the world with meaning and potential reward. The better the understanding, the higher the probability of a constructive working relationship. This ability to understand others means developing sensitivities as to how others work, learning about others' personal styles, and developing an appreciation of their perceptions and concepts of the world.

Understanding how others work individually or within groups enables one to engage constructively in working relationships with others. This in turn furthers an understanding of how to join with others to create a desired social/business organization's result. It is critical to be able to work with others in the many social and interpersonal relationship areas, while at the same time buying into the organizational direction (vision and mission of the group). This type of approach often leads to positive relationships that are maintained far beyond the project for which they began. This approach allows the creation of a respected friend who happened to be found at work.

Today's employees are asked to work collaboratively, in teams, as resources, as part of multiple work groups, and so on. These different roles and circumstances can be challenging. The ultimate goal is for the employees to fulfill their roles and provide the required services or products. This means that each employee, based on personal style, needs to develop strategies to work with others constructively.

In many cases, organizations are attempting to create collaborative win/win relationships to help ensure the growth and development of their employees, to help fulfill some of their personal and professional needs, and to ensure they cooperate and collaborate so that everyone can be productive on all fronts. Many employees have adopted a collaborative style so they can increase their knowledge, skills, and worth, while at the same time benefiting the organization. This willingness to work for the mutual welfare and benefit of the group, rather than just self-interest, is considered a higher level of employee development. These employees develop themselves as a result of working for the organization's good; consequently everyone benefits—the worker, co-workers, and the organization (ultimately the customers and even the shareholders).

Futuring

Futuring is the ability to position yourself for a potential opportunity based on that open and creative personal style above. Soothsaying used to be a profitable profession—especially if you could successfully predict the future! In today's world a newer version of soothsaying is surfacing as a critical skill for both personal and professional survival. The quest is equipping yourself with the necessary knowledge, skills, attitudes, and behaviors required for success, along with some good guessing.

Many of today's predictions have to do with being able to recognize patterns, observe evolution, know the right people, and be at the right place at the right time with the right resources required for entry into the playing field. The ability to recognize and interpret trends properly is a valuable trait as well. This trait allows one to position himself or herself for the future.

Another critical trait is the ability to understand that business evolution is an organic process. This process is driven by many factors, such as environmental and economic factors, resource availability, and leadership direction. These influences create a very dynamic and often chaotic environment in which different ideas and opportunities emerge. Opportunities abound if one is in the right place at the right time.

Today's employee builds social capital that can be used to cultivate productive professional contacts. Social capital can be used to help create one's future. For example, as one sees emerging trends one can create new contacts for personal and professional opportunities, and, if one is very lucky, perhaps even make that valuable contact with a future trend setter and capitalize on being in that part of the network.

The worker of today not only needs to be vocationally flexible but "locationally" flexible as well. Today workers share both physical space and cyberspace, frequently moving to new physical locations and/or working from a computer across great distances. The old paradigm of working in a community near where you live is slowly fading. The world is shrinking as it globalizes.

Many workers are confronted with challenges due to several simultaneously emerging events. The worker, in order to create a preferred future, has to determine for himself or herself the probability of a trend as well as the professional fit for his or her self-development. This ability to predict a future that meets one's needs and goals is a new concept for many.

Another critical skill is to create or influence others to create a preferred path for the future. Whether it is garnering support for a project you want to work on, finances for a new venture, or gathering resources for a collaborative effort, influencing is becoming a critical factor. Being able to understand social systems and to determine leverage points (areas in which to apply pressure to create a desired result) is a major dynamic in creating opportunities for a desired future.

How Do You Fare for Tomorrow and Beyond?

Having considered these four foundation stones, it's time to move to the next step, self-analysis. This procedure assists in identifying one's perceptions of one's present position. It also helps reveal where one wants to be in the future.

The self-assessment inventory that follows is designed to help you, the reader, consider what may be necessary for your current work environment and what level of expertise you possess. Next, the inventory helps assess how you are positioned to provide this expertise in tomorrow's work world. This information can then be used to create a map of your "destiny" according to the chosen growth path and where you see yourself now.

Self-Assessment Inventory

Instructions: For the four foundations, consider each of the listed "driving dynamics." Rate your skill level for today's environment using a scale of 1 to 5. (1 should be considered minimal and 5 maximal.) Enter your self-assessment number in the "Where Do I Fit Today" column. After that is completed, assess how you are "Positioned for Tomorrow." Enter a separate score of 1 to 5 for each of the driving dynamics in the Tomorrow column.

Area	Definition	Driving Dynamic to the Future	Questions	
			Where Do I Fit Today?	How Am I Positioned for Tomorrow?
Professional Mastery	An individual's ability to develop a knowledge base and rapidly apply it to the discipline of choice	Foundational, intellectual knowledge in my field of specialization		
		Rapidly applying knowledge, technologies, and related processes		
		Incorporating new thoughts and concepts beyond the current discipline		
		Track record of successful experiences in the field		
		Responding flexibly to rapid changes in the work environment		
		Keeping up with requisite knowledge so as not to encounter obsolescence or aging of knowledge		
		Total		
Personal Style	Understanding your work style and personal growth needs and how these impact the organization in which you are working	Knowledge of my personal learning style(s)		
		Knowledge of my performance style(s)		
		Ability to lead		
		Ability to follow		
		Cultivating self as a growing, lifelong learner		
		Maintaining a balance between my work life and my personal life		
		Total		

Area	Definition	Driving Dynamic to the Future	Questions	
			Where Do I Fit Today?	How Am I Positioned for Tomorrow?
Understand-ing Others	Constructively engaging in interpersonal relationships within profes-sional settings	Ability to understand the differences of others		
		Knowledge of strategies for successfully working with the learning and perfor-mance styles of others		
		Ability to engage in work with varying groups of people		
		Ability to create and maintain relationships		
		Ability to collaborate and work with others		
		Willingness to work for the mutual welfare and benefit of the group rather than self-interests		
		Total		
Futuring	Creating assumptions and predictions, positioning yourself for a potential opportunity	Knowledge of trends and patterns in the field		
		Perceiving the organic nature of the evolution of this field		
		Cultivation of productive professional contacts		
		Being flexible in order to go where I need to go when I have to go		
		Being able to gauge probability of trends and my professional fit		
		Knowing where to influence for desired results		
		Total		

Interpretation Instructions

Total your scores for each of the areas on the Self-Assessment Inventory. Use the graph below to chart your scores. For *Professional Mastery*, enter your Today score as an X and your Tomorrow score as an O on the Self-Assessment Graph. For *Personal Style,* enter your Today score as an X and your Tomorrow score as an O on the Self-Assessment Graph. For *Understanding Others,* enter your Today score as an X and your Tomorrow score as an O on the Self-Assessment Graph. For *Futuring,* enter your Today score as an X and your Tomorrow score as an O on the Self-Assessment Graph.

Self-Assessment Graph				
	Professional Mastery	**Personal Style**	**Understanding Others**	**Futuring**
30				
29				
28				
27				
26				
25				
24				
23				
22				
21				
20				
19				
18				
17				
16				
15				
14				
13				
12				
11				
10				
9				
8				
7				
6				
5				
4				
3				
2				
1				
0				

Tool Interpretation

If a Today or Tomorrow score is 15 or lower, this suggests an area needing concentrated improvement. If a Today or Tomorrow score is above 21, you are positioned well.

Next Steps—Create a Plan

With your scores charted, you are now at a point to create a plan. The form below will help you organize your thoughts and create a plan you can use to go into the future.
First perform an overall analysis.

- Consider what your Today scores suggest about needed skill development in your current position or endeavor.

- Consider what your Tomorrow scores suggests about future skill development.

- What does the overall pattern of your graph suggest about finding a place for yourself in the ever-changing environment of today and tomorrow's work world?

- Observe your pattern on the self-assessment graph. In the space entitled "Overall Analysis/Thoughts" on the form below, write your observations about yourself.

Second, identify each of your needs in the foundational areas and create a set of specific notes. Then determine how you are going to plan to meet those needs and determine a time for your accomplishments.

Overall Analysis/Thoughts			
Foundations	Notes for Improvement	Plan	Timeline
Professional Mastery			
Personal Style			
Understanding Others			
Futuring			

Remember that this plan must be reviewed on a regular basis—the world is an organic, vital place!

Conclusion

Today's workers are subject to a variety of new forces that create an ever-changing work environment. The concept of work stability as we once knew it is a paradigm of the past. In the *new normal* of today's work world, the independent worker is a commodity responsible for planning his or her current and future work life.

Four key areas—professional mastery, personal style, understanding others, and futuring—are seen as key for ensuring success. Confidence and capability in these areas help equip the worker with the knowledge, skills, attitudes, and behaviors that will ensure personal and professional development.

Everyone needs to optimize his or her personal and professional development. This development needs to be carefully planned based on the natural strengths and desires. Knowing who they are and where they fit, today, tomorrow, and beyond, will help ensure and care for the ever-changing global workforce.

References

Greiner, L. (1998, May/June). Evolution and revolution as organizations grow. *Harvard Business Review.*

Maslow, A.H. (1987). *Motivation and personality* (3rd ed.). New York: HarperCollins.

Neil J. Simon *is the CEO of Business Development Group, based in Ann Arbor, Michigan. He has over thirty years' experience in working with organizations and individuals to improve performance. His work focuses on organization leadership, strategic change, and implementation utilizing his A²D⁴ Collaborative Consulting Approach. Mr. Simon works nationally and internationally with organizations to strategize, innovate, design, or redesign processes, departments, divisions, or entire organizations to optimize organizational performance.*

Fred Zimmer *is a senior consultant with Business Development Group, Inc. He has seventeen years' experience in the clinical, medical, and community non-profit sectors, focusing on improving individual and program performance. His emphasis includes working with organizations to envision preferred futures, foster critical alignments, and develop system-wide processes for implementing strategic goals.*

Training Personnel to Use Speech Recognition Software

Martha C. Yopp

Summary

Speech recognition software, a revolutionary new feature in Microsoft Office XP and 2003, makes it possible for users to enter text, control menus, and execute commands by speaking into a microphone. It is easy to use, is readily available at virtually no cost, can increase employee and management efficiency and productivity, and can reduce incidents of carpal tunnel and repetitive stress injuries.

This article promotes the use of the Microsoft Word XP or 2003 speech recognition software over other speech recognition programs because it comes with the Microsoft Office product and does not require any additional cost except for a microphone headset. [This is not intended to be an advertisement for Microsoft products but rather a heads up that most office workers have this resource readily available, but they are not aware of it.]

The Association of Repetitive Motion Syndrome reports that repetitive stress injuries (RSI) occur when people perform the same physical motion over and over. This can result in temporary or permanent damage to cartilage, tendons, ligaments, nerves, and muscles, and it can be painful and debilitating (Hensing, 2001).

One way to alleviate some RSIs is by reducing the amount of keyboarding that people who work with computers must do. Microsoft Word XP and 2003 come with a sophisticated voice/speech recognition feature that is readily available and easy to put to use.

Robert Hensing, a Microsoft product support specialist who suffers from repetitive stress injury, reports that he is "absolutely floored by this technology" (2001). Hensing's job required him to send and receive over three hundred emails per day.

After typing so frequently for two years, he began to experience pain so severe that he could not easily turn the ignition key in his car.

> "I was terrified that I'd done irreparable damage. . . I'm only twenty-five years old and don't know what I'd do for a living if I couldn't use my hands to type."

Hensing began using the voice-recognition software on his computer, and he now sends and receives emails using his voice with minimal keyboard interaction.

> "I'm pleased to report that after several weeks, the pain in my fingers nearly subsided. Office XP [speech recognition software] exceeded my expectations, and I can be pretty tough to please" (Hensing, 2001).

How It Works

Understanding spoken language is something people often take for granted. Most of us develop the ability to recognize speech when we are quite young. Children are usually proficient at speech recognition by the age of three.

Just like people, the computer needs to learn to recognize speech. When you read aloud the prepared training text that comes with the Microsoft software, the training wizard looks for patterns in the way you speak. At any time, you can go back to the training wizard to read additional training text, thus giving the computer more opportunity to learn to recognize speech patterns. When speaking to a computer, you want to speak in a consistent, level tone. Speaking too loudly or softly makes it difficult for the computer to recognize what has been said. Speak without pausing between words. A phrase is easier for the computer to interpret than just one word.

When people first start using speech-recognition software, they discover that the computer sometimes makes mistakes. It records words that sound like what was spoken. The computer is not capable of thinking or translating. Additional training and correcting errors help the computer recognize the words you use and add them to the speech recognition dictionary.

System Requirements

To use the speech recognition software provided with Microsoft Office you need the following:

- Microsoft Office XP or 2003

- A headset with a microphone

- A 400 megahertz or faster computer

- 128 MB or more of memory

- Windows XP or later

- Microsoft Internet Explorer 5.01 or later

Headsets range in price from $10 to $35. The one I use cost less than $10, including shipping, when purchased in lots of ten. Jeff Reynar, a Microsoft program manager, recommends the use of a high quality microphone such as a Plantronics communication headset. Those are available for $20 or $25. This, of course, is minimal when the potential for widespread usage is taken into consideration. When using the microphone, you need to position it so that it is about an inch to the side of your mouth. You do not want it directly in front of your mouth, and you do not want to breathe directly into it.

Getting Started

Once you have Microsoft Office XP or 2003 and a headset with a microphone, you do not need anything else except experimentation and training time. You do not need much training to start, but the more you train the more effectively you and the computer will work together. Very simply, you go to *Tools* on your menu bar and select *Speech*. Then follow the instructions on your computer. I recommend you read all of the beginning training excerpts. It takes about an hour and you do not have to do it in one session. Additional information from Microsoft about using Microsoft Speech Recognition is available at the following website: www.educ.uidaho.edu/bustech. Click on *Keyboarding*, then *Voice Recognition*, and you will find several instructional links.

Another resource is Speaking Solutions, Inc., a company that can provide additional support for a reasonable price. Visit their website at www.speakingsolutions.com. They will sell you a training manual and a good pair of Plantronics headsets for $35. You do not have to have the manual, but it does walk you through the use of all of the commands in an orderly fashion. The website also lists two textbooks that can be used to improve efficiency and productivity.

Two Modes: Dictation and Voice Command

Microsoft speech recognition software operates in two modes: (1) *Dictation*, which allows the user to dictate memos, letter, e-mail messages, etc., and (2) *Voice Command*, which allows the user to select menu, toolbar, and dialog box items. When you are in the voice command mode, you cannot dictate text, and when you switch to the dictation mode, only a few commands are recognized. Microsoft developers, after extensive field-testing, decided that two modes work better than one for most users (Reynar, 2001).

To begin dictating, make certain your microphone is on and click the dictation icon, or say *"Dictation,"* to start voice recognition. Turn the microphone off when you are not dictating. Speech recognition will continue to process sounds until the microphone is turned off.

Voice commands are used to edit or to move around the document after dictation is completed. Microsoft speech recognition works well when used in conjunction with your keyboard and mouse. Over time, however, you may use the mouse and keyboard less and less. Voice commands do work, and they enable you to work in a hands-free environment.

Commands and Formatting

The voice recognition software can recognize a number of commands:

- *Select* allows you to pinpoint words and phrases.

- Add lines by dictating *New Line* for one line or *New Paragraph* for two lines.

- Correct errors by using the *Correct* command.

- The commands *Scratch That* and *Undo That* remove unwanted text.

- Also recognized are commands such as *Cut That, Paste That, Center, Align Left, Align Right.*

- You can format with commands such as *Underscore, Bold, Bullet,* and by indicating *Font* size and style.

- You can add names, unusual words, acronyms, and/or jargon to your dictionary.

Numbers

Numbers smaller than twenty are spelled out when dictated. Numbers greater than twenty are inserted as digits. To dictate all numbers as digits, you must say, *"ForceNum"* before you say the number. When dictating decimals, say the number followed by *Point,* for example, *"Ten Point Six"* for 10.6.

Punctuation

You will also dictate essential punctuation. Use the common name for punctuation marks: period, comma, exclamation point, semicolon, question mark, and so forth.

Symbols and Special Characters

Symbols and special characters such as the ampersand, asterisk, at sign, slash, backslash, hyphen, double dash, plus, dollar sign, pound sign, brackets, fractions, and quotation marks can also be dictated.

Speech recognition can be used to create slideshow presentations using PowerPoint and to enter data and move around in Excel. Speech recognition software can be used for other Microsoft Office applications as well.

User Profiles

Speech recognition user profiles store information about how to recognize your voice. You can create profiles for multiple users on the same computer. You can also create additional profiles for yourself when working in environments with different levels of noise or using different microphones.

Correcting Errors

There are several ways to correct errors using speech recognition software. You can right-click on an error and a list of alternatives will be displayed. If the correct alternative is not listed, you can spell over errors or you can dictate over errors. You can also add words to the speech recognition dictionary or delete words you no longer use. You can use the Learn from Document features to add words that previously were not in the dictionary.

Improving Your Accuracy

Train your computer to recognize your voice by reading aloud the prepared training text. Additional training, and the correcting of mistakes, increases speech recognition accuracy. As you dictate, don't be concerned if you do not immediately see your words on the screen. Continue speaking and pause at the end of your thought. The computer will display the recognized text on the screen after it finishes processing your voice.

The ultimate goal of speech recognition training is to increase accuracy to 98 percent when speaking familiar words at a controlled pace. A pace of 110 to 170 wpm with 98 percent accuracy is much better than the very best typists in the world can maintain.

Reduce Keyboard and Mouse-Related Injuries

The mission of Speaking Solutions, a company that specializes in training people to use voice recognition software, is to greatly reduce carpal tunnel syndrome (CTS) and repetitive stress/strain injuries (RSI) caused by the keyboard and the mouse while, at the same time, increasing productivity through the use of speech recognition software (*About Speaking Solutions*, n.d.).

Speaking Solutions executives are asking educators and workforce trainers to promote a program that teaches students and personnel to use speech recognition software. They advocate ending the epidemic of keyboard and mouse related injuries by adopting five goals for injury prevention (*About Speaking Solutions*, n.d.):

1. Reduce keystrokes and mouse clicks among healthy computer users by 50 percent by 2009, while improving overall productivity.

2. Reduce keystrokes and mouse clicks among RSI and CTS sufferers by 95 percent immediately, while improving their productivity.

3. Encourage the implementation of continuous speech recognition instruction in every K-12 school and college by 2009.

4. Establish a continuous speech recognition "trainer of trainers" program in every state.

5. Assist corporate and government agency human resource departments as they implement speech recognition training in the workplace.

Using a computer should not be painful. The future of millions of hands, wrists, shoulders, and necks depends on the ability to pass along essential speech recognition skills: basic reading skills, enunciation skills, and composition and communication skills (Barksdale, 2003a, 2003b).

Speech recognition software has been used very successfully with handicapped adults. In many respects, able-bodied adults are benefiting from the research by and commitment of disabled adults in using and perfecting this technology so that we all now have access to it at minimal cost. Public opinion has also changed. Speech recognition is receiving greater acceptance. Educators and business people are no longer asking "Why?" They are asking, "How do I get started? What do I need to begin?"

Summary

Speech recognition enables people to voice-write between 110 and 170 words per minute with 95 percent accuracy after only a few hours of training. The use of speech recognition software can increase productivity of computer users and reduce incidents of carpal tunnel and repetitive stress injuries caused by excessive and frequent use of the keyboard and mouse.

There are few, if any, legitimate reasons not to incorporate speech recognition into the training agenda for all organizations using computers for inputting data and information. Doing so does not mean that most people will use speech recognition exclusively, but they will have a viable alternative, particularly for large documents or if they are experiencing any of the early warning signs of repetitive stress injuries or carpal tunnel.

References

About Speaking Solutions. (n.d.). Speaking Solutions: Speech recognition resources for everyone. Retrieved October 12, 2004, from www.speakingsolutions.com/about/index.html.

Barksdale, K. (2003a). *Safer keyboarding: Fifteen principles of safer keyboarding instruction.* Speaking Solutions, Inc. Retrieved October 12, 2004, from www.speakingsolutions.com/news/art16.htm.

Barksdale, K. (2003b). *Speech recognition's role in reducing injuries.* Speaking Solutions, Inc. Retrieved October 12, 2004, from www.speakingsolutions.com/news/art16.html.

Hensing, R. (2001, April 18). *Office XP speaks out: Voice recognition assists users.* Redmond, WA: Microsoft Corporation. Retrieved December 8, 2004, from www.microsoft.com/presspass/features/2001/apr01/04–18xpspeech.asp.

Reynar, J. (2001, April 18). *Office XP speaks out: Voice recognition assists users.* Redmond, WA: Microsoft Corporation. Retrieved December 8, 2004, from www.microsoft.com/presspass/features/2001/apr01/04–18xpspeech.asp.

Martha C. Yopp, Ed.D., *is a professor of adult and organizational learning at the University of Idaho, Boise Center. She earned a B.S. from Oregon State University, an M.S.T from Portland State University, and an Ed.D. in higher education with an emphasis on human resource development from George Washington University. Dr. Yopp has been a faculty member at the University of Idaho for eighteen years. Her background includes community college teaching and workplace training, and she currently serves as president of the Idaho Lifelong Learning Association.*

Reluctance to Role Play*

Susan El-Shamy

Summary

Role playing is a valuable training technique that develops skills, builds confidence, and increases the possibility of behavioral change. However, many people are reluctant to role play, and their reluctance can impede their own learning and the learning of other participants in the class as well. This article investigates some of reasons that people are reluctant to role play and then generates simple steps instructors can use to address these reasons and reduce participant reluctance.

Have you ever been in a situation in which you were reluctant to role play? Perhaps you were a participant at the time and you were asked to demonstrate an unfamiliar concept in an impromptu role play with someone you didn't know in front of a group of strangers. Now, that's enough to make anyone reluctant. Or maybe, as an instructor, you found yourself hesitating to use a role-playing activity. You knew that the activity was good and that participants could benefit from doing it, but a blinking yellow light went off somewhere in the back of your mind. "Watch out," came the warning. "Some people don't like to role play."

And it's true; some people don't like to role play. Being asked to assume a role and behave in a manner that does not come easily can put a person in an extremely difficult situation. No one likes to feel vulnerable, awkward, and exposed in front of other people. And many people feel self-conscious about making mistakes and doing poorly in public. But what's their alternative? Refusing to go along and not taking part in the role play is not an acceptable option.

So what do reluctant role-playing participants do? They will often go along half-heartedly, participating to a point, but not taking any risks or pushing themselves beyond their comfort zones. And their reluctance and lack of enthusiasm will not only

---

*Editor's Note: For a more in-depth discussion about this topic, see *Role Play Made Easy*, by Susan El-Shamy, published by Pfeiffer.

impede their own learning, but can affect the general mood of the class, lower the energy of other participants, and obstruct the learning of other participants in the class as well.

Reluctance to role play is really quite unfortunate because role playing is an extremely effective skill-building technique. This structured, goal-directed technique, which uses the acting out of a part in a given context, allows participants to immediately apply information and practice behaviors presented in class material. It's immediacy, flexibility, and great learning advantages make it the method of choice for many of today's popular training topics. Be it performance improvement, leadership, communication, customer service, coaching, mentoring, or management development, role playing is a valuable tool for the building of key skills and the practicing of new behaviors.

What can be done to ease reluctance? If we can ease our participants' most basic fears and apprehensions, if we can make the road to role playing safe and secure, then the reluctance to role play will be greatly reduced and we can fully employ the many advantages and benefits of this fine tool for learning. Let's begin by investigating some of the reasons that people are reluctant to role play and then generate simple steps and easy strategies that instructors can use to address these reasons and reduce participant resistance.

Causes of Reluctance

When it comes to the question of why people are reluctant to role play, there is no single, simple answer. In fact, there seem to be a number of reasons for such reluctance, ranging from fear of making mistakes and looking stupid, to worries about putting oneself in the vulnerable position of being judged by others, to concerns about handling spontaneous and extemporaneous situations. Add to these reasons the fact that many people at one time or another may have been exposed to some rather bad role-playing experiences at the hands of less-than-effective instructors, and you get that spontaneous gasp of, "Oh, no, not role playing!"

When you find participants hesitating and balking to take part in role playing and you ask what the problem is, you may or may not hear the real reason for their reluctance. Some people will make comments like, "I'm afraid of looking like a fool," "I hate being the center of attention," or "I hate having strangers critique my performance." But just as often, or maybe even more often, you will hear comments like, "I just don't like role playing," "The whole thing is so silly," and "Role playing is boring." My guess is that these latter concerns are not always people's real concerns. It could be that people who are reluctant to role play may also be reluctant to share their deeper apprehensions.

Be that as it may, in discussions with various colleagues and numerous participants over the years, I have found that a few key reasons for resisting role playing always come up. I'd like to review these reasons and delve into the concerns that are being expressed. Then I'll present some basic steps that you can take to overcome this reluctance to role play.

Fear of Making Mistakes

A good deal of role-play reluctance can be attributed to the need to appear competent at all times and its corollary: the fear of making mistakes. This need to appear capable and knowledgeable is particularly strong in the workplace and is bound to arise in situations in which colleagues and co-workers are brought together for learning purposes. Since most role-playing activities require the learner to "perform" in some way, usually by applying new information and trying out new behaviors, fear of failure and fear of looking stupid are certain to come up. The more anxious and fearful the participant feels, the more reluctant he or she will be to do the role play.

Fear of Feedback

Add to people's fear of making mistakes and looking incompetent the fact that they will receive feedback from other people in the class, and the reluctance to role play becomes even more pronounced. While the concept of feedback in its purest form can be quite appealing—to receive accurate, helpful information about your performance—the reality of receiving feedback in a classroom role-playing activity is quite another matter. Participants who are inexperienced in giving feedback may miss important information, focus on inconsequential aspects, and/or deliver feedback in an inappropriate manner. And even when feedback is done well, many participants are reluctant to have other participants listening in and perhaps chiming in with further comments.

Feeling Vulnerable

Many people attribute their reluctance to role play to their feelings of being vulnerable and exposed in role-playing activities. They do not like to draw attention to themselves. They don't like being the focus of an activity and being watched and observed by other people. Their basic nature is more introverted; they prefer to take in information and think about it for some time before discussing it with someone else or acting on it. Of course, there are other more extraverted people who enjoy interaction and don't mind being in the spotlight. But if you are one of the quiet types, a more private person who does not like to discuss your problems or take on an unreal persona in front of a group, then role playing can be a dreaded ordeal.

Receiving Poor Instructions

Reluctance to role play can be increased considerably by confusing and unclear instructions. There is nothing worse for an instructor and the participants than to begin a role-playing activity and see the whole classroom turn into a bewildered, muddling mess. When participants don't know exactly what they are supposed to do and how they are supposed to do it, their fears and stress levels increase. And when participants don't know what they are supposed to do or how they are supposed to do it, they are likely to proceed in a variety of ways—some will do it right, some will do it wrong, and some won't do it at all.

Feeling Pressed for Time

Being put on the spot time-wise can also increase a participant's sense of vulnerability and apprehension. Participants will sometimes complain about the lack of time to plan for role playing. They become stressed in situations that are too spontaneous and where they lack sufficient time to "think it through" and "plan what they are going to say and do." This issue of time, and how much time is spent doing what, is a complicated one. Too much time and participants become bored. Too little time and participants feel rushed.

Feeling Trapped

As instructors, when we introduce a role-playing activity, we often do so quickly and enthusiastically and hope that no one balks too much. We divide participants into small groups, give individuals numbers or letters and a sequence of events to follow, and pretty much expect people to do what they're told. They have few options and not many choices to make. Some participants report feeling trapped by such circumstances. They feel they have to do the role playing—that there is no graceful way out. To refuse or withdraw would make them "look bad," so they go along half-heartedly, sometimes begrudgingly.

A Combination of Reasons

As you have probably noticed, these reasons tend to overlap and compound one another. Time pressures and poor instructions add to stress levels and contribute to the fear of failure and make people feel more vulnerable. An excellent feedback system can be impaired if there is not enough time to use it properly. Fear of making a fool of oneself in front of strangers may impede a person's ability to take in and digest complicated instructions.

But just as these reluctance factors can negatively compound one another, the reverse is true also. By addressing even one factor and easing that reason for reluctance, the others factors will lighten just a bit. If two or three factors are addressed, overall reluctance is reduced. And if you can deal with all of the factors to some degree, you will see and feel a much more positive acceptance of your role-playing activity.

Overcoming Reluctance

How many times have you announced an upcoming role-playing event to your class and had your announcement met with cheers of delight? Somehow the response, "Oh boy, we're going to role play!" seldom occurs. But there are things you can do, simple steps that you can take, to address reluctance factors and win over the hearts and minds of your participants to embrace this valuable tool of role playing.

Because reluctance to role play is so common, most participants in your programs will be reluctant to one degree or another. Their reluctance may range from slight hesitation to allout stubborn resistance. But it's there, and it diminishes the potential for optimum learning. Therefore, a good strategy for instructors is to plan for resistance and begin addressing it immediately.

From the moment you start the program, begin a thorough campaign to win over your participants to the upcoming role-playing activities. You can do this by increasing their comfort levels with one another and building trust within the group; selling them on the advantages and benefits of role playing; supplying structure and organization to all activities; and providing choices and flexibility within the role-playing experience. The more understanding, involvement, and ownership participants have of the role-playing activity, the less vulnerable they will feel and the more willing they will be to take risks and learn as much as possible from the activity.

Increase Comfort Levels

One of the first things you can do to lower resistance is to make sure that the participants spend some time getting to know one another before becoming involved in role playing. Even people who work together will benefit from becoming better acquainted. A short warm-up activity at the beginning of class, and perhaps a team-building type of activity right before role playing, can help increase people's comfort levels.

For example, in a class on managing meetings, a twenty-minute warm-up activity in which individual participants determine their top three problems in managing meetings and then circulate among themselves comparing and discussing their problems can do a great deal to increase comfort levels. Participants get to meet one another, build sympathy and empathy for one another's problems, find many problems that they have in common, and realize that they are not alone in the difficulties that they face—all of which make it easier to role play with one another later in the program.

Address Confidentiality Issues

People need to have some assurance that their comments and "mistakes" will not go beyond the classroom. It is important that you discuss confidentiality and issues around privacy well before you introduce any role-playing activity. Explain to the participants that the information they share with one another during the training is confidential and is not to be shared outside the classroom. This includes personal and work-related information that is shared in class activities, group discussions, feedback sessions, and even informal discussions with one another throughout the program.

Obtain some type of agreement from the group. For example, you might ask the group, "Can we all agree that the personal and professional information that is shared in class today will not go outside the class?" Look around at the members of the group as you ask this question and give them time to nod or verbally indicate their agreement. If you see some hesitation, questioning looks, or any indication of discomfort, ask for questions and comments and conduct a short discussion. The bottom line here is to address their concerns and win their wholehearted participation in the learning activities to come.

Sell Them on Role Playing

This seems like an obvious thing to do, but I have to admit it was years before I realized that every other person on earth did not hold my own understanding of the great value of role playing. For some reason I just thought it was obvious why role playing was a great technique and never really explained it to participants. Please don't make the same mistake. Tell your participants why you want them to role play and go over the many advantages and benefits of role playing.

My big three selling points for role playing are its immediacy, flexibility, and potential for real learning. With role playing, participants can try out new behaviors right away—they don't have to wait until they get out of class and back at work or wherever. They can apply what they are learning, receive feedback, and develop those new behaviors on the spot. And there is flexibility in role playing. Participants can ask their role-playing partners to respond in specific ways, to make the activity more difficult, or to ease up a bit. And in role playing, participants have the opportunity to learn from their fellow participants; they can listen to other people's situations and problems, observe how others apply classroom information, and see different people try out new behaviors.

Encourage Risk Taking and Making Mistakes

Explain to your participants how much they can achieve by becoming involved and working hard in the role-playing activities. Tell them that role playing should not be easy. If it is too easy, then they should take responsibility to make it more difficult. Encourage them to take risks and push themselves. Challenge them to make mistakes and learn from those mistakes.

I like to do a "warm-up round" of role plays and then give participants a pep talk to push harder and try something more difficult. I'll say things like, "When it comes to building skills and competencies through role playing, if you are not making some mistakes, then you're not pushing yourself hard enough and taking full advantage of the situation. Let's do another round, and this time choose a more difficult situation and advise your role-playing partner to be harder on you."

Provide Structure and Direction

Good structure and precise directions are imperative for effective role playing. Participants need a clear understanding of what they are supposed to do and how they are supposed to do it. This means that you need a thorough understanding of the procedures they are to follow. Think through and write out what you want them to do. Prepare a one-page handout of directions that is clear, straightforward, and easy to follow. Make copies of these directions and prepare a flip-chart page that covers them.

Understanding the process will provide the structure and organization that participants need to feel secure in what they are doing. Distribute your handout with the step-by-step instructions and then, using the flip-chart page, state the purpose of the role play and go through each step of the role-playing activity, explaining what will take place. Check for understanding with the group and answer any questions. You can post these instructions on the wall, where you can refer to them during the activity if necessary.

Minimize Fears of Feedback

You will want to do everything you can to minimize the fear factors inherent in feedback. It will help immensely to first explain exactly what feedback is and is not. In role-playing activities, feedback is limited, specific, non-judgmental information about the behavior being developed through the role-played interaction. It is not anything at all that the observer wants to say.

To ensure effective feedback, you may need to teach your participants the basics about giving and receiving feedback by incorporating a short module on feedback, perhaps with a demonstration and a short feedback practice activity. The time spent in developing feedback abilities will pay off in the success of your role-playing activities. You can also make feedback more private and less threatening by using written feedback forms and having no feedback discussions. Or you can limit feedback content to very specific behaviors, such as the use of a certain model or the following of particular guidelines.

Offer Choices and Flexibility

All people like to have a certain sense of freedom and flexibility within any given situation. No one likes the feeling of being trapped in a situation with no way out and no viable options. In fact, many people report that, once they have options and choices in a situation, their reluctance lessens and they are more likely to remain in the situation. And I have often seen this to be the case in role playing. People respond better to role playing when they are not forced to participate.

Don't rush people into participation; give them time to think and plan. Be flexible about just how much a participant is required to do. Provide your participants with choices in regard to situations to role play, the order of role playing, type of feedback used, and level of difficulty. Giving your participants choices and options, even the option of opting out, will do wonders for eliminating feelings of entrapment.

In Summary

Role playing is an extremely effective skill-building technique. It's immediacy, flexibility, and numerous learning advantages make it an excellent method to use in many of today's most popular training programs. However, many participants are reluctant to role play because they feel self-conscious about making mistakes and doing poorly in public. Or they may feel vulnerable, awkward, and exposed trying out new behaviors in front of other people.

You can reduce role-play reluctance in your programs by increasing participant comfort levels and building trust within the group; informing class members of the advantages and benefits of role playing; supplying structure and orderliness to all activities; and providing alternatives and flexibility within the role-playing experience. Such steps will reduce reluctance, yours and theirs, and make your participants more open to taking full advantage of their role-playing experiences. Good luck!

Susan El-Shamy *is senior partner at Advancement Strategies, Inc., where she designs and delivers training products and programs for a variety of U.S. companies. Dr. El-Shamy is also a regular guest lecturer at the Indiana University School of Business. Her other Pfeiffer publications include* Diversity Bingo: An Experiential Learning Activity *(1994);* How to Design and Deliver Training for the New and Emerging Generations *(2004); and* Role Play Made Easy *(2005).*

Nuts and Bolts
Checklists for a Faultless Workshop
Lois B. Hart

Summary

The learning part of a workshop is most important and yet, if we don't pay attention to the critical categories of administrative tasks, the very foundation of the planned training event can collapse. The essential checklists presented in this article cover tasks to develop a workshop program, to prepare learning materials, and to arrange for the site, room set-up, supplies, equipment, food and beverages.

Ted, a trainer from St. Louis, flies into Dallas only to discover that his box of handouts cannot be found at the site of tomorrow's workshop. Unfortunately, he does not have a set of the originals with him.

Sally forgot to outline the kind of room she needs for her workshop and discovers, on arrival, that the room is so small that there is barely room to move among the participants' tables and absolutely no open space for her structured activities.

A discussion about the causes of conflict is interrupted, ironically, by the nearby rat-tat-tat of a jackhammer. No one told Ray that the training center was in the midst of remodeling!

Susan worked for days on upgrading her PowerPoint visuals. She was quite proud of the result as she rolled out the new presentation—until the bulb on the LCD projector blew. She had no spare bulb!

These nightmares actually happen to trainers; believe me, I know! When we first start out as trainers, we have so much on our minds that these administrative details can easily be forgotten. In-house trainers, who can rely on a workshop coordinator, may assume that he/she will provide every supply and piece of equipment needed. Even experienced trainers can get so caught up in preparing a new workshop design that they neglect to send directions to the participants until the last minute.

The learning part of a workshop is most important; yet, if we don't pay attention to the nuts and bolts, the very foundation of the planned training event can collapse. Help is on the way with these checklists for independent trainers, a lead trainer who is coordinating a team of trainers, and the in-house trainer and workshop coordinator.

The following are the six critical categories of administrative tasks that, if attended to, result in a faultless and successful workshop.

1. Confirm the Training Event

2. Workshop Design and Follow-Up

3. Participants' Learning Materials

4. Site and Room Arrangements

5. Supplies and Equipment

6. Food and Beverages

It is worth the time to follow every one of the following checklists.

1. Confirm the Training Event

The first step toward a successful workshop is to obtain confirmation of the scope, goals, objectives, and budget by completing these six tasks:

☐ Establish need for training on this topic.

☐ Prepare proposal and budget for this event.

☐ Establish the preliminary verbal agreement (with client or training manager).

☐ Review possible dates for the training.

☐ Get final signed agreement on the training goals, objectives, scope, target group, and budget (from client or training manager).

☐ If you need to travel to the training site, confirm your airline reservations, rental car, and hotel.

2. The Workshop Design and Follow-Up

The second category includes eighteen tasks that ensure an effective workshop design. Most occur before the training event; however, there are additional tasks after the training event.

Program Tasks Before the Workshop Starts

- ☐ If creating a new workshop, conduct a needs assessment. If adapting a previously used design, look at evaluations and trainer's notes.

- ☐ Draft a workshop design that includes the time allotment for each module.

- ☐ Review the design with the client, training manager, or perhaps a focus group (if this training is new to the company or organization).

- ☐ Decide who will facilitate each module (you, other trainers, guest speakers).

- ☐ Invite trainers or guest speakers. Ask for a description of their presentations with a goal, objectives, and amount of time needed. Also ask what supplies, equipment, and room set-up they will need.

- ☐ Send other trainers or guest speakers a confirmation of the date, time, and location for the training event.

- ☐ Finalize the workshop design and distribute a copy to everyone who will be training or speaking at the event.

- ☐ Determine whether pre-workshop homework is required. If so, create an explanatory memo and send it out to participants in enough time before the event but not too far out (10 to 20 business days).

- ☐ Compile a list of the participants for registration and to be used as a handout.

- ☐ Create an evaluation form.

- ☐ Create (and collect) handouts, checking that the correct template and footnotes are used. (See the next list of tasks for more on the participants' learning materials.)

- ☐ One week before the workshop, send to all participants the directions, a final agenda, and a reminder about the assignment.

- ☐ Purchase guest or speaker gifts and write thank you notes.

Program Tasks After the Workshop

☐ Tabulate evaluation results and send to the client, your manager, other trainers, guests, and perhaps the participants.

☐ Make notes to yourself regarding suggestions for improvement.

☐ Send participants one or more follow-up emails with suggestions that will ensure application of what they learned and to reinforce the learning.

☐ Send handouts to any participants who missed the workshop.

☐ Send gifts (if purchased) and thank you notes to other trainers or guest speakers.

3. Participants' Learning Materials

The third category includes eight tasks that enhance participants' learning:

☐ Establish a template for handouts. Include font style and size, capitalization, and justification (for heads, subheads, and text) and guidelines for use of bullets and numbered lists. Provide examples of correct copyright citations.

☐ If working with other trainers and/or guests, send the handout template to them. Establish agreement about who prepares and copies their handouts.

☐ Remind each person about obtaining permission and including copyright citations.

☐ Provide deadline for submission of handouts for copying.

☐ Arrange for copying handouts. If you use a notebook, remember to ask to have the handouts three-hole punched.

☐ Purchase, collate, and prepare the notebooks.

☐ If you ship the handouts or notebooks, be sure to hand carry the masters.

☐ Create a Master List of Handouts for the entire workshop. Some general handouts needed include:

    ☐ Agenda

    ☐ List of participants

    ☐ Evaluation form

    ☐ Assignments

    ☐ Bios of guests

4. Site and Room Arrangements

The fourth category includes nine tasks that ensure the most appropriate training site and room set-up. This enhances rather than distracts from learning.

☐ Develop criteria for selecting the most appropriate site. (See Exhibit 1.)

☐ Review options for sites (in-house training room, hotel, conference center). Request brochures or literature if the site is new to you.

☐ Visit sites (if they are new to you).

☐ Select site and negotiate terms (as needed). Get written confirmation.

☐ Obtain clear directions to send to participants, trainers, and speakers.

☐ Confirm your own and others' preference for room set-up(s), reviewing the types shown in Exhibit 2. Once selected, sketch the room set-up and give to appropriate person(s).

☐ A week before, double-check room set-up and food arrangements and solve any problems.

☐ The day before the training, check the room and solve any problems. (See Exhibit 3.)

☐ Collect bills and submit to client or accounting.

Exhibit 1. Site Selection Criteria

Attractive and Comfortable: Is the training room(s) attractive? Does it have windows and comfortable chairs?

Audiovisual Capacity: Is the space set up for use of all audiovisual equipment you might need such as PowerPoint, overheads, video? Can you rent any of this equipment at the site?

Costs: What are all of the costs involved? Be sure to include room rental, food and beverages, equipment rentals, and parking.

Customer Service: Does the site provide testimonials from previous clients or other documents of their commitment to serving you?

Food and Meals: Can they be provided at this site?

Handicap Access: Has the site made accommodations for access to the building, training room, and bathrooms?

Location: How convenient will this be for participants?

Noise: Are there any potential noise problems from adjacent training rooms? Any construction plans?

On-Site Coordinator: Will there be an on-site coordinator to solve problems, adjust the heat and AC, and change the room set-up?

Overnight Accommodations: Are there sleeping rooms at this site or nearby?

Parking: Is there ample parking?

Security: Are there posted directions in case of fire or bomb threat?

Space: Is the space adequate? Sufficient for the required set-up, display of books and other resources, trainer's staging area of materials, supplies, and for breaks?

Exhibit 2.   Four Types of Room Set-Up

Theater

In this style, participants face forward toward one point, usually someone who is speaking to them. This can be arranged with chairs perfectly lined up in rows or, for more eye contact, the rows can be arranged in a concave, slightly rounded fashion.

Theater Styles

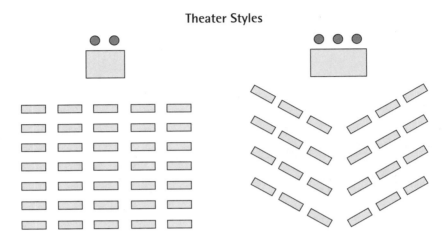

Schoolroom

An odd name for today's training world, but it merely means adding tables to the theater style pattern; thus the tables and chairs can be perfectly lined up in rows facing the front or angled forming a herringbone effect. This variation allows more eye contact among participants.

Schoolroom Styles

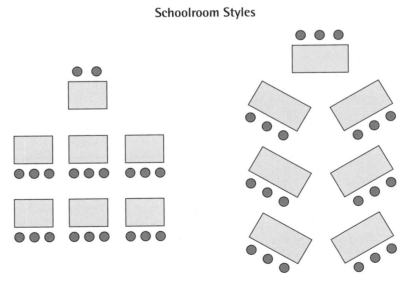

(continued on the next page)

Exhibit 2.   Four Types of Room Set-Up, *continued*

Conference

This style evokes the traditional boardroom with a large table, either oval or rectangular, with chairs on the outside. Variations include arranging the tables into a T shape or a U with participants on the outside edges, allowing the trainer to walk into the U's opening.

Conference Styles

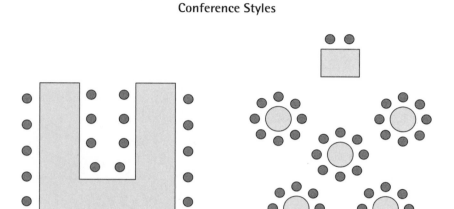

This Author's Choice

After years of training, this author has a preference for an arrangement of round tables, of sufficient size and with enough chairs for six people each, to optimize eye contact and participation. These tables are scattered throughout a room with space between them for privacy and for an easel by each table (if needed). Off to the side are tables for food and beverages (nearest the door for quick dashes for a smoke or trip to the loo), a display table for books and other resources pertinent to the workshop's content, and a table for handouts, supplies, and equipment (best off to a side out of participants' line of sight). This spacious room set-up allows for rearranging the furniture for occasions when you want chairs in a circle or for an open space for a structured activity.

Exhibit 3.   Training Room Last–Minute Spot Check

☐ Is the room set up as sketched out previously?

☐ Is all of the necessary equipment in the room and ready to use?

☐ Are all the supplies accounted for?

☐ Are the notebooks and table tents distributed as requested?

☐ Can you access the lights and thermostat?

☐ Does the food and beverage table have what was requested for the first phase of the workshop?

☐ Were the signs posted as requested?

5. Supplies and Equipment

The fifth category includes tasks that support the training design with exactly the right supplies and equipment.

☐ Contact trainers and guests about supplies and equipment they will need.

☐ Beyond the typical supplies (see Exhibit 4), you may want one or more of the following for your workshop:

  ☐ books and article for a resource display

  ☐ colorful items to jazz up the room such as crepe paper, balloons, vase of flowers, and/or banners

  ☐ gifts for prizes or for closing ceremony

  ☐ posters supporting the workshop topics

☐ Arrange for the equipment needed (schedule with your clients or your own organization, rental) (See Exhibit 5.)

☐ Check availability of supplies (in your own organization, at your client's site, or at hotel/training center).

☐ Submit request for supplies or buy supplies.

☐ Deliver supplies and equipment to training room. Check that equipment is working properly.

☐ Post directional signs.

☐ Afterward, arrange for pick-up of supplies, signs, and equipment.

Exhibit 4. Supplies Checklist

☐ 3" x 5" cards

☐ colored dots

☐ extension cords

☐ folders

☐ glue sticks

☐ hole punch

☐ markers for flip chart in multiple colors

☐ markers for whiteboard

☐ nametags

☐ paper clips

☐ paper: blank, lined, notepads

☐ pencils

☐ pencil sharpener

☐ pens

☐ pointer for overheads

☐ sticky notes

☐ stapler

☐ stars

☐ power strip

☐ table tents for names

☐ tape: masking, duct, adhesive

Exhibit 5. Equipment Checklist

☐ audiotape recorder and tapes

☐ camcorder

☐ camera

☐ calculator

☐ computer

☐ computer and LCD for PowerPoint

☐ copier

☐ flip charts on easels and extra pads of paper

☐ microphone and speakers

☐ overhead projector, acetate and pens, extra bulbs

☐ screen

☐ slide projector

☐ stereo

☐ CD player

☐ tape recorder, cord, blank tapes, and batteries

☐ VCR or DVD

☐ whiteboards and correct pens

6. Food and Beverages

The sixth category includes eight tasks that provide food and beverages throughout the workshop to refresh the participants during their breaks.

☐ Review your options: in-house cafeteria, hotel food and beverage, caterer, or eat out in a restaurant. Review the availability, menus, and prices for each. Determine whether they can meet any special food needs like no sugar, vegetarian, vegan.

☐ Finalize your best option. Confirm all details in writing.

☐ Review special food needs from participants, trainers, and guests.

☐ Finalize menus for all meals plus for morning and afternoon snacks and beverages. (See Exhibit 6.)

☐ Provide purchase order form, check, or credit card for deposit and/or final payment.

☐ If food and beverages are not provided through your company cafeteria, hotel, or caterer, see the Food and Beverages Checklist (Exhibit 7) for what to borrow, purchase, and pack.

☐ Forty-eight hours beforehand, provide final counts for meals.

☐ Collect bills and send to the client or accounting.

Exhibit 6.   Menus for Workshop

Continental breakfast

Morning snack: juices, fruit, nuts

Lunch

Afternoon snack: cheese plate, crackers, veggie with dip, popcorn

Exhibit 7.   Food and Beverages Checklist

☐ baskets for snacks

☐ carafes for hot drinks

☐ cocoa

☐ coffee pots, two kinds of coffee, and filters

☐ cooler

☐ cream/milk

☐ cups for hot and cold beverages

☐ glasses

☐ ice

☐ knives for cutting food

☐ napkins

☐ pitcher

☐ plates

☐ soft drinks: diet and regular, with and without caffeine

☐ sugar

☐ tablecloths

☐ tea: variety of herb and caffeinated

☐ utensils: serving and silverware

☐ water: bottled or filtered

☐ water pot, electric, for tea and/or cocoa

Lois B. Hart, Ed.D., *is executive director of Courageous Leadership Consortium, founder of the Women's Leadership Institute, and president of Leadership Dynamics. Dr. Hart has thirty years of experience as a trainer, facilitator, and consultant, presenting programs on leadership, teams, conflict, and facilitation. She has written twenty-three books, including* Connections: Saying Hello and Saying Good-Bye, 50 Activities for Developing Leaders *(Vols. I and II),* Learning from Conflict, Training Methods That Work, *and* Faultless Facilitation.

Connecting Training to Performance

Tyrone A. Holmes

Summary

Human resource development (HRD) has a long history in American organizations. Today, virtually every company provides learning activities for employees. According to the American Society for Training and Development, U.S. organizations spend an average of $820 per employee on training and education. This number increases to nearly $1,200 per employee for large Fortune 500 companies and public sector organizations (Sugrue & Kim, 2004).

Unfortunately, this training and education does not always live up to expectations, especially when it comes to improving individual and organizational performance. One reason for this is that many organizations fail to take the steps needed before and after an educational event to make sure training content is transferred to the workplace in a way that significantly enhances performance. This article addresses this problem by offering a three-phase Performance-Based Training Model that outlines the specific steps that must be taken before, during, and after a training event to ensure that it has a positive impact on employee performance.

The Performance-Based Training Model described in Table 1 is based on three fundamental principles:

1. The success of any training event must be defined in terms of employee performance.

2. The training event itself, while important, is not enough to facilitate a significant and sustained increase in employee performance.

3. The only way to ensure that a training event leads to improved performance is to specifically plan for that improvement well in advance of the event.

Table 1.   The Performance-Based Training Model

Before the Training Event	The Training Event	After the Training Event
Clarify the benefits of training		
Define performance expectations		Implement support and rein-forcement activities
Communicate performance expectations to learners	Implement the training inter-vention using skills-based learning strategies	Evaluate the impact of training on individual and organizational performance
Identify support and reinforce-ment activities		Provide additional learning opportunities

Before the Training Event

The most important element of the training and development process involves those activities that take place prior to the training event. The success of any training intervention will be determined by how effectively you clarify the benefits of training, define performance expectations, communicate those expectations to learners, and identify support and reinforcement activities.

Clarify the Benefits of Training

Your first step is to clarify the benefits you expect to gain for the learners, their managers, and the organization as a whole. Before you can effectively design a training program, you must be clear about what each of these parties will gain from the experience. For example, if you are facilitating a leadership education program, the learners may benefit by developing skills that will improve their performance as leaders. This in turn can lead to rewards such as promotional opportunities and raises. Managers can benefit by developing a talent pool of employees that will be ready to fill the positions that will open in the near future. They may also benefit by having employees who can take on more leadership responsibility within their units (e.g., team leaders), thus reducing workload. The organization benefits by improving its human capital, by reducing the cost of hiring leaders, and by improved leader performance. Likewise, if you are facilitating a customer service training program, the learners can benefit by developing skills that will allow them to successfully manage difficult service problems. Managers benefit by the reduction of customer service complaints, and the organization gains by having more satisfied customers. (For more information on the identification of training benefits, see Forman, 2004.)

Define Performance Expectations

Before you implement any training activities, you should be clear about what you expect learners to be able to do as a result of the training. For instance, if employees will take part in communication skills training, you need to clarify what skills they will be expected to develop and how these skills are to be used on the job. You must also determine how the performance expectations will connect to the performance management process. This makes the customization of training much more effective, and it helps learners connect the educational process to their jobs.

Communicate Performance Expectations to Learners

Once you have defined performance expectations for the training participants, communicate these expectations to the learners *prior to the training event.* If you wait until the actual training program, it is too late. The participants must understand why they are participating in the training program and how they will benefit. They should be clear about what they are expected to be able to do as a result of their training and how they will be supported once they are back on the job. This can have the added benefit of increasing the learners' interest in the training program.

Identify Support and Reinforcement Activities

Once the training is complete, there should be activities that support and reinforce the skills that were developed during the session. The most effective way to do this is to provide the learners with continuous opportunities to apply their new skills on the job. For example, if a group of supervisors has completed behavioral interviewing training, they should have an opportunity to participate in employee interviews as soon as their training is complete. Likewise, if an organization's salespeople have participated in an advanced sales training course, they should have a chance to apply their newly developed sales techniques as soon as possible. Participants should also have an opportunity to receive feedback on their performance and to receive continuous on-the-job "practice." Simply stated, if you fail to give learners a chance to apply their new skills once they are back on the job, they will lose them.

The Training Event

The most important aspect of the actual training event is the use of skills-based learning tools and methods. As the name suggests, skills-based training is designed to enhance job-specific behaviors that have a direct impact on performance and to positively impact participant awareness, knowledge, and skills (Holmes, 2004). Awareness is the affective domain that involves learning about oneself and the impact that one's behavior, style, and values have on overall effectiveness. Knowledge consists of the cognitive domain that focuses on learning information, concepts, and theories that contribute to effective performance. Skills, which is the most significant learning domain, consists of developing behaviors and abilities needed to perform at the highest level possible (Pedersen, 1994).

Skills-based training includes classroom sessions and workshops that involve one or more of five basic methods: lecture, case study, role play, behavioral modeling, and self-assessment activities (McDonald-Mann, 1998).

Training for Knowledge

Lectures and case studies can have a significant impact on the *knowledge* domain. Lectures can be used to present content-specific information to a large group of people over a relatively short period of time. They can also incorporate two-way interaction through the use of small group discussions. However, pure lecture can diminish the effectiveness of a classroom learning experience. That's because adult learners have a relatively short attention span. Therefore, it is important to make sure lectures are no more than fifteen minutes and are used in conjunction with other skills-based learning techniques.

Case studies present participants with a specific organizational situation or scenario. The participants review the situation, the outcome, and the behavior of the individuals involved to determine whether alternative actions might have yielded a superior result. They are very effective at provoking thought, engendering discussion, and enhancing overall knowledge. Case studies offer several advantages when it comes to facilitating learning (Eitington, 2002):

- They offer real situations in which participants become active learners, as opposed to passive observers.

- They are specific. Participants deal with explicit facts and circumstances rather than vague or general situations.

- They allow participants to work cooperatively to resolve problems and make decisions.

- They enhance problem-solving and decision-making skills.

- They help participants understand that different people can see the same situation in very different ways, and that there can be multiple solutions to a problem.

- They bring about a better understanding of the complexity of human behavior and the fact that people do not always behave in a logical, predictable manner.

- They can help improve communication and listening skills through the facilitation of group discussion.

Training for Skills

Role plays and behavioral modeling are excellent for facilitating development in the *skills* domain. Role plays are highly participative exercises in which participants act out characters assigned to them in a specific scenario (Thiagarajan, 1996). They provide each trainee with the opportunity to practice skills that have been learned during the educational program. Because of this practice component, role plays are very effective at helping participants to develop new skills, to learn new information, and to change attitudes.

Behavioral modeling, which is based on social learning theory (Bandura, 1986), takes role playing one step further. It provides participants with an opportunity to observe behavioral models, to practice the desired behavior, and to receive feedback on their performance. Of all the skills-based training methods, behavioral modeling is the most important because it provides the learner with an opportunity to observe the desired behavior and to continuously practice the behavior in a relatively safe environment. Generally speaking, the behavioral modeling process involves the following steps:

1. Prior to the classroom training session, create role-play situations that the participants can relate to. One of the most common problems with this form of training is the use of scenarios that fail to link with the audience. The issues outlined in the situation should connect directly with the participants' experiences and development needs.

2. Facilitate a role-play demonstration (the behavioral model) that all of the participants can observe. One way to do this is to facilitate a "bad" performance and then facilitate a "good" performance and let the audience discuss the performance differences. It is important to highlight the specific skills that participants will be practicing.

3. Form triads, which consist of two role players and one observer, who will participate in fifteen-to-thirty-minute "rounds." The two role players will consist of one person acting out a role and one person practicing the skills (e.g., customer service, sales, communication).

4. Disseminate background data regarding the scenario to all participants. Give participants a chance to review their roles.

5. Start the exercise and give the role players at least fifteen minutes to act out the scenario and practice the skills. Conclude the round by having the observers give both positive and constructive feedback to the role player who was practicing the skills.

6. Repeat Steps 4 and 5 with different individuals serving as role players and observers.

Training for Awareness

Finally, skills-based training can also have a positive impact on the *awareness* domain by incorporating self-assessment activities. Self-assessment activities consist of paper-and-pencil inventories that evaluate the respondent's current status and functioning in a specific area such as communication skills or coaching effectiveness. These inventories give workshop participants insight into their attitudes and behaviors and the impact these have on performance. This is turn allows participants to modify their behavior in ways that will increase their overall effectiveness.

After the Training Event

If you have done a good job of facilitating the pre-training activities and implementing an effective skills-based training program, the post-training activities are relatively simple. Specifically, there are three things that must be done to ensure that the training content is transferred to the workplace in a way that significantly impacts performance: implement support and reinforcement activities, evaluate the impact of training, and provide additional learning opportunities.

Implement Support and Reinforcement Activities

As previously discussed, it is very important to provide learners with an opportunity to apply the skills they learned during the training program once they are back on the job. Therefore, a strategy should be created that describes how these support activities will be implemented for each training participant. This will require the support and active involvement of the participants' managers, since they will be identifying the potential reinforcement activities and providing performance feedback on an ongoing basis.

Evaluate the Impact of the Training on Individual and Organizational Performance

Much has been written on training evaluation and the various tools and methodologies that can be used to facilitate the assessment process (for example, see Kirkpatrick, 1998). However, for our purposes, the approach is relatively simple. Evaluation should address two basic questions. First, are the training participants applying their new skills in a way that improves individual and, potentially, organizational performance? Second, have the participants met the performance expectations defined prior to the facilitation of the training program? Both of these questions can be addressed through the administration of an organization's formal performance management system. In other words, the observations of the participants' managers will be crucial in determining the overall effectiveness of the training program.

Provide Additional Learning Opportunities

Finally, if the training participants have had a positive learning experience that has been transferred to the workplace in ways that improve individual and organizational performance, then it is a good idea to provide additional developmental opportunities to support their learning. This can be done through a variety of learning methods such as classroom training, developmental assignments (e.g., on-the-job training), developmental relationships (e.g., coaching and mentoring), or self-directed learning activities (e.g., Internet, CD-ROM, distance learning).

Conclusion

Facilitating training and education programs that have a significant impact on performance is not a complicated process. However, many of today's training programs fail to influence performance in any discernible manner. The Performance-Based Training Model outlined in this article will help you successfully facilitate training that has a direct impact on employee performance.

References

Bandura, A. (1986). *Social foundations of thought and action: A social cognitive theory.* Upper Saddle River, NJ: Prentice-Hall.

Eitington, J.E. (2002). *The winning trainer: Winning ways to involve people in training.* Woburn, MA: Butterworth-Heinemann.

Forman, D.C. (2004). The triple win: The missing link in improving the effectiveness of training programs. *Performance Improvement, 43*(5), 20–26.

Holmes, T.A. (2004). Designing and facilitating performance-based diversity training. *Performance Improvement, 43*(5), 13–19.

Kirkpatrick, D.L. (1998). *Evaluating training programs: The four levels* (2nd ed.). San Francisco, CA: Berrett-Koehler.

McDonald-Mann, D.G. (1998). Skill-based training. In C.D. McCauley, R.S. Moxley, & E. Van Velsor (Eds.), *The Center for Creative Leadership: Handbook of leadership development* (pp. 106–126). San Francisco, CA: Jossey-Bass.

Pedersen, P. (1994). *A handbook for developing multicultural awareness* (2nd ed.). Alexandria, VA: American Counseling Association.

Sugrue, B., & Kim, K-H. (2004). *State of the industry: ASTD's annual review of trends in workplace learning and performance.* Alexandria, VA: American Society for Training and Development.

Thiagarajan, S. (1996). Instructional games, simulations, and role plays. In R.L. Craig (Ed.), *The ASTD training and development handbook* (4th ed.) (pp. 517–533). New York: McGraw-Hill.

Tyrone A. Holmes, Ed.D., *is the president of T.A.H. Performance Consultants, Inc., a full-service human resource development consulting firm specializing in the enhancement of individual and organizational performance. As a dynamic speaker, trainer, consultant, and coach, Dr. Holmes has helped countless individuals enhance their ability to communicate, resolve conflict, and solve problems in culturally diverse settings. He has created and copyrighted numerous training systems and speaks on a variety of communication, diversity, and consulting topics.*

The Inside Track

Ajay M. Pangarkar and Teresa Kirkwood

Summary

What does it take for an internal manager, specifically those responsible for the training function, to obtain "buy-in" for training solutions? Although many organizations are realizing the value of equipping their employees with the knowledge they require to be competitive as well as leveraging the knowledge they possess, when budgets are tight, and they almost always are, what do you need to do to get your share of the proverbial pie to ensure proper employee development?

Training and learning initiatives are under tremendous scrutiny at all levels of the organization. It is important to understand how a proposed solution will not only impact the organization as a whole but how it fundamentally cascades down to those directly affected.

In this article we will identify the three primary levels of stakeholders within an organization, what they believe is important to gaining their support, and techniques on overcoming resistance in gaining buy-in at every level for the proposed training solution.

Walk into almost any company and you will hear management proclaim that people are its greatest asset. In reality, however, intellectual capital development is rarely a primary focus, and it's often viewed as an expense rather than an investment.

Training managers and consultants are challenged to sell the benefits of an intangible need to those who want to see tangible results. External consultants understand this obstacle, but when managers, especially those responsible for training, have to propose training solutions, they often encounter significant resistance. This resistance usually stems from a fear of change or fear of failure.

Selling training internally is all about being prepared, involving the appropriate individuals, and clearly understanding what executive management wants to hear. The focus must be on the benefits of the proposed training, not the features. For example, if you are proposing a customer service program for front-line workers, one feature would be resolving client problems. But the benefit would be an increase in customer satisfaction or an increase in repeat sales. Applying the feature/benefit principle will help you sell your program to the biggest critics.

Know Your Audience

When seeking buy-in for training-related projects, training managers often focus on obtaining support from the high-level decision makers, executive management. But there are only two possible outcomes to this—either management approves or rejects the project. If it's approved, then only one level of decision makers is sold on the idea. The training, more often than not, is doomed to fail because those directly affected were not consulted. Resistance from that group can kill the project.

Successful training managers recognize early who they need to approach to get a training program off the ground. Essentially, there are three groups to address: the training participants, mid-level managers, and executive management.

Training participants will accept any training if it provides them with value-added resources and doesn't take time away from their immediate responsibilities. The training must be easy for them to absorb and incorporate into their daily activities if it's to change behavior. It's important to balance the needs of the participant with the need for performance improvement. Effectively doing this aligns their goals with the needs of business managers and broadens the scope of training.

When dealing with mid-level managers, it's important to recognize their requirements. They need to leverage their employees' ability to achieve specific departmental or production objectives. At this level, managers are involved in budget planning and the allocation of funds directly affecting their environment. Being directly on the front lines of business, they are accountable for pre-set performance benchmarks on many levels, which places high demands on resources. Taking these concerns into account, business managers have little patience for training solutions that don't produce immediate results and that take employees away from their daily responsibilities.

Decision making at the executive level focuses on maximizing profitability and minimizing expenses. These managers want to create an environment that increases sales through improving product quality and customer and employee satisfaction. Their objective is to optimize the return on their investment in every business-related activity, especially when investing in employees. In the knowledge economy, ideas, innovation, and synergy are critical to long-term success. Every training investment must ensure that the performance of the organization improves by developing a knowledgeable team of employees to effectively serve clients and to capitalize on new opportunities. It's at this level that many training managers and consultants pitch their proposal, ignoring the other participants involved in a program's execution.

Success depends on how a manager addresses the concerns of each decision maker and how the decision makers are involved in developing the training solution. Knowing your audience is essential to gain support, and the first step to selling training solutions internally.

Essential Questions to Answer

It's easy to find critics for any training solution. Even if you justify the need for training, there will always be individuals at every level of management challenging your reasons. As an athlete prepares for an important event, you should do the same to sell your solution. The following are common questions you'll be faced with when proposing a training solution. Understanding the questions will help you defend your position and will help you better understand how training can be effective within the organization.

Is There Really a Need for Training?

Training professionals often overestimate the value training can provide. If the poor perception of training is to change, then training managers, and consultants, need to be honest about its effectiveness. There are many instances in which a formal training program isn't necessary. For example, your company has recently upgraded existing software. Is there a need for training or are employees capable of learning it on their own? Perhaps they only require coaching in some of the new features of the software.

Do All Employees Need Training?

Management believes that every person must pass through training if they are to maximize their investment. This is a myth. Training is most effective only when the right individuals are involved. Focus your training efforts on the people with the need and those who will benefit most. For example, if you are introducing a new product, then the production team may require training in quality procedures, whereas customer service employees would require training on the use of the product.

What Are the Expected Outcomes?

This is one question that management will surely ask. Training professionals often misdiagnose the problem that the required training is attempting to solve. Training's primary goal is to improve on existing processes and outcomes. This leads back to the benefits mentioned earlier. When attempting to build a case for training, you must ensure that the benefits answer the needs of your audience and the investment delivers on the actual expected returns.

How Will the Training Move Us Closer to Our Goals?

Executive managers expect that every business decision should move them closer to a desired goal. Human capital investment is no exception to this rule. Managers recognize that their people are the key to their success or failure. Even more important, they also recognize that the investment they make in people is also unpredictable and volatile. Your responsibility is to assure and show management that the proposed training solution will lead them one step closer to their goals.

What Are Management's Expectations?

Each level of management has certain expectations from their investment. Clearly understanding what they are will help you in marketing training internally. At the top level, managers expect to see links between productivity and profitability. Setting up clear benchmarks against both internal and industry measures will certainly improve your case for training. Mid-managers want to see immediate outcomes and short-term results. Work closely with them to develop an implementation plan that minimizes workplace disruption and provides the necessary skills to move them closer to their immediate objectives.

What Resources Will the Training Require?

All organizations are constrained by limited resources. Many managers believe that there are more critical issues to resolve with these resources before they will commit to training. To avoid this objection, you need to know what resources are required. Do not underestimate your needs, and prepare to justify your position. Then present this case to the decision makers and those who are affected by the training.

What Will the Training Cost?

Cost/benefit and profit/loss are terms that aren't always familiar to training professionals. If not handled carefully, this question can be a trap. The key to selling your training internally is to speak in terms that management understands. Prove to them that training employees is an investment that will result in measurable and profitable outcomes. Clearly determine direct and unforeseen costs and relate them to expected results. Provide real tools that measure your training's returns.

Conclusion

The perception of training is changing, and the need for training is growing. If real change is to take hold, training professionals, both managers and consultants, must find effective ways to ensure that true learning leads to results. Training is about developing abilities and knowledge that translate into sustained performance. Building organizational requirements and employee needs into the proposed training solutions is essential to gain acceptance at every level.

Ajay M. Pangarkar *is founder of CentralKnowledge, leaders in comprehensive strategic learning solutions. He is recognized for his experience in helping companies implement training evaluation and ROI strategies and the training of new trainers and subject experts. He writes for several HR and training publications, is government accredited, and delivers learning programs for professional orders and business institutions. Mr. Pangarkar is the founder of the Quebec ROI Network, is a founding member and president of the CSTD Quebec chapter, and is a member of the CSTD national board of directors.*

Teresa Kirkwood *is vice president of CentralKnowledge. She works with businesses, educational institutions, and community groups to develop custom learning solutions. She mentors business start-ups for youths in the community, regularly speaks for women entrepreneurial groups, and was nominated for the Ernst & Young Canadian Business of the Year award. Ms. Kirkwood is an accredited trainer with the Quebec government and has been published in many business and training-related magazines. She is a founding member and vice president of CSTD Quebec and is actively involved in the development of the Quebec ROI Network.*

Applying Recognition to Training and Development

Bob Nelson

Summary

The business adage that "you get what you reward" is a universal yet often underutilized principle in day-to-day management, and the training and development function is no exception. There are lots of ways that recognition can be used to make the training function more efficient, learning more effective, and the training staff more appreciated. In this article, we'll examine some of these possibilities to show how you might get the most out of the training investment that's made in your organization.

Before Training

All performance starts with clear goals, and this is true for the training activity as well. We know that adult learning requires any training to be highly relevant to the learners' needs. To me, the most effective training today pulls an attendee's job, with its challenges, opportunities, and applications, into the classroom as much as possible. Why are employees sent to a specific training session? What are they supposed to gain from the experience? How will this help them in their jobs? What questions do they have prior to the program that they would like to have answered in the training? All managers should be urged to take some time with every employee to answer these questions before the employee is sent to a training session.

This simple discussion with one's manager prior to training is itself a form of recognition for most employees: it provides dedicated time and attention with the most important person in any employee's job that is focused on the employee's learning and development, involving them in the goal-setting process for the training activity. Increasingly, the most powerful forms of recognition as reported by today's employees are exactly these type of intangible, interpersonal forms of management support. The more that individuals are involved with establishing learning goals for training, the more they are apt to learn and the more the learning activity will be valued by them.

During Training

Recognition can be a powerful tool within the classroom as well. The more the training environment can be a positive, nurturing experience, the more—and faster—attendees are apt to learn. From complimenting a question that is asked to thanking a volunteer who has offered to share a perspective, recognition is fundamental for helping trainees to lower their defenses and *risk* participating and learning something new. You can also have more fun and be more explicit in creating rewards that can be used in the classroom, such as tossing miniature candy bars to students who answer a question correctly or having participants applaud after someone "reports out" from a group activity. Other examples of the use of recognition in a training setting include the following:

- Using an in-class pass-around trophy such as a water gun for certain positive classroom behaviors (compliments of Peg Murray, trainer, Skillpath Seminars).

- Creating an on-the-spot award, such as a flexible straw or piece of crumpled paper, and asking participants to make the award meaningful in reinforcing the use of newly learned behaviors back on the job (compliments of Amelia Armitage, principal, Performance System Associates).

- Providing certificates for participants to complete about something they have learned in the training and having the certificate presented to the person by a partner (compliments of Toni La Motta, author of *Recognition: The Quality Way*).

Every training session should include some discussion and brainstorming by attendees as to how learnings in the session can be reinforced back on the job and ways attendees can hold themselves *accountable* to their commitment to apply what they've learned back at work.

After Training

For learnings to become used and ingrained, they must be reinforced back on the job. The more the learnings from the training can be discussed, shared, and practiced, the greater the chance that a transfer of learning will take place. Ideally, each attendee should have a post-training meeting with his or her manager to discuss how the training went, whether the employees' questions were answered, and ways the training will be implemented in the person's job. This simple discussion with one's manager does not have to take a lot of time, but is important in highlighting the importance of the training and the expectation by the manager that the learnings from the training actually will be used.

The manager plays a significant role in reinforcing learning, both by having this discussion and by systematically looking for ways to notice and thank the employee as that person uses learnings from the training. Progressive managers would even discuss the employees' preferences for how they would like to be recognized as they apply things they've learned in training.

Another effective way to call attention to learnings after training is to make it a standard practice for employees to share one or more of the learnings they received from any training they attend with the work group. In addition to helping those employees crystallize their learnings, this again encourages the group to value the training experience and what can be learned from it, promoting an attitude of constant learning and improvement among staff.

The Training and Development Staff

Last but not least, recognition can and should be used to build the morale and pride of the training staff as they make progress toward departmental goals. A good example of this is found with Elsie Tamayo, who used recognition to turn around the morale, pride, and productivity of the training department when she was training director for the City of San Diego, Department of Social Services.

When Elsie started in her position, employee morale was low and the group's identity in the organization was weak. She met with the thirteen employees in her department and asked how they wanted to be perceived by the organization. The group created its own identity as the "Training and Development Center" and created a logo and painted it on the outside and in the lobby of their building. Everyone also received business cards for the first time with the new department logo on those cards.

At each department meeting, Elsie solicited the help of one employee to come up with some type of fun way of rewarding another employee in the group. For example, to announce one employee's promotion, the group made a parade through the building; another employee was presented with an Energizer Bunny "because they kept going and going and going, helping others when needed"; a toy roadrunner was presented to someone who worked fast. She also started each department meeting by reading letters written to her praising the department or people in it. At all times, she gave the group the latest information she had about developments in the organization.

Once a week, every person was given an hour to meet with her to talk about anything he or she wanted to discuss. Initially many of the meetings were less than ten minutes, but over time everyone came to use a full hour. Employees would discuss results from a training session and how they could improve, problems they were having with other employees, ways to improve their skills and career potential, and so forth.

Elsie used numbers as recognition to increase the visibility of achievements of the group. For example, the number of employees trained each month was tracked, as were cost savings ideas, and progress was communicated throughout the organization. In the department, flip charts were hung publicly that tracked progress toward different goals, and "master's degrees" were awarded to trainers and managers who trained 1,000 hours.

She used extensive spontaneous rewards, such as quick handwritten notes or a note on a flip chart that read "you really handled the meeting well yesterday" (with specifics and why the activity was important) and then posted the flip-chart sheet on the person's door. She often let people come in late the next day after finishing a training session. She bartered her training services with other training companies to get training slots for her group members or facilities for an off-site retreat. She also started a self-development library and positioned use of it as a reward.

She hosted a fake "marathon" with all project members and provided T-shirts and awarded "records"—actual LPs with new labels and jackets to fit the achievements of individuals in the group—that were handed out during a mock marathon celebration. Elsie even announced that the team was going to spend one half-day a month as a Reward and Recognition Day (R&R Day) in which the group would come up with things they wanted to do together to celebrate their successes along the way. In subsequent months they did such things as taking the train to Los Angeles to visit a museum, going shopping in Tijuana, going to the zoo, and so forth.

Since all rapport comes from shared experiences, this activity not only reinforced desired performance, but helped to build a sense of group pride and cohesiveness.

All these activities were conducted with little or no budget, and throughout employees knew they still had to put in the hours needed to do their jobs. Within several months, the morale, excitement, pride, and energy of the department skyrocketed, and the group was viewed with greater esteem by the rest of the organization.

Conclusion

Recognition: It's what matters. Recognition is all around us every day, just waiting to be used to encourage the behavior and performance you most need from those you work with. Prioritize what you most want from your group and start recognizing those things when you get them!

One final note: Don't forget to recognize and thank those managers who support individual learning and development among their staff and the training department and the ongoing value of learning and development in your organization. Make them role models that other managers can emulate to help make the overall organization more successful.

Bob Nelson, Ph.D., M.B.A., *is president of Nelson Motivation Inc., in San Diego, California; a popular presenter to management groups, conferences, and associations; and a best-selling author of* 1001 Ways to Reward Employees *(now in its forty-third printing);* 1001 Ways to Energize Employees; The Management Bible; Managing for Dummies; *and* The 1001 Rewards and Recognition Fieldbook: The Complete Guide.

Where Are the Grown-Ups?
Developing Mature Leaders*
Lisa J. Marshall

Summary

Our current stories about leadership are inadequate. Not that a new story is needed; instead we must return to an old one, invented every time the world reaches a certain level of complexity. To paraphrase Lao Tzu, the Chinese philosopher in 6th Century BC China (another time of great social complexity), "Bad leaders are hated and feared, good leaders are loved and admired, and with great leaders, the people say, 'We did it ourselves.'"

Those great leaders lead through their being, their presence. They open a space inside of which people seem to enlarge, to glow with the illumination of a shared call to action, and to resonate together powerfully. The result is the magic of focused and coordinated action. Fully themselves, they invite others into a story of deep commitment and profound results.

In this article, we look at three overlapping stories about leadership. The first is the old story of heroic leadership. The second is the more current story of collaborative leadership. The third is the story of leadership when things must be made to make sense before action can be taken—dialogic leadership. We explore what prevents us from reaching maturity in all three of those stories and how to address such obstacles.

The Old Story

The oldest leadership story is the hero who slays the monster. It is the equation of leader with superhero, whose legacy we still struggle with. Wilfred Drath, in *The Deep*

---

*Adapted from *Speak the Truth and Point to Hope: The Leader's Journey to Maturity* (Kendall/Hunt, 2004).

The 2006 Pfeiffer Annual: Training

Blue Sea: Rethinking the Source of Leadership, names this story "First Principle Leadership." He notes that such a leader, "being the exemplar of what is right, good, powerful, intelligent, is naturally the best person to provide direction and to know what needs to be done" (2001, p. 39).

Drath adds that this story, like all stories about leadership, is jointly created and held between leader and followers. "Dominance and charisma come from this perfect attunement between leader and follower in the shared creation of a kind of leadership that creates a leader who is irreplaceable" (2001, pp. 65–66). In that irreplaceability, of course, lies the weakness of such leadership. If the leader single-handedly embodies all that the community wants and needs, then insufficient capability is developed within the community or organization: there is no leadership pipeline. Family-run businesses, Fortune 500 companies, and start-ups alike struggle with these issues of succession.

The Current Story

As society becomes more complex, demands on leaders also become more complex. Leadership is no longer the purview of the one who can best define the community's "beckoning, collective future" (Whyte, 1996, p. 164). Instead, many people must contribute their information and insight for that future to be clear, and they work to influence one another in that process. Drath's "Second Principle Leadership" story thus is one of collaboration and influencing. The most influential person becomes the leader. "If commitment in the first principle can be called loyalty, commitment in the second principle is alignment" (2001, p. 87).

This emphasis on collaboration and alignment has been widespread in both the public and private sectors in the last few decades, reflecting the influence-driven nature of large organizations. Leaders are expected to build alignment in their organizations, publicly seeking opinions from all sides before setting a direction. That direction is then understood to have taken into account all those points of view. Such leadership is seen as interpersonal and influential, as well as more tolerant of ambiguity (Drath, 2001). This story, too, is jointly created and held between leader and followers.

The Future Story

In the old stories, the slaying of one monster often provokes the waking of the next, as it did in *Beowulf*, when slaying Grendel awakened Grendel's mother. So, too, must our old and current leadership stories recognize that, in succeeding, they have generated a new monster—that of a world grown too complex for First and even Second Principle stories of dominance and influence.

We now stand on the cusp of a third story about leadership, "Third Principle Leadership." It is the story we need when leading in a world too confusing to continue making decisions and solving problems, because we no longer know what the problems actually are or what decisions to make. We have to make sense of this world before we can solve problems and make decisions. As Drath observes, now leaders must engage in "a search for shared understanding (which is not the same as agreement) on which the hard work of problem solving and decision making can be built" (2001, p. 159).

The Power of Story

In Third Principle Leadership, stories are the tool for making meaning out of the data flood. Told and retold, framed from one point of view and then another, stories become the vehicle for sense-making (Drath, 2001). Shared stories let us see, hear, and feel one another's experiences, allowing us to taste and smell new possibilities. Weaving disparate stories together, we intuitively sense what is and is not working and what might or might not work in the future. Such stories become living entities, "living stories" for which, knowing the past and the present, we work together to influence and form the future.

These living stories invite everyone into a new and different kind of conversation, a conversation for meaning-making and possibility. They can prevent both analysis paralysis and premature action. Because they invite entry into the experience in ways that standard PowerPoint presentations never do, stories also protect us from the naysayers and critics, who always have reasons why something will not work and never suggestions about how it can work.

Love: A Different Path to Leadership Development

It seems almost taboo to talk about love and leading in the same sentence. Yet it is precisely the shift that needs to take place for Third Principle Leadership to occur. At the heart of mature leadership is love: love of life, love of one's work, love of truth, love of learning, and love for other people. This does not mean leadership is some sort of superhuman feat. These forms of love are felt every day, by literally hundreds of thousands of people all over the world, people just like you and me. They are people who have accessed the power of loving their work and loving the people with whom they work.

What's Love Got to Do with It?

"Why aren't you focusing on the hard stuff, like truth-telling or integrity, the messages our leaders really need to hear today?" "Nobody wants to hear about love." "You're on dangerous ground here if you want to be taken seriously," people have repeatedly warned me. "You may be right, but you can't talk about love in this organization."

Yes, it is dangerous ground. If we understood that love was at the core of all truly great leadership, leadership that creates the worlds we yearn for, we would indeed pose problems. Because we would not settle for the leadership we currently have in our organizations, in politics, in education, or in our faith communities.

We would ask our leaders to ask us the hard questions. We would ask our leaders to invite us into conversations in which meaning is made and value established. We would see that the famous leaders are rarely the great leaders. We would recognize the great leaders because they make us feel more competent, capable, and committed. We would know that "the bottom line" is merely a metaphor for a yearning for greatness and that companies do not exist to make money any more than human beings exist merely to make blood. In both cases, their purpose must always be something larger.

So if love is a major part of leadership, what is love? The dictionary offers this definition, among others: "unselfish concern that freely accepts another in loyalty and seeks his good." It also means "to thrive," with roots in Old English and Germanic words that mean to esteem and trust, as well as belief and faith.

Here is what defines love in a workplace setting: a deeply felt caring for the work we do and the people we do it with, a zest for the life we are leading, and a passion for the world in which we are doing it. This love is not soft and fuzzy. It is rigorous, demanding, and unwilling to be "nice" when tough kindness is required. It sets high expectations and then enables people to meet them. Love requires truth and integrity. It asks us to grow up, let go of our egos, know when to hold our boundaries, and when to fold them. Love asks us to ask the bigger questions—is this just good for me or is it good for the team, the division, the organization, the community, the planet?

So why is love unspeakable? Maybe because we use that one word to mean so many different things. Probably because the workplace, frankly, is designed to be a "manly" place, and real men do not talk about love. Possibly because we have so deeply subscribed to the "rational man" view of economics, to Frederick Winslow Taylor's notion that every activity can be deconstructed to its smallest part and then reassembled, and to the machine metaphor of work, that we do not see any room for love in those models.

But I would submit that, ultimately, we do not talk about love and leadership together because the hardest thing in life is to learn to act from love instead of from jealousy (competitiveness), ego, fear, and greed (fear of scarcity). We are afraid we will not measure up, so we shut off the conversation and blind ourselves to the loss.

Yet the hard, cold truth is that the only community most of us have these days is our workplace. If we do not find and give love in our workplace, we starve emotionally. It is not enough (although enormously important) to go home to a loving family. The reality for most people is that the best part of their waking life is spent at work. If their hearts are not nourished there, how will they have anything left to give when they get home?

It is often argued that love, in its behavioral forms of conversation, clarity, and compassion is (1) not actually a valid leadership tool; (2) without standing in the workplace; and (3) insufficient to engage whole organizations in meaning making and problem solving. Yet these arguments long ago lost their validity.

There are decades of solid research confirming the positive bottom-line impact of manifestations of love, such as service, integrity, trust, and respect. *Fortune* magazine's "100 Best Places to Work" issue consistently reports that companies where people feel valued and respected make healthy profits. One study showed a 756 percent increase in net profits over eleven years in companies that valued multiple internal and external stakeholder satisfaction and involvement (Kotter & Haskett, 1992). In *Working with Emotional Intelligence*, Daniel Goleman (2000) cites literally hundreds more studies with similar results.

Why is the research ignored? Why are our businesses in the shape they are in? Why are our communities in the shape they are in? Why are our schools in disrepair? Why is the idea of public office anathema to so many bright, educated, ambitious people? If they know what needs to be done, why are our leaders not doing it?

Finding the Leaders We Need

The answer is deceptively simple: they are not really leaders. Whether in the public or private sector, we do not promote leaders; we promote managers. Managers do things that can be measured; leaders change the agenda. Managers seem safer. In addition, we have made the role of leader untenable: we expect leaders to be perfect. We demand that they lead everywhere, not just in their own domain. We do not accept leaders as human beings with flaws and gifts.

Because they are fundamentally not leaders, but managers, many of our so-called leaders just do as they are told. And what they are told is primarily, "Make money, now" and "Don't rock the boat politically." So our "leaders" sacrifice ethics and long-term thinking on the altar of generating 20 percent per year ROI, or govern via polls, addressing themselves only to what the majority think they want this week. And yes, it is just that simple.

And it is just that complex. Because, for this to change, we must all begin to address the hard issues of growing up. We must step up to our own individual leadership responsibilities. No matter our age or stage, we must acknowledge the captaincy of our own lives; no one else decides how to live our lives. We must accept that there are times to recognize the call to lead and times to simply give wise counsel to whoever is leading.

The closest analogy today to a mature leadership role is an unlikely one: that of the community organizer. Ernesto J. Cortes, Jr., a member of the national staff of the Industrial Areas Foundation (IAF), a source of much of the organizing tradition in the United States since the 1930s, notes, "The ethics of power really hovers around the question of how you go about obtaining consent. You can obtain consent by force or violence. You can obtain consent by deceit, by lying to people. You can obtain consent by manipulating people, withholding information, rendering them incompetent. But finally you can learn to obtain consent through informed judgment" (Moyers, 1999, p. 144).

Many who lead today do so by obtaining consent through force or deceit or withholding. These are not the leaders we need. The training that community organizing offers might be the best training we could offer in our leadership programs today. Its emphasis on serving, on promoting others instead of yourself, and on asking the hard questions would serve today's leaders—and their followers—far more than courses on supply chain management or global econometrics.

For, if as Joe Jaworski, co-founder of the Global Leadership Initiative and author of *Synchronicity: The Inner Path of Leadership*, says, "Leadership is all about the release of human possibilities," then teaching leaders how to "obtain consent through informed judgment" means that we release the power of leadership that enrolls, leadership that invites the world to participate in the making of meaning and the taking of action without scapegoating or blaming (1998, p. 66). In a time when most leaders shift attention away from their own responsibility by pointing fingers at others, this leadership is truly needed.

Self-Authorizing Leadership

Third Principle Leadership, the sense-making and story-building form of leadership, offers us a new leadership voice. It is a self-authorizing voice, one that says, "I am responsible for my own fate" (Carol Stoneburner, personal communication, April 22, 2002). With self-authorizing leadership, there is, paradoxically, more and less of us. As David Whyte notes, "One of the outer qualities of great captains, great leaders, great bosses is that they are inutterably themselves. . . . The best stay true to a conversation that is the sum of their own strange natures and the world they inhabit, and do not attempt to mimic others in order to get on" (2002, p. 47).

Strangely, these leaders do not achieve their identity at our expense. By being absolutely who they are, such leaders also give us room to be absolutely who we are. And when we can be who we are, egos dissipate. We focus instead on the larger demands, a compelling vision of what wants and needs to happen in the world. As one Intel executive observed, "The key to having an apolitical environment is that you have a burning vision of success for the organization and the ability to subordinate yourself to that vision. That vision is more important than your other personal goals. If you can't do that, then no one who's following you can be asked to or will do it" (Noury Al-Khaledy, personal communication, October 15, 2001). This subordination to the larger goal reflects a profound developmental step. It is the step where we move into service and belonging, a step toward maturity.

One example of such a leader is Joe Ehrman, former linebacker for the Baltimore Colts, who is now a minister and a high school football coach at Gilman School in Baltimore. When his young teams assemble before a game, the coaches call out, "What is the coaches' job?" The boys call back, "To love us." "What is your job?" "To love each other."

No Gilman football player is allowed to enter the cafeteria and see another student eating alone without going to sit and eat with him or her. This team has taken the city championships five years running. It is not about being soft—it is about the rigorous discipline love requires. Such loving leadership is hard work and demands consistently high behavioral standards. It also produces superb, highly competitive results (Marx, 2004).

The Biology of Leading

How does this process work? What are such leaders actually doing? They are actually activating the neurological processes that allow us to change. As Drs. Fari Amini, Richard Lannon, and Thomas Lewis note in *A General Theory of Love*, "Who we are and who we become depends, in part, on whom we love" (2001, p. 144). By love, they also mean that capacity to care deeply about others and seek their best interests.

Such deep caring, they conclude, carves new neurological pathways, literally redesigning the way our brains work. These neurological revisions that love makes possible, in what is known as our limbic system, are central to effective individual and collective leadership. They generate the increased capacity—emotional, intellectual, moral, and spiritual development—that underlies almost any form of leadership maturity.

Jim Collins concludes his chapter on leadership in *Good to Great* by discussing the question of whether one has to sacrifice having a great life in order to work for a great company. Just the opposite, he concludes: The leaders of great companies "clearly loved what they did, largely because they loved who they did it with. For no matter what we achieve, if we don't spend the vast majority of our time with people we love and respect, we cannot possibly have a great life" (2001, p. 62). In leadership, love, as defined earlier, becomes both cause and effect, both source and action.

Finding the Grown-Ups

Mature leaders are people who can act in all three leadership stories (heroic, collaborative, and dialogic) as needed. Another part of maturity is that you can be fully responsible for saying what needs to be said (or doing what needs to be done) without grandiosity, the secret belief that you are responsible for *everything*. Grown-up leaders understand that there are others to help. They invite collaboration. They speak of possibilities with clarity, compassion, and gratitude, acting in these ways as well, creating the space in which we can operate at our finest.

Comfortable with facing reality and confident that once the sense-making is complete, all things can be (collectively) handled, the great leaders become almost transparent, a kind of ego-less force in whose presence all blossom. These are people who tell us the future by being that future. They make possible a new story.

Obstacles to Leadership: Facing Our Monsters

What gets in the way of being leaders, whether in our own life or in our organization's? What prevents us from fully owning our potential for greatness, whatever form that might take? The external obstacles are easily identified: limited resources, negative attitudes, lack of organizational commitment, unexpected changes in the environment, constant crises, etc. Yet at root, each of these obstacles simply masks deeper issues. For it is never the issue itself that is the real obstacle to our success.

Ultimately, the real monsters we face on our leadership journey are the ones carried inside, the monsters illuminated by our responses to those crises or issues. Do we declare defeat the first time it is announced that there are not enough resources, or do we decide to get creative? Do we allow ourselves to be defeated by difficult bosses, or accept that taking flak is part of our job if we want to see something bigger accomplished? Are the changes in the environment really the crisis, or is it us—our lack of resilience, unwillingness to learn, failure to see the opportunities that also accompany the changes?

The Monster of Who We Are

The real monsters are internal. At the end of the day, the central question is not what "they" did to us. It is and will be "How did I prevent/minimize/respond?" There is a line from an old cartoon strip called "Pogo" that captures this monster's essence: "We have met the enemy and he is us." It seems intrinsic to human nature that we get in our own way far more than anyone else ever can. Some of us recognize this early in life and begin to address it; others spend most of their lives discovering the power of their self-fulfilling prophecies. And, of course, some die blaming others for self-induced misery.

How exactly are we our own monsters? Let us look again at the neurology of our limbic systems, our mammalian brains. When frightened or threatened, primates suffer from what Daniel Goleman calls an "amygdala hijacking" (2000, p. 74). That is when two small glands called the amygdala, located in the mammalian brain, end-run or overpower the thinking brain (the neocortex) because they sense danger. They activate the oldest part of us, the brain stem or reptilian brain, engendering the "fight, flee, or freeze" response. (Which one is activated depends both on circumstances and on the specifics of your individual neurological wiring.)

While those three choices have served to keep us alive for thousands of years, there is no denying that they instantly bankrupt the leadership role. Blood is rerouted from the brain to the hands if the message is "fight," to the legs if the message is "flee," and to neither if it is "freeze." Muscles around the rib cage tighten so that the predator cannot hear you breathing. Adrenaline and cortisol are pumped into your system. These chemicals support short-term, intensive activity—but can kill if they remain at elevated levels for too long.

Choice and creativity disappear. With a full-blown amygdala hijacking there is only reaction. The leader rushing blindly into battle because he or she has no biological choice no more provides great leadership than the leader who freezes or flees the field.

It is the rare grown-up who can prevent a personal amygdala hijacking in the midst of a group panic attack. Nigel Morris, founder and CEO of Capital One, the financial services company, credited his personal coach for the increased maturity that enabled him not to lose his head during a week in which the company's stock lost 40 percent of its value. After three years of coaching, Morris recognized that, as a leader, he could not succumb to terror, but had to hold the boundaries and create the container of assurance within which everyone else could mentally return to work.

The dilemma in this dynamic is that the amygdala is a "coarse" sorter, that is, *any* element in the current situation that harkens back to *any* element in *any* past situation in which you experienced threat, humiliation, embarrassment, or shame will alert the reptilian brain, home of the fight, flee, or freeze response. Does someone remind you of a bully from fourth grade? Does the boss's behavior remind you of your dad at his worst? Even triggers as subtle as these will "awaken the reptile." If that past memory relates to something truly traumatic, it can induce a full-blown amygdala hijacking.

This reaction is complicated by gender differences. Both women and men have fight or flight responses to life-threatening situations. Men tend to have reptilian responses to not only life-threatening, but to a wide variety of stressful situations. When not faced with threat or humiliation, however, women's response to stress is very different. Labeled "tend and befriend" by scientists, it appears that women's affiliative natures cause them, under stress, to be more likely to reach for connection than to fight, freeze, or withdraw (Dess, 2000). While probably more useful in the workplace, "tend and befriend" responses also come at a cost—taking on relationship responsibility when you may not have the resources to sustain it.

Male or female, such reactive responses are not inevitable. However, it takes considerable insight and self-discipline to prevent amygdala hijackings. Not only must you be able to recognize vulnerabilities and hot buttons in yourself, but you must also consciously develop strategies for preventing reptilian responses. For some, the path to such self-knowledge and self-discipline may lie through coaching or therapy. For others, practice in the martial arts or meditation may be more effective.

Monsters All Around

Beyond the biological, there are a large number of other opportunities to be your own monster, your own worst enemy. In fact, there are monsters in four key domains of life: emotional, intellectual, moral, and spiritual. Chief among the emotional monsters is ego: that driving need to be the one in charge, the one in the spotlight, the one who has all the answers, the one who has the most, the one who does it all. And perhaps for a time it may actually happen just that way. Yet no one wins every battle.

When Andy Pearson was CEO of PepsiCo, *Fortune* called him one of the ten toughest bosses in America. Twenty years later, as founding chairman of Tricon Global Restaurants (KFC, Pizza Hut, and Taco Bell), Pearson (now in his seventies, which only proves you are never too old to learn) has developed new leadership skills. He has come to realize that the heart is the key to a company's competitive edge, and that if limbic needs are fundamental to human beings, then addressing those needs is not a weakness. Pearson's view of leadership has altered: "Your real job is to get results and to do it in a way that makes your organization a great place to work—a place where people enjoy coming to work, instead of just taking orders and hitting this month's numbers" (Dorsey, 2001, p. 84).

For Pearson, that change had to do with reining in his ego. "I think I've gone from making my way by trying to be the smartest guy in the room to just asking questions and insisting that the answers be reasonable and logical" (Dorsey, 2001, p. 85). His move toward maturity was not about *not* asking those hard questions. It was about no longer asking them to prove his smarts, but doing it in service of the larger good. "There's a big difference between being tough and being tough-minded. There's an important aspect that has to do with humility" (Dorsey, 2001, p. 86). Pearson reports that he's been surprised at how difficult it is to get Tricon leaders to behave this way, primarily due to the lack of role models.

Arrogance is probably the most common form of intellectual monster. It often manifests itself as locking into a system of thinking that prevents other possibilities from being recognized until too late. Investment in a specific style of analyzing the world lends itself to "ownership of the parts" rather than "stewardship of the whole" (Joe Dyer, personal communication, March 19, 2002) and tends to generate rigidity, making organizations vulnerable to new competitors, disruptive technologies, or market changes.

Depression is a spiritual monster that more and more rears its ugly head in the work world. As a 2003 *Psychology Today* article reports, "One top executive who 'met the monster and made it through' contends that being crowned king is itself the problem" (Marano, 2003, p. 60). He found the fear of losing what he had was a very different game than the work of getting it and didn't like the person he became in his efforts to hold on to "it." At the senior management level, he says, "Depression is rampant among people who have achieved their goals—and even worse among those who have not" (Marano, 2003, p. 60).

Ultimately, depression is a failure to have found meaning in life. It is especially unspeakable in the workplace: one must appear tough, competent, and clear-headed at all times. The fear of being "discovered," when the price may be a literal one, as when the organization's market value is affected, or less direct, when a plum assignment is directed elsewhere, feeds a vicious cycle of loneliness and despair.

Greed is perhaps the ugliest moral monster, one that can seduce us into self-betrayal, the Faustian bargain that excuses behavior that corrodes us from the inside out. It may be greed for money, for power, or for the trappings of power. In all cases, the need behind the thing you are greedy for—whether power, perks, or dollars—is a sense of self-worth that cannot ultimately be filled by such symbolic forms. Sooner or later the sense of accomplishment gives way to the gnawing of the greed monster, and the search begins again. Breaking free of greed often requires an especially brutal wake-up call—loss of a loved one, loss of family and friends, or even a near-death experience—accompanied by the recognition that the hole is not being filled by greater wealth or higher status.

The Monster of How Far One Has Come on the Journey

What is the source of all these monsters? It is, ironically, our own growth and development. As humans, we spend our emotional lives caught between twin poles: (1) a powerful desire for autonomy, for independence, for self-hood, and separation and (2) an equally powerful desire for connection, for community, for affiliation, and intimacy. In this push/pull lies the wellspring of our monsters.

"Our experience of this fundamental ambivalence may be our experience of the unitary, restless, creative motion of life itself" (Kegan, 1983, p. 107). In the process of maturing, we spend our lives spiraling upward between these two poles, touching base with each and then pushing off to a higher level that absorbs and integrates everything that has come before. For some, it is a path punctuated by significant experiences; for others it is more gradual. Either way, this movement is the deep structure of the leadership journey.

Defining Maturity

Maturity is a word that falls into the category of "I know it when I see it." The dictionary defines maturity as "fully developed in body or mind, as a person." But what does "fully developed" really mean? Maturity is the place where the twin poles of development, our need for autonomy and our need for connection, no longer pull us apart. We no longer feel our true self only when resting comfortably on a pole. We come to understand, consciously or unconsciously, that the space between them represents possibility and we open into it.

If, or when, we stop maturing, we become stuck, unable to move beyond our current position in autonomy ("I don't need anyone else, I can do this by myself!") or connection ("I need help; I can't do anything by myself"). But the pull to move on will never really go away, and much of our energy is sapped just resisting it.

When we are truly on the leadership journey, however, we awaken one morning to find our "self" moved off the pole, drawn inexorably to the next stage, and then suddenly we have a very different experience. Our old stories about our self, about whom and how we are, no longer work. We have not yet evolved new stories to replace them. "I'm just not myself," is a phrase that, as a coach, invariably tells me that life has bumped that person off a position on one of the poles. Thrown unwillingly into transition, specifically Bridges' (2003) "neutral zone," where all things are possible and nothing predictable, most of us panic, at least until we better understand what is happening. Frightened and grieving at the loss of the old self, we often revert to the dynamics of the reptilian brain described earlier.

Facing Essential Pain

Robert Kegan, in his powerful integration of human development theory, *The Evolving Self*, notes that growth involves "a redrawing of the line where I stop and you begin, a redrawing that eventually consists in a qualitatively new guarantee to you of your distinctness from me (permitting at the same time a qualitatively 'larger' you with which to be in relation)" (1983, p. 131). This construction of a new and larger self and other occurs over and over, whether we are moving from the autonomy pole, convinced of our independent capabilities and fundamental aloneness, or from the connection pole, deeply committed to relationship and community. Each time it involves a powerful (and often terrifying) period of "not knowing"—not knowing where the boundaries are and not knowing what should be brought (or not) from the old self to help constitute the new one.

We are all familiar with the childhood cycles of this experience, whether it is the "terrible twos" or the more complex and painful push-pulls that characterize the adolescent's path. It also describes us when we are called to the next level of leadership development. The young leader, receiving criticism from his manager, finds himself suddenly unable to discern the boundaries between himself and his work or what he truly knows to be right, let alone the meaning of the apparent loss of approval from such a significant "other." Even a mature leader, faced with a crisis, can quickly find herself deeply thrown to a state of siege, losing sight of the fact that what happens to her is not the same as what happens to her organization. Pulled from the pole on which he or she had been resting comfortably, each must now experience the profound discomfort of learning a new way to be, a higher way to function in the world. This is the essential pain of leadership growth.

At other times in our lives, the next step on the journey may be internally generated through a call to find a deeper self or a more meaningful role in the world. As Carol Pearson puts it, then "our seeking takes on a different, deeper quality. Suddenly, we are seeking spiritual depth and authenticity, and we know it is not just a change in environment—mates, work, place—we seek, but a change in ourselves" (1991, p. 128). Again we must face the essential terror of not knowing, having to relearn both the world and our self.

Ultimately, maturity changes our perspective on this process. Instead of fearing "not knowing," we relax into it, embrace it for the possibilities it brings, and quit fighting to return to one of the poles. A kind of internal spaciousness develops that allows us to trust that our identity, our fundamental "self," will survive this period. Others later note that we seem much more "at ease in our own skin" and are more drawn to being in our presence.

Performer or Learner: How Will You Face the Journey?

Research on children's approaches to learning by Carol Dweck, a professor of psychology at Columbia University, holds an important key to how we take this journey. Dweck (2000) observed that children who believed performance was a measure of ability quickly became discouraged when they ran into difficulties. Such "performer" children assumed that experiencing difficulty indicated an innate lack of ability, since ability was, by definition, fixed and permanent. Children who did *not* assume that ability was fixed were stimulated or challenged by difficulties and threw themselves into resolving them. Experimenting with both greater effort and different strategies, they saw (and experienced) their effort as a way to increased capability.

As adults, these attitudes persist. Performers stick to what already comes easily (their natural abilities), thereby inhibiting the development of new capabilities. As a result, they do not commit to endeavors that might require a higher level of performance than they believe themselves capable of offering.

Learners focus differently: They are driven far more by curiosity than by concern with how others perceive them. Their concern thus is with action ("What happens if I try this?"), rather than with performance ("How will I be judged?"). Learners tolerate a lot of frustration and mistakes on the road to accomplishing what they want. Consequently, their capabilities continue to expand.

Most leaders function as performers in some arenas and learners in others. The dilemma is that, if at critical moments we revert to performer mode, our focus is on how we are perceived by others. We lose the opportunity to listen to and discover our new and evolving self, the opportunity to mature. We may even lose the possibility of discovering the leader emergent within.

If, on the other hand, we can face such moments as learners, if we can access our hunger to understand and "participate in the grandeur of the universe—whether it is through a great love, a great work, the ultimate experience, personal transformation, or the attainment of wisdom" (Pearson, 1991, pp. 127–128), then the difficult moments are more easily managed. When we are fascinated by what we are learning, the simple shift in where we put our attention reduces the discomfort—and the terror—and we move more easily and gracefully through difficult times and learnings.

Later in Dweck's career, she began to see that feedback had an enormous impact on the performer/learner dynamic. Having assumed that the preferences for learner or performer were innate, she was startled to discover that she could turn performer children into learners by the way she gave them feedback. Feedback that focused solely on results created performers. Feedback that focused on the process—how hard they worked, how creative or imaginative they were, and how persistent—created learners. In other words, feedback that focuses on the process of exploration and learning makes us learners. Feedback that focuses solely on results creates performers.

This at least partially answers the question about whether leadership is innate or can be taught, as well as addressing the questions about whether there are clear ways to grow and develop leaders. Clearly leadership can be "untaught" through the ways in which organizations recognize and reward certain behaviors. When only short-term results matter, bullies become perceived as leaders. If curiosity, innovation, and generativity are rewarded in our performance management systems, then we get a deeper, richer version of leadership. Thus, when we encourage or reward learning and growth, we develop leaders.

Much of the current ill health of corporate, non-profit, and political leadership can be traced to this dynamic. We have become so focused on immediate results that we inexorably press our leadership into being performers and squeeze the learner out of them. In this way, Wall Street is its own monster.

Metamorphosis

In Joseph Campbell's architecture of the great stories, known as "the hero's journey," heroes inevitably must confront monsters. In so doing, they are forced to greater levels both of competence and of self-awareness. Again, in Beowulf's story, when the hero slays Grendel, he must then fight Grendel's mother, a far more fearsome monster. So too, when we slay the easy monsters as young leaders, we awaken larger forces that will not be denied if we are to mature. We must confront our biological and character weaknesses, as well as our yearnings for greatness, for being part of something larger than ourselves. Those are our true monsters.

Inherent in the hero's journey is the notion that a change, a metamorphosis, is what is required to face down monsters. Metamorphosis means "a transformation, as if by magic or sorcery, a marked change in appearance, character, condition or function." The caterpillar spins a cocoon, hides inside, and returns a butterfly. I have chosen the concept of the "wormhole" to describe these powerful change experiences. It is a term from physics that refers to a "tunnel in the fabric of space/time," that fits the metaphor of a magical and bewildering change that drops us into an utterly different world than we expected.

Four distinct categories of wormhole showed up in my research with leaders, each with its own unique qualities:

- Accepting the call

- Letting go of doing it alone

- Living under the microscope

- Not having all the answers

Obviously, these four are not the only possible wormhole experiences. Getting fired, the loss of loved ones through death or divorce, a deeply felt spiritual experience, nearly dying oneself, having to fire people, even an organizational collapse of some kind, can all precipitate a trip through the wormhole. What all such experiences have in common is the sense of a tectonic plate shift, after which life is never quite the same again.

Not all leaders go through all four wormholes, but all go through at least one. Wormholes have several elements in common. They each trigger abrupt discontinuity, a stunning "pattern interrupt" for the person who undergoes them. Each has a humbling impact. The leader who experiences them is knocked off his or her current developmental pole and endures that period of not quite knowing himself or herself before the old identity can be transcended and included in a new, fuller, richer one.

This is exactly the metamorphosis from caterpillar to butterfly that Mort Meyerson described when he became head of Perot Systems after being CEO of EDS: "There was a time during that first year at Perot Systems when I would go home and look in the mirror and say to myself, 'You don't get it. Maybe you ought to get out of this business. You're like a highly specialized trained beast that evolved during one period and now can't adjust to the new environment'" (1996, p. 71). Myerson had to recognize that what was asked of him now was leading through presence, through who he was, not what he did. It was up to others to *do*; it was up to him to *enable* them to do. It was an exceedingly difficult recasting of his self-image.

Wormhole 1: Accepting the Call

For some people, just accepting that they are leaders, that others perceive them that way, is a stunning pattern interrupt. It requires a dramatically different sense of self than the one they were previously carrying, and their world is never the same again. For one person, it is the moment when a question is asked and all heads turn in her direction. For another, it is the moment of realizing that if there is bad news to be given, he would rather be the one to do it. Suddenly a new story begins.

Wormhole 2: Letting Go of Doing It Alone

The second wormhole is facing that we cannot go it alone. This is the move past our oldest leadership story—heroic leadership—into something more flexible. It may be that the projects are too big or the complexity too great; the result is the same. We recognize that we cannot work through the situation alone, that a team is needed to succeed. There is often a major crisis of confidence when young, technically gifted leaders realize that they can no longer hold the plans inside their heads because the project scope has gone beyond their capacity. This may seem blindingly obvious, but for many young leaders, it is a painful moment, and feels like failure: "How can I be a leader if I need other people?"

Wormhole 3: Living Under the Microscope

A reality of leadership is that you are watched, every move and every word. Your perceived mood becomes the organization's mood. In a profound way, your "self" is not just yours anymore: It belongs to everyone. The higher one goes in an organization, the truer this is.

In this wormhole, you become exquisitely aware of your own behavior and its impact. As Carly Fiorina, former CEO of Hewlett-Packard, is said to have observed, "You may as well pay attention to your behavior; everyone else is." The leader is the one who models keeping promises and allowing people to tell the truth. He or she makes it clear that discipline matters by delivering on promises, making clear requests, expecting clear responses, and holding people accountable. The result is muscularity in the story, a robustness that makes it clear: this story *will* happen.

Wormhole 4: Not Having All the Answers

The fourth wormhole has to do with the reality that you do not have all the answers and never will. There are dark places, shadow sides in you, in others, and in the situation that make it hard to see with clarity. To see in the shadows we need a new set of conversations, ones that enable people to discern which way is true north, what questions need to be asked, what issues need to be defined.

This wormhole requires humbly accepting the limits of your knowing and learning to live with ambiguity and paradox. It is about learning to trust, as well as to step into others' shoes and open yourself up to new possibilities. This wormhole most directly leads to leadership through presence, getting work done by enabling others rather than through your own actions. A *Sloan Management Review* article by Kate Sweetman commented that "people working for managers who openly express uncertainty and who seek employee input in resolving ambiguous challenges are more satisfied with their jobs, more committed to and less cynical about their organizations, and more likely to identify with the companies they work for" (2001, p. 8). No longer needing to control outcomes, such leaders trust that the people and processes they have put in place will produce the necessary results.

The Courage to Change and Mature

Wormholes demand courage of us. As Peter Koestenbaum notes, "No significant decision—personal or organizational—has ever been undertaken without . . . a commitment to wade through anxiety, uncertainty, and guilt" (Labarre, 2000, p. 230). Whether choosing how to approach a layoff, where to allocate scarce resources, or whether to take a new assignment, these difficult decisions can change us.

Notice that we can only change ourselves. If we are to be leaders who "obtain consent through informed judgment" (Moyers, 1990, p. 144), then other people must make their own choices. As Koestenbaum says, you do not motivate people with techniques, "but by risking yourself with a personal, lifelong commitment to greatness—by demonstrating courage. You do not teach it so much as challenge it into existence" (Labarre, 2000, p. 230). When we face our wormholes with courage, others can as well. Wormhole experiences generate a profound shift in attitude, bringing us to a deep understanding that our story, like our attitude, is our own. Trapped by it or enlarged by it, the decision is ours.

Ultimately, the changes that mature us as leaders have the paradoxical effect of simplifying us while increasing our embrace of ambiguity. We know ourselves—what we value, for what or for whom we will take a stand—and we have accepted both our own strengths and weaknesses. We increasingly know when to step up and when to step down and are comfortable with both. At the same time, we no longer need to simplify the world, to insist on a black-and-white, either/or reality. Perhaps as we make peace with our monsters and, in so doing, accept our own shadow sides (without empowering them), we have less of a need to polarize the world into "them or us" or "right or wrong." The answer to "either/or" becomes "both/and." Inevitably, this is accompanied by a growing sense of the whole, a vastly deepening appreciation for the interconnectedness of all aspects of life. From here we can reach for maturity in our emotional, intellectual, moral, and spiritual domains.

In 1974, General George Lee Butler was assigned to the Air Force Directorate of Plans and asked to prepare positions for the Strategic Arms Limitation Talks (SALT). The more he came to understand American nuclear strategic planning, the more he questioned the underlying rationale.

When named commander of the Strategic Air Command in 1991, Butler drastically reduced the number of nuclear strike targets. When arms talks resumed, he openly urged negotiators to lower ceilings on nuclear weapons, a position that many believe resulted in his not being appointed Colin Powell's successor as chairman of the Joint Chiefs of Staff. Since retiring, he continues to lobby for an end to nuclear weapons.

Intellectual maturity allowed Butler to question our nuclear military strategy; emotional maturity allowed him to take the unpopular positions that his moral maturity required; and spiritual maturity was reflected in his deep desire to be of service by preventing a world nuclear holocaust (Public Policy, 2002). Ultimately, Butler changed the thinking of the next generation of military leaders. This is the impact of a grown-up leader.

Conclusion: Simplicity, the Other Side of Complexity

True maturity in leadership requires that we indeed attain that "paradoxical mixture of personal humility and professional will" that Jim Collins (2001, p. 67) found in leaders of companies that went from being good to great. It has been said, "The mind cannot endure paradox; the heart can." What we inevitably sense in mature leaders, people who have faced their monsters, is that their hearts are wholly engaged with life. Through their capacity for love, they have come to understand that paradox is indeed, "the last illusion before the reality of wholeness" (Darya Funches, personal communication, March 6, 2002). Whole human beings, such leaders lovingly invite the wholeness in us all.

References

Amini, F., Lannon, R., & Lewis, T. (2001). *A general theory of love.* New York: Vintage Books.

Bridges, W. (2003). *Managing transitions: Making the most of change.* New York: Perseus Publishing.

Collins, J. (2001). *Good to great.* San Francisco, CA: HarperCollins.

Dess, N. (2000, September/October). Tend and befriend. *Psychology Today.*

Dorsey, D. (2001, August). Andy Pearson finds love. *Fast Company,* p. 84.

Drath, W. (2001). *The deep blue sea: Rethinking the source of leadership.* San Francisco, CA: Jossey-Bass.

Dweck, C. (2000). Believing in fixed social traits: Impact on social coping. In *Self-theories: Their role in motivation, personality, and development.* Philadelphia, PA: Psychology Press.

Goleman, D. (2000). *Working with emotional intelligence.* New York: Bantam Doubleday Dell.

Jaworski, J. (1998). *Synchronicity.* San Francisco, CA: Berrett-Koehler.

Kegan, R. (1983). *The evolving self.* Boston, MA: Harvard University Press.

Kotter, J., & Haskett, J. (1992, June 6). The caring company. *The Economist,* p. 75.

Labarre, P. (2000, March). Do you have the will to lead? *Fast Company,* p. 230.

Marano, H.A. (2003, May/June). The depression suite. *Psychology Today,* p. 60.

Marx, J. (2004). *Season of life.* New York: Simon & Schuster.

Meyerson, M. (1996, April/May). Everything I thought I knew about leadership is wrong. *Fast Company,* p. 71.

Moyers, B. (1990). *A world of ideas II: Public opinions from private citizens.* New York: Doubleday.

Pearson, C. (1991). *Awakening the heroes within: Twelve archetypes to help us find ourselves and transform our world.* San Francisco, CA: HarperCollins.

Public Policy: George Lee Butler. (2002). The Heinz Awards. Available from www.heinz awards.net/recipients.asp?action=detail&recipientID=67; internet (last accessed January 13, 2005)

Sweetman, K. (2001, Fall). Embracing uncertainty. *MIT Sloan Management Review,* p. 8.

Whyte, D. (1996). *The heart aroused: Poetry and the preservation of the soul in corporate America.* New York: Currency/Doubleday.

Whyte, D. (2002). *Crossing the unknown sea: Work as a pilgrimage of identity.* New York: Riverhead Books.

Lisa J. Marshall *is a nationally recognized expert on leadership maturity and organization development, and principal of The Smart Work Company. A best-selling business author, Ms. Marshall's newest title is* Speak the Truth and Point to Hope: The Leader's Journey to Maturity *(Kendall/Hunt), which presents for the first time her critically acclaimed leadership-development approach.*

Narcissistic Managers
An Impediment to
Organization Development
Marlo E. Ettien

Summary

In a technological age in which participative management is vital to the on-going success of any organization, identification and continual improvement of processes requires top and middle management to be an example through long-term, consistent leadership. With all the management self-help books, seminars, conferences, and mergers, it still seems to elude management teams that favoritism, discrimination, and using the company as a personal playing field are paths leading to stagnation rather than to continual development of the organization. Management does not have the luxury of being narcissistic or condescending. Rather, it must responsibly accept that stagnation in whatever measure begins with them and trickles down to the working level—and not the reverse. This article presents a concern that a lack of leadership skills poses a threat to organizational success. It also presents one author's view about necessary leadership development to overcome the problem.

Studies show that the most successful organizations create an environment of harmony and cooperation, fostering orderliness through unity and building efficient processes that lead to positive outcomes, such as increased productivity, timely achievement of goals, and customer satisfaction (Applebaum & Batt, 1994; Deming, 1995; Emery, 1995; Lawler, 1992; Pinchot & Pinchot, 1994).

After more than fifty years, it appears that what Dr. Edwards Deming, the man who saved Japan's industry after World War II, attempted to get American companies to understand is still necessary guidance. Dr. Deming's Profound Knowledge Theory states

The 2006 Pfeiffer Annual: Training

that, "[a] leader must understand the system he or she is attempting to manage. Without this understanding the system cannot be managed or improved. A system cannot understand itself or manage itself. Optimization of the parts does not optimize the whole. System optimization requires coordination and cooperation of the parts, which requires leadership" (Deming, 1995; www.maaw.info/DemingExhibit.htm).

Organization Development

Organization development is the process through which organizations seek to raise performance levels by understanding the people who operate the systems. These people are responsible for organizational viability, so organization development encourages management to act responsibly, rather than bask in the prestige and privileges afforded them.

Related to the concept of organization development are the concepts of human capital management, employee research, and leadership development, which require those in management to demonstrate the same emotional, creative, intellectual, and intuitive intelligence they expect other personnel to mirror in daily operations as partners in the organization. The same principles uniformly used at the upper management level need to be implemented at the working level to ensure that approaches to improvement are consistent. For example, results of management brainstorming sessions or high-level meetings with customers that change business practices or that would increase productivity at the working level should not be hoarded as exclusive benefits for management. Such information hoarding is disruptive and counterproductive.

Human Capital Management

To prevent disruption in an organization's development, human capital management must guarantee that the person hired fits the position for which he or she is hired. Adequately trained personnel must understand their role in supporting and fully embracing their mission, particularly those hired to be managers. Promoting personnel to management positions who have not demonstrated they have the emotional, creative, intellectual, and intuitive abilities to perform at that level causes dysfunction. If potential managers have not demonstrated intelligence in its varying forms at the supervisory level and below, they cannot be considered for a management role. Wrong choices lead to employee frustration. Multiplication of small obstacles over time brings about large-scale stagnation for the organization. Management selections and decisions must be made in the best interest of the organization, never in the interest of individuals.

Leadership Development

In the interest of the organizational whole, leadership development seeks to identify the following three abilities in managers:

1. The flexibility of leading and managing interchangeably;

2. Ability to adjust to the changes of the organization's goals; and

3. The consistency to function at the management level.

Despite lack of seniority or previous managerial experience, personnel who demonstrate such talent should be considered for decision-making positions. Talent, understood as leadership, is the most accurate measuring rod for advancement to the management level.

In a highly competitive global market, companies that lack cohesion and waste intelligence in its varying forms will stagnate. Managers who place their own interests ahead of those of the organization will necessarily make poor choices. Such management hubris leads to financial ruin, whereas management humility and cooperation lead to health for the organization. The very countries American companies are increasingly outsourcing to have taken the business knowledge they have acquired in America to surpass them in producing quality products and providing gracious customer service. If American companies cling to a narcissistic management approach instead of benefiting from the depth of "profound knowledge" of their own employees, other companies based in Africa and Asia will gladly replace them. Perhaps American companies would not have to outsource at such alarming rates if management did not use the company as its personal playing field. Instead, managers should develop the potential of employees with training, fair rewards, and advancement. These are lessons that Dr. Deming taught to the Japanese in the 1950s. Management should correct itself or face the consequences.

Addressing the Problem

Solutions for self-correction should include the following:

1. Requiring all managers to have at least a master's degree with an area of specialization. By having an area of specialization, the manager demonstrates the ability to study a problem in depth and look at it from various angles; this translates into flexibility in the workplace and the ability to set aside glib answers;

2. Upper management should meet with employees individually to discuss the organization and compare their experiences with the data collected as feedback from surveys. This method serves as oversight to curtail any possible abuses of power. Further, it promotes the sharing of knowledge from the bottom up;

3. Middle managers as coaches need to understand that work is to be handled—never people; and

4. Supervisory managers need to examine the resumés of all employees to know how to best utilize their skills. Appropriately matching skills with tasks helps to foster employee fulfillment, while at the same time furthering the goals of the organization.

Conclusion

Respect for the abilities of employees and humility in management promote the health of the organization. Narcissism and self-seeking lead to inefficiency, which in turn leads to financial failure. To manage is to take on responsibility, not to take on an ego-satisfying position of prestige.

References

Applebaum, E., & Batt, R. (1994). *The new American workplace: Transforming work systems in the U.S.* Ithaca, NY: ILR Press.

Deming, W.E. (1995). *The new economics for industry, government, education* (2nd ed.). Cambridge, MA: MIT Press.

Emery, F. (1995, January). Participative design. *Quality and Participation*, pp. 6–9.

Lawler, E.E., III. (1992). *The ultimate advantage: Creating the high-involvement organization.* San Francisco, CA: Jossey-Bass.

Pinchot, G., & Pinchot, E. (1994). *The end of bureaucracy and the rise of the intelligent organization.* San Francisco, CA: Berrett-Koehler.

Marlo E. Ettien *is a contracting officer for the Office of Naval Research in Atlanta, Georgia. She has a bachelor's degree in communication from Chatham College and is pursuing a master's degree in organizational management at the University of Phoenix.*

Emerging Knowledge Management Trends

Worachat Buranapunsri, Robert Jordan, and Zane Berge

Summary

As learning enables employees to work more effectively and efficiently, organizations must adopt necessary technologies or tools that offer employees a better way to learn so that the employees can achieve organizational goals. Training is not the only method by which organizations can provide learning to employees. Knowledge management and performance support are alternatives. Organizational leaders must understand when each method should be used. While training provides instruction, knowledge management systems capture and disseminate information throughout the organization. Performance support provides a way for employees to complete tasks while on the job. This paper focuses on knowledge management. To be able to successfully implement a knowledge management system, organizations need to choose technologies that are simple and compatible with their infrastructure and employees. Organizational culture, technology, and employees are the most prominent factors that determine organizational success or failure in implementing knowledge management. The effective combination of training, knowledge management, and performance support allows employees to enhance their capability to learn and work better.

With the growth of Internet technology, learning is no longer limited to the classroom. Employees also learn when organizations incorporate knowledge management (KM), online training, and other performance support systems. This paper defines KM, highlights why organizations need it, and describes the shift away from training to KM. Challenges of KM and factors affecting its successful implementation are also addressed. Finally, distinctions between KM, training, and performance support systems are explored.

The Shift from Training to Knowledge Management

Learning and *training* are often used interchangeably. Their meaning is not the same, however. Training is a process in which instruction is provided to learners. It supports learning, an internal method of processing information into knowledge. An effective organizational learning strategy encompasses more than training. Broadly defined, learning in the workplace is a process by which employees obtain new knowledge and skills to increase their performance and productivity. Learning empowers employees to work more efficiently. Organizations benefit from a comprehensive learning strategy, which often includes, but is not limited to, training (Rosenberg, 2001).

Many organizations use training as a default approach to facilitate and improve employee performance. Training may be delivered via several methods, including online, in the classroom, and through satellite (Rosenberg, 2001). In today's world, however, strategic business needs rapidly change. Organizations must ensure that their employees are continually learning so that they can react quickly to changes and increase their productivity. At the same time, as technology evolves, it alters the way we learn, manage, and leverage knowledge (Zwart, 2002). While advances in technology-based learning may ultimately reduce the need for traditional classroom-based training, new learning methods are now possible. For organizations to thrive today, they must be prepared to transform their perceptions and preconceptions of the learning process and develop new learning tools, approaches, and organizational principles (Rosenberg, 2001).

Many organizations realize that training is no longer sufficient to stimulate learning. Smart organizations realize that learning should be available to employees when and where they need it (Rosenberg, 2001; Rossett, 2002).

As intellectual capital becomes more valued by organizations, KM has become more prevalent. Organizations that value intellectual capital recognize information as a factor of production and knowledge as a resource to be fostered, sustained, and accounted for (Srikantaiah & Koenig, 2000).

Even though training can effectively transfer knowledge and improve performance, it is often not efficient for organizations to train everyone to do everything. Not all learning needs to be acquired by training. Employees also learn by reading, observing, experimenting with trial and error, and communicating with their co-workers. Organizations create knowledge management systems to offer employees access to information that incorporates the collective knowledge and wisdom of the organizations (Rosenberg, 2001). Organizations also need to focus on how employees can access information and find a way to make it easily accessible when needed (San Diego State University, 1999). KM is an excellent way to empower employees to learn by obtaining the information they need when they need it.

Overview of Knowledge Management

KM is defined as a means to assist individuals, groups, teams, and organizations to learn what an individual knows, what co-workers know, what the organization knows, and what employees need to learn. It assists employees and organizations to organize and disseminate knowledge by sharing information, expertise, and insight throughout the organization. Learning, information, and expertise are then applied to new business strategies and endeavors (Gorelick, Milton, & April, 2004; Rosenberg, 2001).

KM includes identifying and mapping intellectual assets within the organization (Barclay & Murray, 1997). It also encompasses generating new knowledge for competitive advantage within the organization, making a great deal of corporate information accessible, and sharing of best practices and technology. Ultimately, KM means getting the right knowledge to the right people whenever it is needed through a variety of technologies, tools, and philosophies (San Diego State University, 1999).

KM provides a strategy and structure for increasing return on intellectual and information resources. It relies heavily on cultural and technological processes of creation, collection, sharing, recombination, and reuse of information. The goal of KM is to generate new value by improving the efficiency and effectiveness of employees and stimulating collaborative knowledge, which enhances innovation and effective decision making (Barth, 2002). KM focuses on improving working relationships and effective communication. Teamwork, collaboration, and interaction are essential in creating the right balance between information and employee action (Rosenberg, 2001).

Why Do Organizations Need Knowledge Management?

Several factors drive organizations to adopt KM systems:

- There is a transition from industrial-based to information-based systems.
- The amount of time available for people to experience and gain knowledge has been reduced.
- Life-long learning is becoming necessary.
- Most work is now information based.
- There are competitive pressures for market and talent.
- With the rapid changes, increased turnover increases the need to capture and disseminate information and knowledge among employees.

- Companies must compete on the basis of knowledge and information they possess (American Society for Training & Development, n.d.; Barclay & Murray, 1997; Gorelick, Milton, & April, 2004).

KM provides a potential solution to all of these challenges. Increasingly, it may be one of the most important factors in determining organizational success. Knowledge is a critical business resource, and KM systems support personal employee growth and enhance organizational effectiveness in gathering, organizing, distributing, and converting knowledge into action (Montano, 2005). It provides a timely way for employees to acquire knowledge and information. Finally, it offers organizations the opportunity to achieve substantial savings, improvements in human performance, and other competitive advantages (Barclay & Murray, 1997).

When deciding whether to initiate KM, organizations often consider the following business goals:

- Retaining key talent
- Improving customer service
- Increasing revenues and profits
- Capturing and sharing best practices
- Managing customer relationships
- Delivering competitive intelligence (Schneider, n.d.)

When Do Organizations Need Knowledge Management?

In order to make a justified decision as to whether training or KM is appropriate, an organization should first conduct a training needs analysis to determine the cause(s) of the problem to be addressed. Training needs analysis can help indicate which solutions, tools, or learning delivery methods are more applicable, since not all problems can be solved by training. Training is appropriate when there is an absence of skills, knowledge, or motivation to perform a job (Rossett, 1987). More specifically, when organizations have a learning need that requires instruction, they generally provide their staff with training.

When the need is for information, KM plays a potentially important role. There are many instances when employees need to learn but do not have to be trained. Although employees are knowledgeable and skilled in what they do, they still have to learn about new customer preferences, their co-workers' activities, or the competition. KM is an approach for providing accurate, well-designed, and easy-to-access information that enhances the learning process (Rosenberg, 2001). For instance, technology is changing at such a constant pace that organizations often cannot afford to have their employees miss work to attend classroom-based computer or software training. An effective KM system can provide employees with the information they need regarding new or updated software without ever taking them completely away from their jobs.

What to Consider When Choosing Technology

Technology enables KM by disseminating information throughout the organization (Montano, 2005; NELH, 2001a). KM tools and technologies supporting the identification of new knowledge opportunities include sophisticated group ware, web retrieval software, and recommender systems (Montano, 2005).

When technology decreases the cost, time, and effort required for people to share knowledge and information, it adds value. If technology is not aligned with organizational and employee needs, or if technology results in information "overload," KM may be useless, even if it incorporates the best technology, since employees will not be able to easily find the knowledge and information they need (NELH, 2001a). Poor tools and technologies undermine the success of organizational efforts in implementing KM. Therefore, choosing technology that aligns with the organizational infrastructure and needs is important.

Simplicity and Power

It is imperative that organizations employ technology that can be simply and inexpensively modified (Figallo & Rhine, 2002). The KM system designer must understand how comfortable users are with the technology (NELH, 2001a). Using simple technology often lowers the barriers to adaptation. Complex technology may be acceptable as long as the complexity offers power for experienced users; however, basic user interface with KM systems should be simple to keep knowledge flowing (Figallo & Rhine, 2002).

Compatibility

When selecting the tools and technologies, designers must make sure that the tools and technologies they will use are compatible with the infrastructure across the organization (Rosenberg, 2001). The technologies must support the system and not obstruct it. Compatibility also refers to whether the users' technological knowledge is compatible with the proposed KM technology. If the users' knowledge is not compatible, they must be trained to use the tools. Designers must carefully assess how much training will be required for employees to effectively use the KM system (NELH, 2001a).

Selecting Tools to Fit Circumstances

When selecting the tools, the designer should realize that different tools have different benefits. One tool will not fit all situations. The choice of tools is influenced by time and place (distance) variables. "The greater the time difference, the more difficult real-time communication can be. The less opportunity there is for physical meetings, the more work must be done on building familiarity and trust" (Figallo & Rhine, 2002, p. 168). Tools that can be used to support communication include email, discussion boards, videoconferencing, project support tools, and virtual working tools, among others (NELH, 2001a).

Matching Technology with Purpose

Technology should be tied to the purpose of knowledge network. KM systems are primarily applicable to learning. However, it may be used for other purposes, such as managing and completing projects or generating new ideas or innovations. KM software design may need to serve various interactive and collaborative purposes (Figallo & Rhine, 2002).

Group Size

The designer must know the number of participants. When choosing suitable technology for a knowledge network, the scale of its usage makes a difference. The choice of platform and its configuration options are important when a company expects hundreds or thousands of conversations to be going on among a great numbers of employees. The appropriate conversation technologies for a KM knowledge network vary depending on different group sizes. For a small group, email or chat works fine, but, for the department level, message board and portals may be better (Figallo & Rhine, 2002).

Duration of Activity

Knowledge sharing conversations may last only two hours, days, a month, or even longer. Conversations may occur in asynchronous (e.g., email, message boards) or synchronous (e.g., chat, real-time event facilities) communication. The shorter the duration of the communication, the more suitable are the real-time interfaces (Figallo & Rhine, 2002).

Challenges of Knowledge Management

To ensure successful implementation of KM, organizations have to overcome challenges related to people, culture, quality control, and acceptance.

People

One of the most serious obstacles to KM is people (*CIO*, 2000). KM is a challenge for many companies because the organizational culture and employee beliefs and attitudes often inhibit knowledge sharing. Some employees doubt the KM paradigm and do not want to share knowledge. Some beliefs and attitudes that constitute barriers to KM include the following:

- Knowledge is power.

- I do not have time.

- That is not my job/responsibility.

- You are just using other people's ideas and taking credit.

- I do not trust them.

In addition, people who compete for jobs, salaries, promotions, status, and power usually believe that if they share their knowledge, they will lose their self-identity and value and, as a result, believe that sharing is counter to their best interests. However, studies have shown that people are generally willing to share but need a supportive and safe environment (NELH, 2001b; Rosenberg, 2001).

Culture

Culture is another challenge (Liebowitz, 1999; Schneider, n.d.). Many organizations try to implement KM, focusing solely on the technological solution, and fail because they overlook the importance of a sharing culture. The absence of a sharing culture and employees' lack of understanding of what KM is and what benefits it offers are the biggest failure of KM initiatives (Schneider, n.d.).

Changing organizational culture is not easy. Studies, however, report that culture can be changed with a great deal of effort and time (Gorelick, Milton, & April, 2004; NELH, 2001b). A knowledge-friendly culture has to be created and nurtured to support knowledge sharing (Gorelick, Milton, & April, 2004).

Quality Control

Another challenge of KM is to determine what information is worthy of capture and qualifies as valuable. Not all information is valuable (DoD, n.d.; Sullivan, n.d.). If the knowledge captured is not carefully validated, employees may waste time and expend energy searching through useless information to locate useful knowledge (Singh, 2004). Obtaining too much information without filtering out the unnecessary information may result in information overload and frustration for the employees.

Acceptance

The acceptance challenge is another concern, since it affects the implementation process. An organization has to realize that an organization's adoption of a KM system does not mean employees' adaptation to it. Ultimately, employees decide whether they will use the system and in what way. They must perceive KM as relevant (Coakes, 2003).

The Success Factors for Knowledge Management Implementation

In order to effectively implement KM, organizations must take success factors into consideration: culture, leadership and senior management support, reward and recognition, technology and gaining IT support, community of practice, and education and training. These factors are very important and cannot be overlooked.

Culture

"An organizational culture is a set of values, beliefs, assumptions and attitudes that are deeply held by the people in the organization" (NELH, 2001a). Culture affects the way people behave and work within the organization. A strong learning and knowledge sharing culture is required in order for KM to be successful and effective (Rosenberg, 2001). Organizational culture greatly affects KM initiatives. For KM to be successful, the culture must recognize learning and knowledge sharing as valued parts of what people do. The culture must be aligned with the values of knowledge sharing. KM requires a culture in which people realize that the knowledge they work with is not merely their personal knowledge, but it is organizational knowledge to be shared. Knowledge must be managed, maintained, and not wasted (Gorelick, Milton, & April, 2004; Rosenberg, 2001). In addition, employees have to realize that training is not the only way to gain knowledge. They can learn and acquire knowledge by participating in KM and learning from one another.

Nevertheless, building a learning and knowledge sharing culture is not easy (Gorelick, Milton, & April, 2004; Rosenberg, 2001). Strategies for changing and building a learning and knowledge sharing culture are grounded in a clear understanding of the true organizational culture and the mental model that shapes people's beliefs. This culture has to encourage experimentation and risk taking; it must not punish failures (Montano, 2005). Moreover, it should promote trust, openness, and shared values among employees so that they will have proactive knowledge sharing across time and space. People need to be able to trust the information they receive to be the best (Rao, 2002).

Leadership and Senior Management Support

Leadership plays an important role in identifying the knowledge that an organization has to obtain and use. Leaders must define the organization's mission in terms of knowledge. They must determine to what degree the knowledge is disseminated throughout the organization. Furthermore, leaders examine and determine the basis for rewarding employee performance for sharing knowledge (Montano, 2005).

Leaders also need to allocate resources, including time needed for the initiative. Another role of leaders is to communicate and model basic values related to the importance of knowledge capturing and sharing. Excellent leaders are committed to creating and offering learning opportunities for employees within the organization (Gorelick, Milton, & April, 2004).

Building a culture that embraces KM requires support from senior management for that culture. Gaining management buy-in is an integral part of the process to create a shared vision for how KM will be implemented within the organization (Liebowitz, 1999; Rosenberg, 2001; Srikantaiah & Koenig, 2000). Without support from the top management, the KM project will never succeed.

Reward and Recognition

When people are asked to do something, they want to know what's in it for them. When employees believe they will personally gain benefit from sharing knowledge, they are more likely to share their knowledge with others (NELH, 2001b). A common method employed to guarantee implementation is the development of a system rewarding and recognizing people who understand, value, and participate in knowledge sharing (Srikantaiah & Koenig, 2000). It is also important to realize that different people are motivated by different things. Some people are motivated by extrinsic rewards—money, bonus, position, etc.—but some needs are intrinsic, such as recognition, knowledge, freedom, etc. Rewards can be both formal and informal, and do not need to be financial. Several studies have proposed that one of the most effective incentives is recognition. Organizations must ensure that they reward knowledge used in meeting business strategies (NELH, 2001b).

Technology and IT Support

Technology consists of infrastructure and collaborative applications. Infrastructure is the hardware and software enabling people to communicate with others from any place and at any time. Knowledge sharing will not possible without the technical infrastructure that supports communication. Once infrastructure is in place, collaborative applications must be implemented to ensure communication across time and space (Gorelick, Milton, &

April, 2004). It is vital that technology be designed to support collaboration and facilitate the flow of information and knowledge throughout the organization. The right technology increases the effectiveness of KM system (Montano, 2005).

To initiate the KM, it is important to gain support from information technology (IT) staff. The designer has to work closely with the IT staff to ensure consistency, scalability, and efficiency of the organizational infrastructure (Rossett, 2002).

Community of Practice

Successful KM depends on communities of practice. In a community of practice, members cooperate in sharing knowledge and information to improve individual performance (Gorelick, Milton, & April, 2004). While they exchange their knowledge and experience with one another, they gain new knowledge and insights, even without being trained.

Employees effectively share information and knowledge when they know and trust one another (NELH, 2001b). Thus, it is important for people in the communities to create personal relationships and mutual trust. Relationships among people in the communities of practice enhance successful implementation of KM.

Education and Training

People must know what is expected of them and what is involved in KM. They should also be provided the skills they require to operate and participate in KM (NELH, 2001b). Formal KM training is one way that an organization can institutionalize KM tools, processes, and behaviors. If the organization decides that KM is a system required to be learned, it can hasten diffusion and increase the adoption of the KM through formal training programs (Gorelick, Milton, & April, 2004).

Knowledge Management, Training, and Performance Support

KM, training, and performance support are ways organizations provide knowledge and information to employees. Understanding each method is important and allows organizations to apply appropriate methods in different situations.

Distinctions Among KM, Training, and Performance Support

KM is online information. It is about *providing the right knowledge and information to the right people at the right time* (Rossett, 2002). KM is one of the best tools to enhance individual performance by providing users the information they need to carry out tasks or a job (Gorelick, Milton, & April, 2004). KM promotes the formation, archiving, and sharing of valued information, expertise, and insight within and across communities of employees and organizations with similar interests and needs. KM is valuable when there is a learning need that requires information (Rosenberg, 2001).

On the other hand, *training* is required when a learning need is about instruction. Training is used when it is essential to shape learning in a particular direction. Training supports learners to obtain new knowledge and skills in a specific level of proficiency or within a specific time frame (Rossett, 2002). However, organizations should conduct training needs assessment before deciding whether training is a suitable solution and when training is needed (Rossett, 1987).

Performance support, sometimes referred to as user support, "includes all of the user-oriented materials, in addition to the user interface, that will support the user in learning and using the system" (Williams, 2004, p. 4). Performance support includes overviews, online help, performance aids, documentation, coaches, wizards, and tutorials. The goals of a performance support system are to reduce the need for formal instruction (i.e., training), improve the quality of work, and enable employees to do the work faster with minimal support from others. In addition, performance support offers users direct information when needed so that they can perform specific tasks successfully (Rosenberg, 2001; Williams, 2004). Performance support offers a way to complete a job or tasks without the need to learn the intricacies of the performance. The focus of performance support is to enable users to become more productive with less effort. The performance support system operates on the basis of providing information and telling users what to do and guides their performance (Rosenberg, 2001). Sometimes, employees just need to know how to perform a particular task; they do not need to be fully trained on the task if it is not part of their normal job responsibility. This is where performance support is more appropriate. The distinctions among KM, training, and performance support are outlined in Table 1.

How Do KM, Training, and Performance Support Fit Together in the Organization?

People are not single-method learners. They are blended learners. When used appropriately, "the combination of training (classroom and/or online), KM, and performance support is a powerful force for learning" (Rosenberg, 2001, p. 77).

A training system is established to meet the needs of organizations that want their employees to acquire new knowledge and skills before beginning their work—or even while working. The organization employs the performance support system to enhance employee performance while on the job. Complete KM systems incorporate both training and performance support in capturing and distributing knowledge (Thai, n.d.).

Table 1.   Differences Among Training, KM, and Performance Support

	Training	Knowledge Management	Performance Support
Goal	The goals are to transfer skill and knowledge to learners and develop learners' capacity and memory	The goal is to be a resource to user	The goal is to assist performance or do it completely
Purpose	Purpose is to instruct	Purpose is to inform and provide information	Purpose is to guide performance directly
Interruption	Requires interruption of work to participate	Requires less interruption of work than training	Requires least interruption of work
User control	Users have less control; instructor or program dictates how users will learn	Users determine how they will learn	Task at hand indicates what the tool will do

Sources: Rosenberg, 2001, p. 77; Rossett, 2002, p. 285.

To survive in the 21st Century business world, Dr. James Z. Li (2000) proposes that organizations need to move their employees from beginners to experts and know how to move knowledge from ones who possess it to ones who need it. Training is the first step toward building employee expertise. Performance support allows employees to perform tasks like experts along the way. Finally, KM accelerates employees' learning by allowing employees to effectively learn from others' experience. The combination of all three approaches offers an organization a powerful tool to compete with other organizations in the knowledge-based economy. The effective integration of KM, training, and performance support enhances the way people learn, work, and share experience and expertise (Rosenberg, 2001; Rossett, 2002).

With KM and performance support, organizations can provide well-structured information and productivity-enhancing tools to enable employees to learn and improve their performance, rather than exclusively depending on training instruction. While an organization may use training (instruction) to teach staffs particular knowledge and skills required to perform a job, it will not need to retrain them when a new product or model comes out; the organization can simply provide the information via KM or performance support (Rosenberg, 2001).

Summary

Learning in organizations happens via many methods, including training, KM, and performance support. Training is not the only way to provide learning. Conducting training needs analysis enables organizations to investigate whether there is a need to provide training and may also suggest other possible methods to solve problems. While training is appropriate when offering instruction, a KM system allows users to access information when needed, and a performance support system provides a path for users to successfully complete tasks. In order to successfully implement KM, organizations must consider the technology they will use, the challenges or problems they may face, and the success factors, as described in this paper. The integration among training, KM, and performance support enhances organizational learning to be more powerful, since it will enable employees to receive timely knowledge, skills, and information to meet all business needs.

References

American Society for Training & Development (n.d.). *Trends in workplace learning: Knowledge management.* Retrieved October 8, 2004, from www.astd.org/astd/Resources/performance_improvement_community/trends.

Barclay, R.O., & Murray, P.C. (1997). *What is knowledge management?* Retrieved October 2, 2004, from www.media-access.com/whatis.html.

Barth, S. (2002, June 19). *Defining knowledge management.* Retrieved October 31, 2004, from www.destinationkm.com/articles/default.asp?ArticleID=949.

CIO. (2000). Cultural barriers challenge KM implementers. Retrieved November 9, 2004, from www.cio.com/sponsors/0600_km/061500_km_side10.html.

Coakes, E. (2003). *Knowledge management: Current issues and challenges.* Hershey, PA: IRM Press.

DoD. (n.d.) *Knowledge management.* Retrieved October 31, 2004, from www.dod.mil/comptroller/icenter/learn/knowledgeman.htm.

Figallo, C., & Rhine, N. (2002). *Building the knowledge management network.* Hoboken, NJ: John Wiley & Sons, Inc.

Gorelick, C., Milton, N., & April, K. (2004). *Performance through learning.* Burlington, MA: Elsevier Butterworth-Heinemann.

Li, J.Z. (2000, August). *The promise of e-learning and the practice of knowledge system design.* White paper. LeadingWay Knowledge Systems. Retrieved March 10, 2004, from www.leadingway.com/pdf/eLearning.pdf.

Liebowitz, J. (1999). *Knowledge management handbook.* Boca Raton, FL: CRC Press.

Montano, B. (2005). *Innovations of knowledge management.* Hershey, PA: IRM Press.

NELH (National Electronic Library for Health). (2001a). *Developing the KM environment.* Retrieved November 2, 2004, from www.nelh.nhs.uk/knowledge_management/km2/developing.asp.

NELH (National Electronic Library for Health). (2001b). *Knowledge management technology.* Retrieved November 2, 2004, from www.nelh.nhs.uk/knowledge_management/km2/technology.asp.

Rao, M. (2002, August 23). *Eight keys to successful KM practice.* Retrieved October 31, 2004, from www.destinationkm.com/articles/default.asp?ArticleID=990.

Rosenberg, M.J. (2001). *E-learning.* New York: McGraw-Hill.

Rossett, A. (1987). *Training needs assessment.* Englewood Cliffs, NJ: Educational Technology Publications, Inc.

Rossett, A. (2002). *The ASTD e-learning handbook.* New York: McGraw-Hill.

San Diego State University. (1999). Knowledge management for training professionals. Retrieved October 8, 2004, from http://defcon.sdsu.edu/1/objects/km/defining/index.htm.

Schneider, J. (n.d.). *Overview of knowledge management.* Retrieved October 18, 2004, from www.jgs.net/resume/overview_of_knowledge_management.htm.

Singh, S. (2004, June 21). *Making knowledge management work on your intranet.* Retrieved November 2, 2004, from www.boxesandarrows.com/archives/making_knowledge_management_work_on_your_intranet.php.

Srikantaish, T.K., & Koenig, M.E.D. (Eds.). (2000). *Knowledge management for the information professional.* Medford, NJ: Information Today, Inc.

Sullivan, M.D. (n.d.). *Knowledge-capturing technologies and the culture of change.* Retrieved November 2, 2004, from www.iabc.com/fdtnweb/pdf/2004KnowledgeCapture.pdf.

Thai, T.H. (n.d.). *Knowledge systems design.* Retrieved October 6, 2004, from http://coe.sdsu.edu/eet/Articles/KSD/start.htm.

Williams, J.R. (2004). *Developing performance support for computer systems.* Boca Raton, FL: CRC Press.

Zwart, D. (2002, November). *The end of training as we know it.* Retrieved November 2, 2004, from www1.astd.org/tk03/pdf/session_handouts/W206.pdf.

Worachat Buranapunsri *received a bachelor's degree in psychology in Thailand and a master of science in industrial/organizational psychology from the University of Baltimore, Maryland. She is pursuing a master's degree in instructional systems development at UMBC.*

Robert Jordan *is an economist with the United States Bureau of Labor Statistics in Washington, D.C. He has been designing and delivering training for ten years. He is currently pursuing a master's degree in instructional systems development at the UMBC.*

Zane Berge, Ph.D., *is an associate professor teaching in the graduate training systems programs at UMBC. His research is in the area of distance training and education.*

Contributors

Kristin J. Arnold, CMC, CPF, CSP
Quality Process Consultants, Inc.
11304 Megan Drive
Fairfax, VA 22030
  (703) 278-0892
  fax: (703) 278-0891
  email: karnold@qpcteam.com

Teri-E Belf
2016 Lakebreeze Way
Reston, VA 20191-4021
  (703) 716-8374
  fax: (703) 264-7867
  email: coach@belf.org
  URL: www.erols.com/belf

Zane Berge, Ph.D.
UMBC
1000 Hilltop Circle
Baltimore, MD 21250
  (410) 455-2306
  email: berge@umbc.edu

Jeffrey P. Bosworth
President
Sales Growth Group
500 Country Club Drive
Longwood, FL 32750
  (407) 786-7330
  fax: (407) 786-7334
  email: jpb@salesgrowthgroup.com
  URL: www.salesgrowthgroup.com

Worachat Buranapunsri
2422 Bibury Lane, Apt. #204
Baltimore, MD 21244
  (410) 944-1223
  email: wanda2521@yahoo.com

M. Sheila Collins
6643 Park Hall Drive
Laurel, MD 20707
  (301) 604-2567
  email: scollins@mscconsultinginc.com
  URL: www.mscconsulting.com

Susan El-Shamy
2502 Browncliff Lane
Bloomington, IN 47408
  (812) 333-1535
  fax: (812) 333-1535
  email: Susanshamy@aol.com

Marlo E. Ettien
Office of Naval Research, Atlanta
  Regional Office
100 Alabama Street, SW, Suite 4R15
Atlanta, GA 30303
  (404) 562-1607
  fax: (404) 562-1610
  email: ettienm@onr.navy.mil

Diane M. Gayeski, Ph.D.
Gayeski Analytics
407 Coddington Road
Ithaca, NY 14850
  (607) 272-7700
  email: diane@dgayeski.com

W. Norman Gustafson
7428 N. Meridian Avenue
Fresno, CA 93720
  (559) 299-2166
  (559) 875-7121
  fax: (559) 875-8848
  email: wngus@hotmail.com

Gail Hahn, MA, CSP, CPRP, CLL
Fun*cilitators
9026 East Minnesota Avenue
Sun Lakes, AZ 85248
  (866) fun.at.work (866-386-2896)
  (480) 802-0103
  fax: (530) 326-2979
  email: gail@funcilitators.com
  URL: www.funcilitators.com

Lois B. Hart, Ed.D.
11256 WCR 23
Fort Lupton, CO 80621
  (970) 785-2716
  fax: (970) 785-2717
  email: lhart@seqnet.net

Tyrone A. Holmes, Ed.D., L.P.C.
30307 Sterling Drive
Novi, MI 48377
  (248) 669-5294
  fax: (248) 669-5295
  email: tyrone@doctorholmes.net
  URL: www.doctorholmes.net

Bonnie Jameson, M.S.
1024 Underhills Road
Oakland, CA 94610
  (510) 832-2597
  fax: (510) 835-8669
  email: BBLjameson@cs.com

Homer H. Johnson, Ph.D.
Loyola University Chicago
820 N. Michigan Avenue
Chicago, IL 60611
  (312) 915-6682
  fax: (312) 915-6231
  email: hjohnson@luc.edu

Robert Jordan
10600 Weymouth Street, #202
Bethesda, MD 20814
  (202) 691-6476
  email: rjordan617@earthlink.net

M.K. Key, Ph.D.
Key Associates
1857 Laurel Ridge Drive
Nashville, TN 37215
  (888) 655-3901
  (615) 665-1622
  fax: (615) 665-8902
  email: keyassocs@mindspring.com
  URL: www.mkkey.com

Teresa Kirkwood
214 Lamarche
Laval, Quebec H7X 3M7
Canada
  (450) 689-3895
  fax: (450) 689-3895
  email: info@centralknowledge.com

Lisa J. Marshall
The Smart Work Company
1365 Hamilton Street, NW
Washington, DC 20011
  (202) 829-0795
  email: lisa@smartworkco.com

Lenn Millbower
Offbeat Training®
329 Oakpoint Circle
Davenport, FL 33837
  (407) 256-0501
  email: lennmillbower@
    offbeattraining.com
  URL: www.offbeattraining.com

Pat Murphy
10153 Maxine Street
Ellicott City, MD 21042
  (301) 592-6672
  fax: (301) 592-6677
  email: Pat_murphy@choicehotels.com

Bob Nelson, Ph.D., M.B.A.
President
Nelson Motivation Inc.
12245 World Trade Drive #C
San Diego, CA 92128
  (858) 673-0690
  fax: (858) 673-9031
  email: bobrewards@aol.com
  URL: www.nelson-motivation.com

Ajay M. Pangarkar
214 Lamarche
Laval, Quebec H7X 3M7
Canada
  (450) 689-3895
  fax: (450) 689-3895
  email: info@centralknowledge.com

Frank A. Prince
Unleash Your Mind LLC
512 N. McClurg Court, Suite #4807
Chicago, IL 60611
  (312) 828-9245
  URLs: 222.speedsleep.com;
    www.unleashyourmind.com

Stephen Randall
1400 Carpentier Street, #202
San Leandro, CA 94577
  (510) 352-5391
  email: steve@manage-time.com

Carrie Reilly
106 Constitution, Building 158
Norman, OK 73072
  (405) 325-0464
  email: creilly@ou.edu

Mark Rose
11729 Cedar Valley Drive
Oklahoma City, OK 73170
  (405) 323-1522
  email: rosemg@oge.com

Jeffrey and Linda Russell
Russell Consulting, Inc.
1134 Winston Drive
Madison, WI 53711-3161
  (608) 274-4482
  fax: (608) 274-1927
  email: RCI@RussellConsultingInc.com

Parth Sarathi
General Manager (HRD)
Human Resource Development Institute
Bharat Heavy Electricals Ltd.
Noida 201301
India
  91-120-2515417
  91-11-22521110
  fax: 91-120-2515417
  email: ps@hrd.bhel.co.in

Neil J. Simon
17340 W. 12 Mile Road, Suite 102
Southfield, MI 48076
  (248) 552-0821
  (248) 552-1924
  email: NJSimon@busdevgroup.com

Steve Sphar
2870 Third Avenue
Sacramento, CA 95818
  (916) 731-4851
  email: sphar1@earthlink.net

Teresa Torres-Coronas, Ph.D.
Rovira i Virgili University
Campus Sescelades
Avinguda dels Països Catalans, 26
43007 Tarragona
Spain
  +34 977 558 777
  fax: +34 977 759 810
  email: teresa.torres@urv.net

Chai M. Voris, M. Ed.
Dynamic Change Solutions, Inc.
6249 Forest Crest Court
Loveland, OH 45140
  (513) 722-4236
  email: cvoris@dynamic-change.com

Martha C. Yopp
University of Idaho
800 Park Boulevard, Suite 200
Boise, ID 83712
  (208) 364-9918
  fax: (208) 364-4035
  email: myopp@uidaho.edu

Fred Zimmer
17340 W. 12 Mile Road, Suite 102
Southfield, MI, 48076
  (248) 552-0821
  (248) 552-1924
  email: FAZimmer@yahoo.com

Contents of the Companion Volume, *The 2006 Pfeiffer Annual: Consulting*

Editor's Choice

Inventories, Questionnaires, and Surveys

Articles and Discussion Resources

**Topic is cutting edge

How to Use the CD-ROM

System Requirements

PC with Microsoft Windows 98SE or later
Mac with Apple OS version 8.6 or later

Using the CD with Windows

To view the items located on the CD, follow these steps:

1. Insert the CD into your computer's CD-ROM drive.

2. A window appears with the following options:

    Contents: Allows you to view the files included on the CD-ROM.

    Software: Allows you to install useful software from the CD-ROM.

    Links: Displays a hyperlinked page of websites.

    Author: Displays a page with information about the Author(s).

    Contact Us: Displays a page with information on contacting the publisher or author.

    Help: Displays a page with information on using the CD.

    Exit: Closes the interface window.

If you do not have autorun enabled, or if the autorun window does not appear, follow these steps to access the CD:

1. Click Start -> Run.

2. In the dialog box that appears, type d:<\\>start.exe, where d is the letter of your CD-ROM drive. This brings up the autorun window described in the preceding set of steps.

3. Choose the desired option from the menu. (See Step 2 in the preceding list for a description of these options.)

In Case of Trouble

If you experience difficulty using the CD-ROM, please follow these steps:

1. Make sure your hardware and systems configurations conform to the systems requirements noted under "System Requirements" above.

2. Review the installation procedure for your type of hardware and operating system.

It is possible to reinstall the software if necessary.

To speak with someone in Product Technical Support, call 800-762-2974 or 317-572-3994, M–F 8:30 a.m.–5:00 p.m. EST. You can also get support and contact Product Technical Support through our website at www.wiley.com/techsupport.

Before calling or writing, please have the following information available:

- Type of computer and operating system

- Any error messages displayed

- Complete description of the problem.

It is best if you are sitting at your computer when making the call.

Pfeiffer Publications Guide

This guide is designed to familiarize you with the various types of Pfeiffer publications. The formats section describes the various types of products that we publish; the methodologies section describes the many different ways that content might be provided within a product. We also provide a list of the topic areas in which we publish.

FORMATS

In addition to its extensive book-publishing program, Pfeiffer offers content in an array of formats, from fieldbooks for the practitioner to complete, ready-to-use training packages that support group learning.

FIELDBOOK Designed to provide information and guidance to practitioners in the midst of action. Most fieldbooks are companions to another, sometimes earlier, work, from which its ideas are derived; the fieldbook makes practical what was theoretical in the original text. Fieldbooks can certainly be read from cover to cover. More likely, though, you'll find yourself bouncing around following a particular theme, or dipping in as the mood, and the situation, dictate.

HANDBOOK A contributed volume of work on a single topic, comprising an eclectic mix of ideas, case studies, and best practices sourced by practitioners and experts in the field.

An editor or team of editors usually is appointed to seek out contributors and to evaluate content for relevance to the topic. Think of a handbook not as a ready-to-eat meal, but as a cookbook of ingredients that enables you to create the most fitting experience for the occasion.

RESOURCE Materials designed to support group learning. They come in many forms: a complete, ready-to-use exercise (such as a game); a comprehensive resource on one topic (such as conflict management) containing a variety of methods and approaches; or a collection of like-minded activities (such as icebreakers) on multiple subjects and situations.

TRAINING PACKAGE An entire, ready-to-use learning program that focuses on a particular topic or skill. All packages comprise a guide for the facilitator/trainer and a workbook for the participants. Some packages are supported with additional media—such as video—or learning aids, instruments, or other devices to help participants understand concepts or practice and develop skills.

- *Facilitator/trainer's guide* Contains an introduction to the program, advice on how to organize and facilitate the learning event, and step-by-step instructor notes. The guide also contains copies of presentation materials—handouts, presentations, and overhead designs, for example—used in the program.

- *Participant's workbook* Contains exercises and reading materials that support the learning goal and serves as a valuable reference and support guide for participants in the weeks and months that follow the learning event. Typically, each participant will require his or her own workbook.

ELECTRONIC CD-ROMs and web-based products transform static Pfeiffer content into dynamic, interactive experiences. Designed to take advantage of the searchability, automation, and ease-of-use that technology provides, our e-products bring convenience and immediate accessibility to your workspace.

METHODOLOGIES

CASE STUDY A presentation, in narrative form, of an actual event that has occurred inside an organization. Case studies are not prescriptive, nor are they used to prove a point; they are designed to develop critical analysis and decision-making skills. A case study has a specific time frame, specifies a sequence of events, is narrative in structure, and contains a plot structure—an issue (what should be/have been done?). Use case studies when the goal is to enable participants to apply previously learned theories to the circumstances in the case, decide what is pertinent, identify the real issues, decide what should have been done, and develop a plan of action.

ENERGIZER A short activity that develops readiness for the next session or learning event. Energizers are most commonly used after a break or lunch to stimulate or refocus the group. Many involve some form of physical activity, so they are a useful way to counter post-lunch lethargy. Other uses include transitioning from one topic to another, where "mental" distancing is important.

EXPERIENTIAL LEARNING ACTIVITY (ELA) A facilitator-led intervention that moves participants through the learning cycle from experience to application (also known as a Structured Experience). ELAs are carefully thought-out designs in which there is a definite learning purpose and intended outcome. Each step—everything that participants do during the activity—facilitates the accomplishment of the stated goal. Each ELA includes complete instructions for facilitating the intervention and a clear statement of goals, suggested group size and timing, materials required, an explanation of the process, and, where appropriate, possible variations to the activity. (For more detail on Experiential Learning Activities, see the Introduction to the *Reference Guide to Handbooks and Annuals*, 1999 edition, Pfeiffer, San Francisco.)

GAME A group activity that has the purpose of fostering team spirit and togetherness in addition to the achievement of a pre-stated goal. Usually contrived—undertaking a desert expedition, for example—this type of learning method offers an engaging means for participants to demonstrate and practice business and interpersonal skills. Games are effective for team building and personal development mainly because the goal is subordinate to the process—the means through which participants reach decisions, collaborate, communicate, and generate trust and understanding. Games often engage teams in "friendly" competition.

ICEBREAKER A (usually) short activity designed to help participants overcome initial anxiety in a training session and/or to acquaint the participants with one another. An icebreaker can be a fun activity or can be tied to specific topics or training goals. While a useful tool in itself, the icebreaker comes into its own in situations where tension or resistance exists within a group.

INSTRUMENT A device used to assess, appraise, evaluate, describe, classify, and summarize various aspects of human behavior. The term used to describe an instrument depends primarily on its format and purpose. These terms include survey, questionnaire, inventory, diagnostic survey, and poll. Some uses of instruments include providing instrumental feedback to group members, studying here-and-now processes or functioning within a group, manipulating group composition, and evaluating outcomes of training and other interventions.

Instruments are popular in the training and HR field because, in general, more growth can occur if an individual is provided with a method for focusing specifically on his or her own behavior. Instruments also are used to obtain information that will serve as a basis for change and to assist in workforce planning efforts.

Paper-and-pencil tests still dominate the instrument landscape with a typical package comprising a facilitator's guide, which offers advice on administering the instrument and interpreting the collected data, and an initial set of instruments. Additional instruments are available separately. Pfeiffer, though, is investing heavily in e-instruments. Electronic instrumentation provides effortless distribution and, for larger groups particularly, offers advantages over paper-and-pencil tests in the time it takes to analyze data and provide feedback.

LECTURETTE A short talk that provides an explanation of a principle, model, or process that is pertinent to the participants' current learning needs. A lecturette is intended to establish a common language bond between the trainer and the participants by providing a mutual frame of reference. Use a lecturette as an introduction to a group activity or event, as an interjection during an event, or as a handout.

MODEL A graphic depiction of a system or process and the relationship among its elements. Models provide a frame of reference and something more tangible, and more easily remembered, than a verbal explanation. They also give participants something to "go on," enabling them to track their own progress as they experience the dynamics, processes, and relationships being depicted in the model.

ROLE PLAY A technique in which people assume a role in a situation/scenario: a customer service rep in an angry-customer exchange, for example. The way in which the role is approached is then discussed and feedback is offered. The role play is often repeated using a different approach and/or incorporating changes made based on feedback received. In other words, role playing is a spontaneous interaction involving realistic behavior under artificial (and safe) conditions.

SIMULATION A methodology for understanding the interrelationships among components of a system or process. Simulations differ from games in that they test or use a model that depicts or mirrors some aspect of reality in form, if not necessarily in content. Learning occurs by studying the effects of change on one or more factors of the model. Simulations are commonly used to test hypotheses about what happens in a system—often referred to as "what if?" analysis—or to examine best-case/worst-case scenarios.

THEORY A presentation of an idea from a conjectural perspective. Theories are useful because they encourage us to examine behavior and phenomena through a different lens.

TOPICS

The twin goals of providing effective and practical solutions for workforce training and organization development and meeting the educational needs of training and human resource professionals shape Pfeiffer's publishing program. Core topics include the following:

Leadership & Management
Communication & Presentation
Coaching & Mentoring
Training & Development
e-Learning
Teams & Collaboration
OD & Strategic Planning
Human Resources
Consulting

What will you find on pfeiffer.com?

- The best in workplace performance solutions for training and HR professionals

- Downloadable training tools, exercises, and content

- Web-exclusive offers

- Training tips, articles, and news

- Seamless on-line ordering

- Author guidelines, information on becoming a Pfeiffer Affiliate, and much more

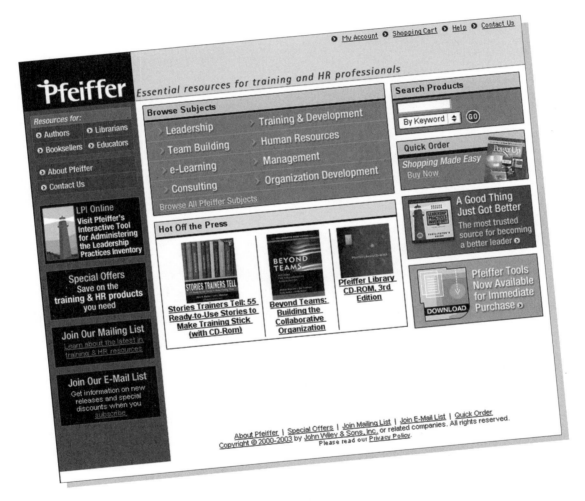

Discover more at www.pfeiffer.com